Promotional poster with various scenes from Cody's autobiography, ca. 1879. Buffalo Bill Historical Center, Cody, Wyoming. 1.69.26.

The Life of Hon. William F. Cody,
Known as Buffalo Bill

THE PAPERS OF WILLIAM F. "BUFFALO BILL" CODY

WILLIAM F. CODY

The Life of
Hon. William F. Cody,
Known as
Buffalo Bill

Edited and with an introduction by Frank Christianson

University of Nebraska Press
Lincoln & London

Support for this volume was provided by a generous
gift from Adrienne and John Mars.

∞

Library of Congress Cataloging-in-Publication Data

Buffalo Bill, 1846–1917.
The life of Hon. William F. Cody, known as Buffalo Bill /
William F. Cody; edited and with an introduction by Frank Christianson.
p. cm.—(The papers of William F. "Buffalo Bill" Cody)
Includes bibliographical references and index.
ISBN 978-0-8032-3619-6 (cloth: alk. paper)
ISBN 978-0-8032-3291-4 (pbk.: alk. paper)
1. Buffalo Bill, 1846–1917. 2. Pioneers—West (U.S.)—Biography.
3. Scouts (Reconnaissance)—West (U.S.)—Biography.
4. Frontier and pioneer life—West (U.S.)
I. Christianson, Frank. II. Title. III. Title: Life of Honorable
William F. Cody, known as Buffalo Bill.
F594.C6745 2011
978'.02092—dc22
[B]
2011015108

Set in Iowan Old Style by Bob Reitz.

CONTENTS

ILLUSTRATIONS

SERIES EDITOR'S PREFACE

In 2006 the McCracken Research Library in Cody, Wyoming, set out to edit and publish the collected papers of William F. "Buffalo Bill" Cody. It seemed like an idea whose time had come; in fact, it was long overdue. William F. Cody was the most famous American of his time. As a cultural figure his influence was unparalleled. And yet Cody's role in our national narrative is largely underappreciated, in part because the relationship between Cody and his public persona has not been adequately examined. Indeed, the familiar Buffalo Bill is perhaps viewed today as a quaint character, if not caricature, whose larger-than-life image obscures the substantive William F. Cody. Because Cody is surrounded by so much myth and lore, it is often difficult to trace the very real contribution that he made to the development of the American West and American culture.

Although the autobiography has been continuously in print and published in various versions, it has never been critically edited or annotated as it is here. In this carefully researched edition, Frank Christianson frames the field of Cody studies by situating Cody within the history, culture, and literature of nineteenth-century America. The Christianson edition and the larger project it anchors elevate William F. Cody to an object of scholarly study while acknowledging and appealing to the

intense popular interest that Buffalo Bill has always gener-
ated. With the addition of substantive appendixes and critical
annotations, this publication offers only a small sample of the
available resources in the extensive but underexplored archive
of Cody material. It is the aim of *The Papers of William F. Cody* to
open and expand that archive through both digital and print
editions of the Cody Papers.

The Christianson edition of Cody's autobiography not only
demonstrates Cody's significance to American cultural studies, it also reveals the extent to which Cody was the consummate self-promoter. He was, as the introduction to this volume
points out, an important innovator in the American art of self-
making, building on and expanding the tradition established by
Benjamin Franklin, P. T. Barnum, and Frederick Douglass, in
casting his personal story as *the* American narrative. Moreover,
Cody's life is an example of how one individual can become
an industry. And, like every other such venture, the success
of Cody's enterprise relied on energy other than his own—it
required boosters, barkers, and skilled handlers. In what can
only be described as the superlative American irony, it turns
out that the self-made man is a collaborative product, the result of a team effort. Fortunately for Cody, his life and times
paired him with the likes of Ned Buntline, John Burke, and
Nate Salisbury (among countless others), all of whom joined
with him in making Buffalo Bill their business.

Just as Cody's nineteenth-century image was nurtured and
promoted by a committed cast, so, too, is the resurgence of
Cody's image in the twenty-first century a collective endeavor.
Many generous donors and talented scholars have contributed
to the success of this documentary project. This new edition of
The Life of Hon. William F. Cody, for example, was underwritten

by a generous grant from Adrienne and John Mars. Naoma Tate, Bill Garlow, and Maggie Scarlett have also been key contributors to the chorus of Cody supporters. Within that distinguished troupe, however, Bob and Dine Dellenback have played the leading role. They have accomplished in the twenty-first century what Buntline, Burke, and Salisbury did in the nineteenth: they made Buffalo Bill possible. And they have done so with generosity, energy, and an enthusiasm that continues to propel this project forward. As William F. Cody takes his rightful place on the expansive and expanding stage of American cultural studies, he is indebted to a long list of patrons and professionals who have made this reemergence possible. At the top of that list are Bob and Dine Dellenback.

Kurt Graham

1. *I Am Coming*. Chromo-lithographic promotional poster, 1900.
Buffalo Bill Historical Center, Cody, Wyoming. 1.69.4922.

A promotional poster from 1900 superimposes the larger-than-life image of William Cody's head and shoulders on the side of a running buffalo. It includes the simple pronouncement, "I Am Coming."[1] The focal point of the advertisement is Cody's face; the semi-profile wears a calm but commanding expression, staring into the middle distance with a long gray mustache and beard to match the flowing hair that pours out from under a gray Stetson. By the turn of the century, the visual association of Cody with the buffalo was almost redundant. Although he went by his birth name his entire life, he was known to the majority of the public as "Buffalo Bill." And, while the lithography of the poster faithfully represents the person of Cody, it also presents the persona (the Latin root means "mask") of Buffalo Bill. That persona was the product of years of careful shaping by Cody and his business associates, whose image-making took the form of dime novels, newspaper stories, stage melodramas, and, of course, the traveling Wild West exhibition. By 1900 Cody had toured the United States and Europe for nearly two decades; he had performed before Queen Victoria and paraded royalty in his Deadwood stagecoach; he had upstaged the Chicago World's Fair, bringing some four million guests to his own exhibition outside the fairgrounds; he had been the subject of countless dime novels and his media machine had inaugurated a new era in mass culture marketing. By century's end millions could identify Cody by his face alone, meaning that millions could *read* the message encoded in the image of Buffalo Bill and assign to it a sweeping narrative that places the American frontier at the center of civilization's progress.

The Life of Hon. William F. Cody, Known as Buffalo Bill is the story of what came before, of the events and experiences that provided the foundation for an image of the American West that would go national and then global in the decades that followed its publication. William Cody's story dramatizes the invention of Buffalo Bill and the relationship between his public and private selves as the author saw them. Along the way we learn how the narrative of frontier and civilization evolved into Buffalo Bill's Wild West, one of the most popular traveling exhibitions in entertainment history. Written when Cody was thirty-three years old, *The Life* recounts his early childhood removal with his family to Kansas Territory, where his father, Isaac Cody, hoped to homestead. It details the deep personal consequences of the "slavery question," which would leave his family fatherless and destitute. From the moment of his father's death, when Cody was just eleven years old, his autobiography recounts a classic American narrative of self-making with a central focus on a life of work. From teamster to trapper, to Buffalo hunter, Army scout, guide, and Indian fighter, Cody's life is a succession of jobs that lead cumulatively to the persona he put forth on both stage and showground for over forty years and across two continents.

Cody's autobiography joined him with contemporaries Frederick Jackson Turner and Teddy Roosevelt in transforming the American frontier into what Richard Slotkin describes as "a *mythic space* [that] began to outweigh its importance as a real place." For these men the frontier became "a set of symbols that *constituted* an explanation of history."[2] The pages of Cody's autobiography draw repeatedly on a frontier iconography that was well-established when he wrote it. The images of Indian fights, buffalo hunting, and the Pony Express reflect popular conceptions of the West. And yet, Cody also anchors his broader popular history in the life of the plains as he experienced it. It is this movement between the personal and the mythic, between plain facts and tall tales—between William F. Cody and Buffalo Bill—that gives this narrative its fascination and its power.

Cody's West

William Cody's seventy-one years were a time of accelerating change in America, and he found himself in the midst of many of the era's most defining events. Like the ever-shifting boundary of the American frontier, Cody's life was characterized by frenetic movement. Among the genres it draws upon, his story is a travel narrative that takes us to a dizzying number of frontier locations. Cody's travel chapters convey the sheer openness that overwhelmed many of the early settlers to the region; much of Kansas, Nebraska, Wyoming, Colorado, and South Dakota lacked geographic markers such as mountain ranges or a coastline, and human settlement was so sparse that Cody could ride for days without encountering any sign of civilization. Although Cody never seems to be lost, GPS-dependent twenty-first-century readers might find their sense of location challenged by the wide-ranging journeys that Cody undertook to explore, hunt, and scout the Great Plains. Like the physical map of the plains, the political map reflected the dynamism of the mid-nineteenth-century frontier. The federal government officially opened Kansas and Nebraska for settlement in 1854;

they became states in 1861 and 1868, respectively. Cody grew up in a place and period that, like Cody himself, was in the process of self-creation. Communities could appear practically overnight and, as Cody would learn from painful experience, in some cases disappear just as quickly.

The phenomenon of westward expansion marked every aspect of Cody's life. In his narrative's opening chapters Cody registers a level of disorientation in the period following passage of the Nebraska-Kansas Act. The law opened the territories for new settlement, it advanced the prospects of the Transcontinental Railroad, and it brought the slavery debate to the western frontier. The Cody family would find their own lives profoundly influenced by all of these factors. While the local population was exploding (white settlers increased by more than ten-fold in the year following passage of the act), nearby Leavenworth was also the throughway to virtually all points west. Although westward migration had declined from its Gold Rush peak in 1849 and 1850, thousands continued to pass through on the Mormon and California Trails en route to the Rocky Mountains and the west coast. Early in his narrative Cody captures his childhood wonder at the sensory chaos of one of the great westbound wagon trains with "wild" cattle, fifteen yokes to a wagon, and the "bull-whips sounding like gun-shots."[3] The Codys found themselves among "rough people" as they tried to negotiate a social and economic environment in constant flux. His family would never find its footing.

The challenges of economic and social transition were subsumed in violent political conflict as the principle of popular sovereignty was applied to the slavery question. Cody's childhood Kansas was made up of homesteads and communities organized along ideological lines. The region was polarized between Free Staters and settlers, primarily from Missouri, who sought to make Kansas a slave state. The upheaval and violence that rocked 1850s Kansas came to a head in 1861 with the Civil War. Although Cody would eventually enlist and serve as a conventional soldier in the Union Army, he first joined a militia group known as the Jayhawkers and later the Red Legs. These guerillas relied on the sale of looted goods to support their enterprise as they fought against pro-slavery militias in Kansas and Missouri. The mixture of revenge and economic opportunism motivating this war on the margins tended to obscure the more clearly defined political imperatives of the national conflict. Even anti-slavery Kansans questioned the Jayhawkers, seeing their motives and means as contributing to a general culture of lawlessness. Cody's mother intervened as a voice of conscience, convincing him to abandon the "jay-hawking enterprise" and urging him to acknowledge, at least indirectly, that "it was neither honorable nor right."[4] Cody's paramilitary career, though short-lived, exemplifies the sometimes morally gray environment of midcentury frontier life.

The Civil War ended the sectional strife over national union, but military conflict remained a dominant fact of life in the territories. With the end of the war, many Americans saw the Plains Indians as the only remaining check on the fulfillment of their Manifest Destiny: the continued expansion of white settlements to the Pacific coast. To address this challenge the United States redeployed its military; those Union soldiers not left to occupy the South were sent west to "pacify" the Plains tribes. The Indian wars continued over the next two decades and ended with the massacre at Wounded Knee in 1890. While sectional conflict brought suffering and hardship to Cody, the U.S. conflict with Plains Indians would provide him, directly and indirectly, with a livelihood for the remainder of his life. By the early 1870s Cody had participated in numerous pitched battles with Cheyenne and Sioux fighters primarily in his role as a military scout.

Cody's scouting career also corresponded with the rise of a mass culture industry that could popularize his alter ego as a dime novel hero. The first novel to feature Buffalo Bill was published serially in 1869. *Buffalo Bill, the King of the Border Men* was written by Edward Zane Carroll Judson under the pen name "Ned Buntline." A story of adventure and revenge in which Buffalo Bill and Wild Bill Hickok team up to defeat a gang of "border ruffians," the novel, which was serialized in *New York Weekly,* initiated the process of making Buffalo Bill a household name. The mass production and distribution of Buffalo Bill published works, along with a series of popular touring melodramas that began in 1872, prepared the way for the Wild West exhibition. By the time Buffalo Bill's Wild West began touring in 1883, Cody's brand was well-established. His legend continued to expand with the emergent myth-making machinery of commercial capitalism, and he remained at the forefront of marketing innovation through much of his life.

Working the Frontier

Cody's working life began at age ten herding cattle for the freighting firm of Majors and Russell (and later Waddell). In key ways this first job established the trajectory for the remainder of his career: it was a nomadic life that put him on horseback. Upon his father's death in 1857, Cody "determined to follow the plains" as a means of supporting himself and his family.[5] He worked for government freighters in various capacities off and on for the next seven years, by which time he was a thoroughly experienced plainsman. He cultivated his skills as a horseman, hunter, and tracker, and these talents were in ample demand in the rapidly developing economy of frontier Kansas.

Cody, like his father, was an indefatigable entrepreneur. He tried unsuccessfully to found a town and manage an inn, both counterintuitive given his acknowledged "restless" tendencies. The two occupations in which he excelled also had the most direct bearing upon his future celebrity: buffalo hunter and military scout. Both activities placed him within the two principle prongs of the country's empire-building enterprise: the extension of the railroad and the Indian Wars. Cody was involved in the work that inspired his nickname for a mere eighteen months. Beginning in 1868 he was hired by a railroad contractor to hunt buffalo as food for the 1,200 workers laying track across Kansas. He later claimed to have killed 4,280 buffalo during that span while developing a reputation as a uniquely skilled marksman from horseback. That reputation was amplified by Cody's participation in a "buffalo-killing contest" against a rival hunter named Billy Comstock. At stake was five hundred dollars, bragging rights to the "championship of the world" (as one promotional bill allegedly declared), and, possibly, the right to use the name "Buffalo Bill." Cody, atop a horse named Brigham and carrying a .50-caliber needle gun named "Lucretia Borgia," claimed victory with 69 kills. The action took place, according to Cody, before a crowd of spectators, including military men from the nearby post who had sponsored the event and tourists from St. Louis. Cody's version of the contest foreshadows the fusion of frontier experience and performance that eventually defined his career: here was an opportunity to exhibit authentic frontier skills before a rapt audience. In this moment the reader sees Cody the showman for the first time claiming to have "raised the excitement" among the spectators to a "fever heat" by choosing to ride to victory without saddle or bridle.[6]

Cody anchors his mythology in buffalo hunting, but his alter ego depended to a much greater extent on his encounters with Plains Indians. In the autobiography Cody first assumes the title "Indian killer" in 1857, at the age of eleven. It is the originating moment in his path to celebrity. On his first journey across the plains as a cattle-herder, Cody's group is beset by Natives and he saves the others from ambush by shooting an attacker. "From that time forward, I became a hero and an Indian killer."[7] This simple declaration establishes the central rhetorical pattern that shapes the remainder of his personal narrative: the confrontation with Indians as the gold standard of frontier heroism. Cody cites an account of the incident in a Leavenworth newspaper that describes him as "the youngest Indian slayer on the plains."[8] Cody infuses the experience with a consciousness-shaping power: "I am candid enough to admit that I felt very much elated over this notoriety. Again and again I read with eager interest the long and sensational account of our adventure."[9] Though one might look for a sense of irony in these reflections, Cody consistently depicts Indian killing as a heroic tableau throughout his autobiography. He reiterates various versions of this primal scene and threads the heroic strand through each phase of his career, most notably with his accounts of the killings of the Indian chiefs Tall Bull and Yellow Hair.

Buffalo Bill was a product of war, and William Cody found ways to commercialize his experience in war like no American before or since. The adversarial phase of Cody's relationship to the Plains Indians culminated during the Great Sioux War in

1876. It was the army's largest military effort since the end of the Civil War, with the conflict spreading over 120,000 miles of western territory and lasting fourteen months.[10] The sensation caused by news of General Custer's defeat at the Battle of the Little Bighorn in late June afforded Cody the ideal platform to stage his most climactic performance of frontier heroism. His participation in the Skirmish at Warbonnet Creek the following month, in which he killed and scalped a Cheyenne chief named Yellow Hair, blurred the lines between Cody's life as a scout and his stage persona. Having embarked on the expedition in full theater costume, Cody ensured that his version of the event was published in newspapers. He also commissioned a play, titled *The Red Right Hand; or, Buffalo Bill's First Scalp for Custer.* In production by the end of that year, the play featured a reenactment in which Cody brandished actual relics from the incident, including his enemy's scalp. Cody's opportunism drew upon Custer's celebrity to enhance his own, while providing him with the raw materials to substantiate his claim as the most genuine frontiersman on the American stage.

Cody's stories of Indian combat reinforce the authenticity of his narrative but depended heavily on many accepted conventions of popular culture. As an army scout Cody was directly involved in numerous combat situations, and yet his depiction of those experiences follows a familiar pattern. His frequent encounters tend to be sudden, preceded by little or no context and followed by fight or chase scenes in which Cody extols the virtues of his horse and displays a special cunning that allow him to triumph or escape. The affinities with stock dime novel plots are unmistakable. Cody parrots the most clichéd language, crowing after one episode in particular, that he and his companions have killed "five 'good' Indians, that is[,] dead ones."[11] These one-dimensional renderings of a military and cultural foe belong to a long tradition in frontier writing that began with the earliest Puritan accounts of confrontations with Native peoples. Descriptions of unprovoked attacks on innocent settlers galvanized readers' sympathies and helped justify the colonizing mission of early European immigrants.[12] By eliding the broader context of territorial issues, treaty violations, and white provocations, Cody concentrates the narrative lens on himself and his reactions to an innately hostile environment.

While simple oppositions govern much of the text, Cody's relationship with Natives is not exclusively adversarial. Trading with the Kickapoo tribe of eastern Kansas provided his father with an economic foothold when the family first arrived in the territory. William Cody writes that he was "much interested" to meet a "real live Indian," and that he spent time among the Kickapoo, "looking about and studying their habits."[13] He even suggests that his primary playmates in Kansas were the Indian boys whose language he learned and who taught him to shoot with a bow and arrow.[14] Cody represents himself as an ethnographer, *studying* the native language and customs of these "friendly Indians." Trade and intercultural exploration became the basis for peaceful social relations in this earliest episode. The scene culminates in a "grand barbecue" hosted by Isaac Cody and attended by two hundred Kickapoos, who treat the white settlers to a performance of one of their "grand fantastic war dances."[15] In the end Cody recollects that the Indians "returned to their homes well satisfied." The episode initiates a secondary theme in Cody's depiction of the Indians that provides a subtext for combat scenes as well: exhibition. Later, Cody concludes his account of the 1869 battle of Summit Springs, in which U.S. Army and Pawnee scout battalions attacked and looted a Cheyenne village, with an appraisal of the "curiosities" amounting to "enough to start twenty museums."[16] This preservationist impulse—Cody as curator—literally at the scene of destruction is one of many ironies that typify his own view of Manifest Destiny, and American expansionism more generally. Cody would later incorporate these adversarial and ethnographic themes into the structure of Buffalo Bill's Wild West by simultaneously staging battles such as "Custer's Last Stand" and the Indian encampment outside the arena, which allowed guests to wander through the authentic reproduction of an Indian village before and after the performance.

Cody's autobiography also emphasizes the role of male mentors in shaping his identity. His impulse to imitate these figures, beginning with his cousin Horace Billings, seems to inspire his development at key stages of his career. Billings offers Cody one of his first experiences in what he calls "practical education," which he contrasts favorably against his brief episodes of formal instruction. Billings embodies the ideal of the restless and independent cowboy, and his horsemanship inspires Cody's first statement of personal ambition: he vows "to become as skillful a horseman" as his "magnificent looking" cousin.[17] Cody's early hero worship anticipates his most formative relationship—his friendship with Wild Bill Hickok—which inspires his ascendance to mainstream middle-class entertainer. Cody makes much of this association, presenting Hickok as a friend, protector, and mentor from early adolescence. Early in the narrative Cody casts Hickok as a romantic hero through his version of an encounter with an outlaw gang. Cody emphasizes his affinities with Hickok to such a degree that it seems a natural fit when the two eventually perform together in a touring Western melodrama. But Hickok's rough edges, including habitual gambling and brawling, undercut his career as a performer, and Cody appears genteel by contrast, a more acceptable, and, ultimately, marketable, version of frontier manhood.[18]

Cody's Auto-American-Biography[19]

After attending a performance of Buffalo Bill's Wild West in 1884, Mark Twain wrote Cody a letter:

> I have seen your Wild West show two days in succession, and have enjoyed it thoroughly. It brought vividly back the breezy wild life of the Great Plains and the Rocky Mountains, and stirred me like a war-song. Down to its smallest details, the show is genuine . . . it is wholly free from sham and insincerity and the effects produced upon me by its spectacles were identical to those wrought upon me a long time ago by the same spectacles on the frontier.[20]

Twain's enthusiasm for the Wild West reflects his sense of shared experience with Cody as well as a deep nostalgia. He had left his home state of Missouri in 1861 to travel and work in the West. After a failed attempt at mining, he worked as a newspaper writer in Nevada and California. Twain's time on the frontier provided the material for one of his earliest works, the semi-autobiographical *Roughing It* (1872), and a number of short stories.[21] Cody and his associates immediately saw to it that Twain's admiring words were reprinted in the newspaper and incorporated into the show's ongoing publicity machine. It was the kind of authorization that was essential to the show's carefully cultivated image; *Wild West* marketing materials consistently shunned the word "show" in favor of "exhibition" to both distance it from lowbrow entertainments and emphasize its educational value. Twain's imprimatur could be viewed as a sign of arrival for a performance that first took formal shape in the autobiography. Both the Wild West and *The Life* consist of narratives that depend on the seamless conjunction of original and reproduction, the paradox of authentic imitation. The appeal of the Buffalo Bill mythology depended on a vivid sense of realism and an ability to convince readers and live audiences that it represented lived experience. Both print and performance stretched images of frontier life across the broadest possible canvas by offering those images as representative of an *essentially* American experience. At the end of his letter, Twain gestures to this possibility when he urges Cody to take the Wild West to Europe, where he might counter British claims about the derivative nature of American culture by presenting something that is "purely and distinctly American." Cody, citing the "repeated suggestions of prominent persons of America" as inspiration, proved Twain right in 1887, when he took the exhibition to London and enjoyed one of the most celebrated and lucrative runs of his career.[22]

Mark Twain's intense nostalgia for the "breezy wild life of the Great Plains" points to another pervasive theme found in the autobiography: the preservation, through narrative, of a vanishing way of life. Twain precisely identifies Cody's formula for success in suggesting that the Wild West embodies an aspect of American life that is both exceptional and ephemeral. Twain was familiar with this dynamic as a founder of American literary regionalism. The regional writing that flourished during the last third of the nineteenth century emphasized local culture through distinct dialect, landscape, and folkways. The 1879 edition of *The Life* was illustrated by True Williams, who provided the art for a number of Twain's novels. Both the visual and verbal portraits in Cody's narrative reflect American regionalism's interest in the ways that material conditions shape individual and communal identity. In his account of his "Boy Days in Kansas" Cody recalls the heady period of early land settlement in Kansas. He describes Missouri emigrants rushing over the border to stake land with whisky bottles—first drinking the whisky and then driving their bottles into the ground to mark their claims. Cody peppers his narrative with such concrete details that vividly evoke the frontier experience.

Like Cody's entertainment career, this "local color" writing depended on a contradiction in terms: a modern mass culture system of production, distribution, and consumption *and* an appreciation for the local culture threatened by the homogenizing influence of that very system. Cody's autobiography, and later his Wild West, exemplifies this logic in the countless ways it foregrounds a distinct culture of the plains. The narrative points to this dynamic directly in the account of his buffalo-hunting work for the Kansas railroad workers. When the Codys first arrived in Kansas Territory the United States contained some twenty thousand miles of railroad track, primarily in the eastern states. As he reached adulthood, railroad building accelerated and pushed west, eventually covering nearly half a million miles of American landscape at the peak of Cody's career. While in Cody's story the railroad signifies progress and mobility, it also serves as a stark reminder that coming changes will render obsolete many aspects of plains life he celebrates.

The "Introductory" to the first edition of the autobiography offers this description from the book's publisher, Frank Bliss: "The life and adventures of Hon. William F. Cody—Buffalo Bill—as told by himself, make up a narrative which reads more like a romance than reality."[23] Bliss claims that "in many respects" the work "will prove a valuable contribution to the records of our Western frontier history."[24] He goes on to promote *The Life* for its high adventure while insisting the story is based on Cody's lived experience. That promise (and disclaimer) of documentary truth mixed with sensationalism sheds light on the version of the frontier mythology that Cody formalized with his autobiography. The narrative's blend of romance and realism interweaves material details with a standardized adventure script that was fast becoming the primary grist in a fledgling American popular culture. Even as it played to popular taste, the autobiography was Cody's most systematic and complete attempt to assemble the various parts of his past in the service of his present public identity. By 1879 Cody was working on the stage and no longer having genuine frontier experiences. *The Life* is a formal summation, a codification of authentic frontier selfhood, and therefore a platform from which to pursue the next phase of his career, one that would complete the transition from original frontiersman to onstage simulator.

William Cody's construction of an American "type" began with a successful use of established genres. The autobiography places Cody within the longest-standing and richest tradition in American literary culture. In what would eventually be the standard for all American autobiographies to come, Benjamin Franklin opens his memoir with a striking remark when he compares his actual life to his life story. Franklin tells the reader that, "the Thing most like living one's Life over again, seems to be the *Recollection* of that Life; and to make that Recollection as durable as possible, the putting it down in Writing."[25] Franklin acknowledges that he hopes to recount a life "fit to be imitated." He suggests that if he had the chance he would choose to live his life over again, reserving the option to "correct" some errors in the second edition. Being denied the opportunity, he settles for the next best thing: the recollection. Franklin's comparison of his actual self to his created persona reflects on the nature of all life writing. Franklin and popular nineteenth-century autobiographers such as Frederick Douglass and P. T. Barnum were engaged in crafting their own versions of American citizenship and manhood. As a cultural project, subsequent autobiographies may rework Franklin's typology but they continue to place the self at the center of a representative American story. In *The Life* Cody imagines himself from the raw materials of his memory while also drawing on the context of the mid-century frontier to give his experiences historical significance. Like Franklin, Cody offers a surrogate of himself, a performance-in-writing that aims foremost to create the impression of authenticity.

Although Franklin's work, first published in 1818, casts a long shadow over the nineteenth century, a more immediate and perhaps more kindred story can be found in Barnum's bestselling *Life of P. T. Barnum*, published in 1854. Both Barnum and Cody aptly begin their autobiographies with the metaphor of birth as entrance onto a stage. Though Barnum was a generation older than Cody, the men's careers ran parallel and, at times, directly converged, as they worked to shape an emerging mass culture. Like Cody, Barnum wrote his autobiography at a relatively young age (Barnum was forty-five, Cody was thirty-three) and, like Cody's, Barnum's *Life* promoted a public persona that advanced a larger business enterprise. Whereas Franklin's narrative provides moral instruction, offering maxims in the wake of his lapses—"nothing [is] useful which [is] not honest"—and attributing success to conscientious application of social virtues, Barnum candidly recounts questionable behavior without a similar didactic framework.[26] His portrait of the American Dream's darker side shows him thriving in a culture of deception. Cody's autobiography navigates a middle ground between Franklin's moralism and Barnum's parody to produce a narrative uniquely suited to late nineteenth-century American sensibilities. Like his predecessors, he candidly acknowledges his failings but identifies them with the culture of the frontier. He counters indecorous images of brawling and drunkenness by displaying the frontier virtues of friendship, loyalty, and bravery, demonstrating these qualities through competition. In essence the autobiography is a series of dramatic set pieces that pit Cody against a variety of opponents. On the one hand he triumphs over civilization's putative enemies through battles with Indians and confrontations with outlaws; on the other he bests his peers through contests such as hunting, shooting, and horseracing. Each incident adds to Cody's bona fides as a frontiersman while at the same time evoking the larger story of America's westward development as a quest for national identity.

A prominent Victorian biographer once stated that autobiography is valuable "in proportion to the amount of misrepresentation it contains."[27] The excesses of Cody's self-dramatization offer as much insight into the man and his context as the "factual" details do. Cody operates securely within the American autobiographical tradition by fashioning an archetype out of his individual and composite experience. Consequently, some events in the narrative may never have happened, others likely happened to someone else, while still others that occurred are either exaggerated or understated. In recent years Cody's biographers have attempted to reconcile Cody's narrative with the historical record, noting the moments when he takes license with his life story. A close examination has shown, for instance, that Cody's claim that he worked for the Pony Express is questionable. Some of the most sensational episodes in the narrative, including encounters with Mormon "Danites" and Indians on the warpath while lying helpless with a broken leg, are also suspect.[28] Cody's style in relating these incidents echoes the language and structure of the popular dime novels which had made his heroic exploits their subject for nearly a decade before he began writing his *actual* story. Cody's adoption of the stilted dialogue and rhetorical flourish characteristic of these westerns to recount some of his more exotic episodes is one indicator that he is drawing on frontier experiences beyond his own. In one of his most dramatic encounters, the dual with Yellow Hair, Cody's version seems more akin to the account in his stage melodrama, *The Red Right Hand, or Buffalo Bill's First Scalp for Custer*, which he commissioned and performed in 1876 after his participation in the events it purported to be dramatizing.[29] Cody's incorporation of popular genres enables him to use a narrative vocabulary already understood by a large readership while at the same time making his story more broadly representative. The autobiography incorporates the expected conventions of dime novels and stage melodramas but also adds a new dimension of realism to the rapidly expanding Buffalo Bill mythology.

The investigative work conducted by Cody scholars is important to a historical understanding of Cody the man. It reveals a dynamic, established early in his career, in which Cody's individual experience and the larger life of his community become fused. In one sense his autobiography, like all life writing, is a creative act, a work of imagination. As he attempts to give shape and meaning to his experiences, he inevitably prioritizes some events over others; he finds significance in events he may not have appreciated at the time; and he presents himself as the central character in a panorama that touches many elements of a broader cultural history.

Cody's version of his life expresses a double vision, or an attempt to interpret his particular past as a representative American experience. He assigns cultural significance to personal experience as far as his understanding allows and in the process offers a form of living American history. For all its excesses, though, Cody's life story nevertheless demonstrates his intimate understanding of the frontier he so successfully mythologized. Indeed, to paraphrase the first edition's publisher, without his "real" life as fuel he could never have produced the "romance" he shared with millions. Every word of the autobiography offers insight into William F. Cody the man while also providing singular access to Buffalo Bill the image and phenomenon. In this sense the autobiography is as much about the future as it is about the past. It establishes who Cody would be, as a public figure, for the rest of his life and for generations of Americans and Europeans who came to interpret American history and the American West through the lens of Buffalo Bill.

A NOTE ON THE TEXT

The authorship of this autobiography has been a source of debate since its first publication in 1879. The fact that other works, namely dime novels, were attributed to Cody but were, in fact, penned by others, has led some to assume that *The Life of Hon. William F. Cody* was ghostwritten as well. The most thorough examination of this question was conducted by Don Russell for the 1978 Bison Books reprint of the autobiography. Russell systematically considers each of the most likely authors and demonstrates why, based on biographical details, none is a credible candidate. He then addresses what he terms "internal evidence," including writing style and diction, to argue that Cody was the exclusive author and concludes that, "the book is about as accurate as most autobiographies written from memory, unchecked by notes or records."[1] This assessment is too general and, probably, too generous. While some of Russell's conclusions about the book's accuracy have been subsequently corrected by more rigorous historical investigation, a consensus has emerged over authorship. Cody's most recent biographer, Louis Warren, demonstrates that *The Life* is "full of what we know to be Cody's own phrasing and tone," leading Warren to conclude that if Cody "did not write it, he dictated it."[2] This judgment does not apply to subsequent editions that appeared during Cody's lifetime. Whatever the degree of editorial intervention in the first edition, intermediaries took a much more active hand in the many versions that appeared between 1879 and 1920.

This edition is based on the original 1879 edition published by Frank Bliss. Without the benefit of a handwritten manuscript, it is impossible to know when printer's errors were introduced into the text. However, obvious printer's errors such as stray punctuation marks have been silently corrected. In addition, silent emendations have been made when typographical and spelling errors are a matter of consistency or when such errors affect clarity. This rule applies to misspelled names when the referent is clear and correction is possible. Misleading punctuation is also corrected when the meaning is not in doubt; this particularly applies to the use of commas and em dashes. A number of idiosyncrasies have been preserved to maintain the character of the document. These include gray areas in terms of unusual spellings and variant spellings such as compound words that are alternately separated, hyphenated, or one word.

Like the autobiography, most of the materials in the appendixes are machine-created documents. The only exceptions are Cody's letters to his sister Julia and wife, Louisa (appendix 2). Although original page breaks are not identified, the transcription of the letters is otherwise literal, even when lack of terminal punctuation and capitalization undermines readability. As a comparison of Cody's letters makes clear, the level of clarity and coherence seems to reflect his emotional state at the time a letter is written. While spelling and punctuation are irregular in the newspaper sample (appendix 3), they do not constitute a hindrance to readability, so transcription has remained literal for these materials as well. Attempts to reproduce varieties of type have been limited to the use of capitalization and italics to show emphasis.

Although William Cody's autobiography has remained continuously in print since 1879, later iterations have consisted primarily of abridgements or reprints, including Russell's 1978 edition. The aim of this edited volume has been to bring the autobiography to a wider and more varied audience. The quantity and specificity of the annotations in this edition reflect an awareness of the needs of a general audience. It is meant to strike a balance that contextualizes and clarifies the text without engaging specialized scholarly debates. The appendixes include representative samples of primary materials from Cody's early life and career. Headnotes offer general historical and thematic contextualization and suggest the potential significance of the material. While publishing parameters limit the extent of the appendixes, the photographs, letters, press coverage, and other samples should suggest the rich range of archival materials available at the Buffalo Bill Historical Center and at other collections as well.

ACKNOWLEDGMENTS

The legacy of William F. Cody is in good hands thanks to a cohort of committed professionals, many of whom lent their generous gifts to this project.

Kurt Graham originated the idea for the The Papers of William F. "Buffalo Bill" Cody series and found in University of Nebraska Press a more than able partner to materialize the project. He also recruited me to join the editorial team and provided astute oversight at each stage, helping to guide this project through to successful completion. His visionary leadership made this volume and the series possible.

This edition would not have been possible without the staff and resources of the Buffalo Bill Historical Center, the McCracken Research Library, and the Cody Institute for Western American Studies in Cody, Wyoming. The most valuable resource on the project was not an archive or a special collection; rather, it was Linda Clark, assistant editor of The Papers of William F. Cody. Her surefooted editorial skills sharpened every aspect of the manuscript and her formidable knowledge of the McCracken Research Library's holdings brought to light many of the key documents in the appendixes. The managing editor, Jeremy Johnston, offered insightful analysis of significant elements of the manuscript. In its later stages the edition also benefited from the research and feedback of research assistants Gary

Boyce and Deborah Adams. Lynn Houze, curatorial assistant at the Buffalo Bill Museum in Cody, also lent her considerable expertise in reviewing annotations. The generous support of the Buffalo Bill Historical Center helped defray a portion of the production costs.

Most of the images included in this volume were drawn from the archives of the Buffalo Bill Historical Center with the help of Mack Frost, the McCracken's digital services technician. However, a number of key images came from other archives. I am grateful for the generous assistance of the staffs at these various institutions, including Mary-Jo Miller at the Nebraska State Historical Society, Jim Fisher at Yale's Beinecke Library, and Coi Drummond-Gehrig at the Denver Public Library. Steve Freisen, director of the Buffalo Bill Museum and Grave in Golden, Colorado, was a great help in providing images of Cody's young family.

In 2009 I attended the Institute for the Editing of Historical Documents sponsored by the National Historical and Publication Records Commission and the Wisconsin Historical Society. The seminar, run by John Kaminski and his staff, offered valuable training in all aspects of the documentary editing process. My experience in Madison has informed each stage of this project.

Heather Lundine, editor in chief at the University of Nebraska Press, caught the vision of the Cody Papers from the start and saw the role of Cody's autobiographical writing within the series. With the help of Bridget Barry, associate acquisitions editor, she steered the project through to timely completion with consummate professionalism. Ann Baker oversaw the copyediting and production stages with care and insight, making this a more presentable volume in the process.

The Brigham Young University College of Humanities under

Dean John Rosenberg and the BYU English Department under chair Ed Cutler provided travel support and research mentoring grants that enabled a number of bright and motivated students to work on the project. The time and efforts of Sarah Campbell, Dave Fife, Hayley Hucks, Kristin Lowe, Ben Miller, and Amy Takabori contributed significantly to the quality of the finished product. Students in my 2010 senior seminar on the frontier in American literature coupled patience and intellectual curiosity in equal parts as I led them through my reading and thinking on this project. In the process the world gained a few new Cody enthusiasts. Dr. Mark Jackson and his research assistant, Thalassa Jones, of the BYU Geosciences and Technology Library, researched and designed the original maps. I am indebted to the Charles Redd Center for Western Studies for a research travel grant.

As always, my wife, Stace, and daughters, Quinn, Teal, and Maggie, provided the most meaningful support, the kind that puts my work in its rightful place alongside the big stuff.

WILLIAM F. CODY'S LIFE:
A CHRONOLOGY

1804–1805 Lewis and Clark's Corps of Discovery expedition charts the Louisiana Purchase of 1803.

1820 The Missouri Compromise becomes law; it divides the land acquired by the Louisiana Purchase into two territories: the north outlawing slavery and the south permitting slavery.

1830 Congress passes the Indian Removal Act, which moved a majority of eastern tribes west of the Mississippi River.

1846 February 26: William F. Cody born to Isaac and Mary Ann Laycock Cody at the family's farmhouse in Scott County, near LeClaire, Iowa.

1847 Mormons begin settling in Salt Lake Valley, Utah.

1849 The California Gold Rush brings 50,000 people west.

1851 The Treaty of Fort Laramie is signed, giving the United States permission to build roads and forts in Indian Territory in exchange for annuity payments to tribes.

1854 Majors and Russell organize a leading western freighting company (which later becomes Russell, Majors, and Waddell). The Nebraska-Kansas Bill becomes law, giving the territories power to determine the legality of slavery by popular sovereignty.

1855 Free-staters' constitutional convention takes place in Kansas; the Topeka Constitution is passed.

1853 Older brother, Samuel, dies after falling from a horse.

1854 Family relocates to Kansas.

1857 Father, Isaac Cody, dies.

1857–1859 Hired by freighting firm Russell, Majors, and Waddell in Kansas; serves on wagon trains and cattle drives.

1860 Russell, Majors, and Waddell organize the Pony Express using riders whose average age is nineteen. The service lasts just eighteen months, being made obsolete by the first transcontinental telegraph line.

1861 Kansas becomes a state.

1861–1865 Civil War.

1862 Congress passes the Homestead and Pacific Railroad acts, which grant Indian land to whites in order to clear the way for a transcontinental railroad.

1860 Claims to have traveled to Colorado to try his luck as a prospector in the Pike's Peak gold rush. Later that year claims to have ridden for the Pony Express at the age of fifteen.

1863 Mother, Mary Ann Laycock Cody, dies.

1864 The Sand Creek Massacre involves an attack on Cheyenne and Arapaho villagers by Colorado Territorial militia.

1864 Enlists in the Seventh Kansas Volunteer Cavalry, known as Jennison's Jayhawkers.

1867 Nebraska becomes a state.

1868 The second Fort Laramie Treaty creates the Great Sioux Reservation; the Lakota are guaranteed the Black Hills region and the Powder River Country in north central Wyoming is closed to white settlement. The treaty ends Red Cloud's War.

1869 The transcontinental railroad is completed. Battle of Summit Springs, Colorado: Fifth Cavalry defeats Cheyennes led by Tall Bull.

1871 Introduction of commercial tanning expands possible commercial uses for buffalo hides.

1866 Marries Louisa Frederici on March 6 in St. Louis and continues to work as an army scout out of Fort Ellsworth, Kansas. Daughter Arta Lucille is born.

1867–1868 Acquires the name "Buffalo Bill" while under contract to provide buffalo meat for Kansas railroad workers. Later claims to have killed 4,280 buffalo during his eighteen-month employment.

1868–1872 Employed as a scout and guide for the U.S. Cavalry, most notably as chief of scouts for the Fifth Cavalry. Takes part in numerous battles including the Battle of Summit Springs, in which he claims to have killed Chief Tall Bull.

1869 Ned Buntline's book, *Buffalo Bill, the King of the Border Men*, is published—the first of more than 550 different dime novels about Buffalo Bill.

1870 Son, Kit Carson, is born.

1872 Receives the Medal of Honor for "gallantry in action" while serving as a civilian scout for the Third Cavalry. Daughter Orra Maude is born. Guides buffalo hunting party and arranges Indian entertainment for Grand Duke Alexis of Russia. Begins eleven-season stage career by playing himself in a melodrama of frontier life, called *Scouts of the Prairie*.

1873 Forms the "Buffalo Bill Combination," a traveling theatrical troupe, with Wild Bill Hickok and Texas Jack Omohundro; confines his scouting to the summer months.

1874 Gold is discovered in the Black Hills tribal area, leading to treaty violations and renewed tensions.

1875 Family lives in Rochester, New York, while Cody travels with the Combination.

1876 The Sioux, under Sitting Bull, and the Cheyennes, under Two Moon, defeat Custer and his troops in June at the Battle of the Little Bighorn, Montana ("Custer's Last Stand"). The Skirmish at Warbonnet Creek takes place several weeks later.

1876 Returns to service as an army scout in the campaign that followed Custer's defeat at the Little Bighorn. July 17: Famous fight with Yellow Hair (later mistranslated as "Yellow Hand"). April 20: Son Kit dies. Produces and stars in *Red Right Hand; or, Buffalo Bill's First Scalp for Custer*, which includes a dramatization of the Warbonnet Creek encounter.

1877 Sitting Bull and his Sioux followers take refuge in Canada.

1878 Indian-manned police forces are established by the U.S. government for supervision of reservations. The southern herd of buffalo nears extinction.

1878 Uses reservation Indians as actors in stage melodramas for the first time.

1879 Publishes *The Life of Hon. William F. Cody, Known as Buffalo Bill, the Famous Hunter, Scout and Guide: An Autobiography.*

1880 The Northern Pacific Railroad is completed.

1881 Artist Frederic Remington (1861–1909) makes his first trip to the West. *A Century of Dishonor*, an indictment of U.S. Indian policy by Helen Hunt Jackson, is published. Sitting Bull returns to the United States from Canada but the Army breaks its promise to grant a pardon, and instead holds him as a military prisoner.

1882 Organizes a Fourth of July celebration in North Platte, Nebraska. Later referred to as the "Old Glory Blowout," the event is a precursor to Buffalo Bill's Wild West.

1883 Sitting Bull participates in the last traditional buffalo hunt of the Sioux; the northern herd is now virtually extinct.

1883 Daughter Irma Louise is born. Stages first Wild West exhibition in Omaha, Nebraska, billed as "The Wild West, Hon. W. F. Cody and Dr. W. F. Carver's Rocky Mountain and Prairie Exhibition." Daughter Orra Maude dies.

1884 Annie Oakley joins the show as "Little Sure Shot;" except for 1888, she remains with the Wild West until 1901.

1885 Sitting Bull joins the Wild West for four months.

1886 Cody builds Scout's Rest Ranch in North Platte, Nebraska.

1887 Congress passes the Dawes Allotment Act, which divides reservation lands on a basis of 160 acres per head of family and results in the Indians' loss of more than three-quarters of their remaining land.

1887 The Wild West joins the American Exhibition at Queen Victoria's Jubilee in London. The show regularly tours Europe until 1906. The three European tours include 1887, 1889–1892, and 1902–1906. Governor of Nebraska bestows the title of colonel.

1889 The Sioux agree to sell nine million acres to the United States, carving the Great Sioux Reservation into six smaller reservations. Only 635 buffalo are reported to be running wild in all of North America.

1890 The Ghost Dance, a religious movement that originated with the Paiute prophet Wovoka, reaches the Sioux. It promises the disappearance of the white man and the return of the buffalo. On December 15 Sitting

Bull is shot and killed by Indian police attempting to arrest him. On December 29 more than 300 Sioux are massacred at Wounded Knee by the Seventh Cavalry. The Census Bureau reports the end of a continuous line of western settlement—the end of the frontier. Wyoming becomes a state.

1893 Frederick Jackson Turner presents his Frontier Thesis at the World's Columbian Exposition in Chicago.

1893 The Wild West show opens next to the World's Columbian Exposition in Chicago; the phrase "Congress of Rough Riders of the World" is introduced as part of the title of the exhibition.

1896 Founds town of Cody, Wyoming.

1898 Spanish-American war breaks out; Teddy Roosevelt leads his Rough Riders at the Battle of San Juan Hill.

1899 Sixteen of Roosevelt's Rough Riders join the Wild West and participate in a dramatization of the taking of San Juan Hill. Cody founds the *Cody Enterprise*, the town newspaper.

1900 Roosevelt becomes president after the assassination of William McKinley.

1902 Forms the Cody-Dyer Mining and Milling Company in Oracle, Arizona; loses much of his Wild West profits in the venture. Irma Hotel, named after daughter, opens in Cody.

1904 Daughter Arta dies.

1905 Sues his wife for divorce. Work begins on Shoshone Dam; renamed in 1946 as Buffalo Bill Dam.

1908 Merges Wild West with Pawnee Bill's Great Far East.

1917 The United States enters
World War I.

1910 Begins a series of farewell
appearances.

1913 The Wild West show goes
bankrupt. The Col. W. F. Cody
(Buffalo Bill) Historical Pictures
Company is formed to produce short
films on the Indian wars.

1914–1915 Travels with the Sells-
Floto Circus.

1916 Joins and makes his final
appearance with Miller Brothers
and Arlington 101 Ranch Wild
West; theme of show is military
preparedness.

1917 Dies on January 10, at age
seventy-one, in Denver, Colorado,
and is buried on Lookout Mountain.
Medal of Honor revoked on February
5, twenty-four days after his death,
because he was a civilian and
became ineligible for the award
under new guidelines. Buffalo Bill
Memorial Association founded.

1918 Daughter Irma Louise dies.

1921 Louisa Cody dies in Cody,
Wyoming.

1989 U.S. Army restores Medal of
Honor to Cody.

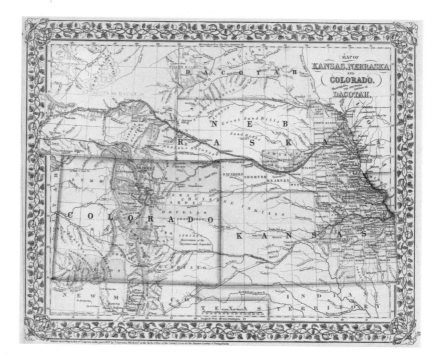

2. Map of Kansas, Nebraska, and Colorado (1867).
Nebraska State Historical Society.

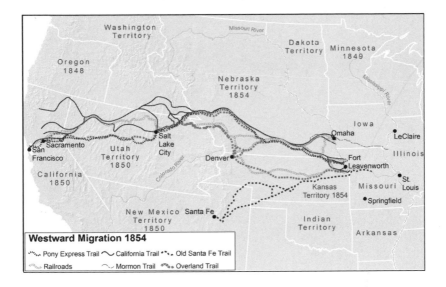

3. Westward Migration Routes, 1854.

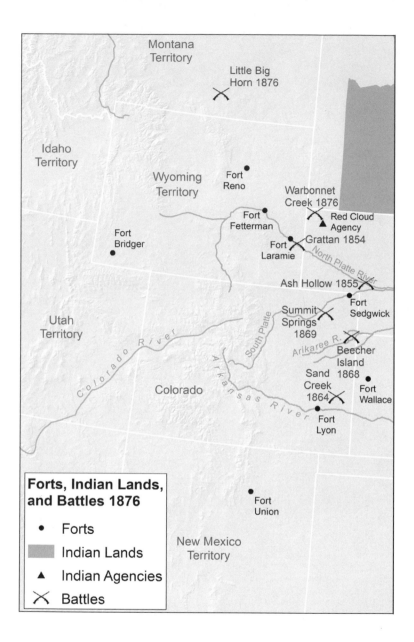

4. Map of military forts, Indian agencies, and key battles, 1854–1876.

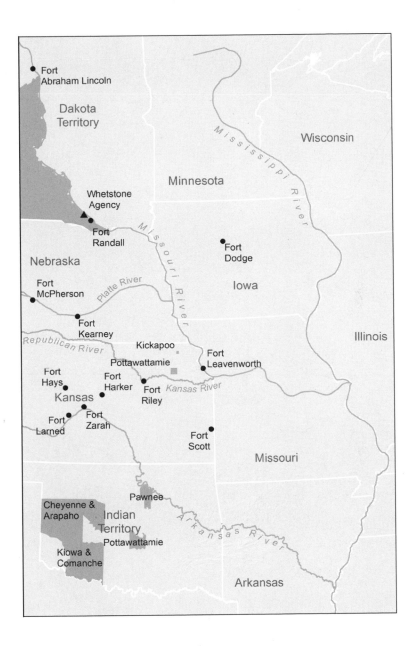

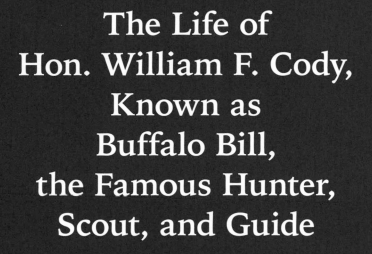

The Life of
Hon. William F. Cody,
Known as
Buffalo Bill,
the Famous Hunter,
Scout, and Guide

AN AUTOBIOGRAPHY, 1879

5. Yours Sincerely, W. F. Cody.

To General Philip H. Sheridan,
This Book Is Most Respectfully Dedicated
by the Author.

Headquarters Military Division of the Missouri,

Chicago. Aug 18th 1879.

My dear Cody,

I have read your books which sketches your life on the plains with much interest. So far as it relate to your intercourse with me I find it scrupulously correct. The scenes that you describe will not again be enacted in this country as the Indians are slowly giving way to civilization, and the railroads have made the exciting life of the mail rider and stage driver of the "overland route" a thing of the past, and books like yours; written as a record of actual daily life will eventually be of real service to the future historians of the country. I hope it will prove enough of a success to reimburse you for the time and trouble bestowed upon it

Very truly yours

P. H. Sheridan

Lieut Genl

to
Mr J Cody Esq

6. Letter from Sheridan

INTRODUCTORY

The life and adventures of Hon. William F. Cody—Buffalo Bill—as told by himself, make up a narrative which reads more like romance than reality, and which in many respects will prove a valuable contribution to the records of our Western frontier history. While no literary excellence is claimed for the narrative, it has the greater merit of being truthful, and is verified in such a manner that no one can doubt its veracity. The frequent reference to such military men as Generals Sheridan, Carr, Merritt, Crook, Terry, Colonel Royall, and other officers under whom Mr. Cody served as scout and guide at different times and in various sections of the frontier, during the numerous Indian campaigns of the last ten or twelve years, affords ample proof of his genuineness as a thoroughbred scout.

There is no humbug or braggadocio about Buffalo Bill. He is known far and wide, and his reputation has been earned honestly and by hard work. By a combination of circumstances he was educated to the life of a plainsman from his youth up; and not the least interesting portion of his career is that of his early life, passed as it was in Kansas during the eventful and troublous times connected with the settlement of that state. Spending much time in the saddle, while a mere boy he crossed the plains many times in company with bull-trains;[1] on some of these trips he met with thrilling adventures and had several hairbreadth escapes from death at the hands of Indians. Then, for a while, he was dashing over the plains as a pony-express rider. Soon afterwards, mounted on the high seat of an overland stagecoach, he was driving a six-in-hand team. We next hear of him cracking the bull-whacker's whip, and commanding a wagon-train through a wild and dangerous country to the far West. During the civil war he enlisted as a private and became a scout with the Union army; since the war he has been employed as hunter, trapper, guide, scout and actor. As a buffalo hunter he has no superior; as a trailer of Indians he has no equal. For many years he has taken an active part in all the principal Indian campaigns on the Western frontier, and as a scout and guide he has rendered inestimable services to the various expeditions which he accompanied.

During his life on the plains he not only had many exciting adventures himself, but he became associated with many of the other noted plainsmen, and in his narrative he frequently refers to them and relates many interesting incidents and thrilling events connected with them. He has had a fertile field from which to produce this volume, and has frequently found it necessary to condense the facts in order to embody the most interesting events of his life. The following from a letter written by General E. A. Carr,[2] of the Fifth Cavalry, now commanding Fort McPherson, speaks for itself:

"I first met Mr. Cody, October 22d, 1868, at Buffalo Station, on the Kansas Pacific railroad, in Kansas. He was scout and guide for the seven companies of the Fifth Cavalry, then under Colonel Royall,[3] and of which I was ordered to take the command.

"From his services with my command, steadily in the field for nine months, from October, 1868, to July, 1869, and at subsequent times, I am qualified to bear testimony to his qualities and character.

"He was very modest and unassuming. I did not know for a long time how good a title he had to the appellation, 'Buffalo Bill.' I am apt to discount the claims of scouts, as they will occasionally exaggerate; and when I found one who said nothing about himself, I did not think much of him, till I had proved him. He is a natural gentleman in his manners as well as in character, and has none of the roughness of the typical frontiersman. He can take his own part when required, but I have never heard of his using a knife or a pistol, or engaging in a quarrel where it could be avoided. His personal strength and activity are such that he can hardly meet a man whom he cannot handle, and his temper and disposition are so good that no one has reason to quarrel with him.

"His eye-sight is better than a good field glass; he is the best trailer I ever heard of; and also the best judge of the 'lay of country,'—that is, he is able to tell what kind of country is ahead, so as to know how to act. He is a perfect judge of distance, and always ready to tell correctly how many miles it is to water, or to any place, or how many miles have been marched.

"Mr. Cody seemed never to tire and was always ready to go, in the darkest night or the worst weather, and usually volunteered, knowing what the emergency required.

His trailing, when following Indians or looking for stray animals or game, is simply wonderful. He is a most extraordinary hunter. I could not believe that a man could be certain to shoot antelope running till I had seen him do it so often.

"In a fight Mr. Cody is never noisy, obstreperous or excited. In fact, I never hardly noticed him in a fight, unless I happened to want him, or he had something to report, when he was always in the right place, and his information was always valuable and reliable.

"During the winter of 1868, we encountered hardships and exposure in terrific snow storms, sleet, etc., etc. On one occasion, that winter, Mr. Cody showed his quality by quietly offering to go with some dispatches to General Sheridan, across a dangerous region, where another principal scout was reluctant to risk himself.

"On the 13th of May, 1869, he was in the fight at Elephant Rock, Kansas, and trailed the Indians till the 16th, when we got another fight out of them on Spring Creek, in Nebraska, and scattered them after following them one hundred and fifty miles in three days. It was at Spring Creek where Cody was ahead of the command about three miles, with the advance guard of forty men, when two hundred Indians suddenly surrounded them. Our men, dismounted and formed in a circle, holding their horses, firing and slowly retreating. They all, to this day, speak of Cody's coolness and bravery. This was the Dog Soldier band which captured Mrs. Alderdice and Mrs. Weichel in Kansas. They strangled Mrs. Alderdice's baby, killed Mrs. Weichel's husband, and took a great deal of property and stock from different persons. We got on their trail again,

June 28th, and followed it nearly two hundred miles, till we struck the Indians on Sunday, July 11th, 1869, at Summit Spring. The Indians, as soon as they saw us coming, killed Mrs. Alderdice with a hatchet, and shot Mrs. Weichel, but fortunately not fatally, and she was saved.[4]

"Mr. Cody has since served with me as post guide and scout at Fort McPherson, where he frequently distinguished himself.

"In the summer of 1876, Cody went with me to the Black Hills region where he killed Yellow-Hand. Afterwards he was with the Big Horn and Yellowstone expedition. I consider that his services to the country and the army by trailing, finding and fighting Indians, and thus protecting the frontier settlers, and by guiding commands over the best and most practicable routes, have been far beyond the compensation he has received. His friends of the Fifth Cavalry are all glad that he is in a lucrative business, and hope that he may live long and prosper.

Personally, I feel under obligations to him for assistance in my campaigns which no other man could, or would, have rendered. Of course I wish him, and his, every success."

E. A. Carr, Lt. Col. 5th Cav., Brev. Maj. Gen'l U.S. Army. Fort McPherson, Nebraska, July 3d, 1878.

Buffalo Bill is now an actor, and is meeting with success. He owns a large and valuable farm adjoining the town of North Platte, Nebraska, and there his family live in ease and comfort. He has also an extensive cattle ranch on the Dismal river, sixty-five miles north of North Platte, his partner being Major Frank North, the old commander of the celebrated Pawnee scouts. While many events of his career are known to the public, yet the reader will find in this narrative much that will be entirely new and intensely interesting to both young and old.

The Publisher.

CONTENTS

CHAPTER I

Childhood

My début upon the world's stage occurred on February 26th, 1845.[1] The scene of this first important event in my adventurous career, being in Scott county, in the State of Iowa. My parents, Isaac and Mary Ann Cody, who were numbered among the pioneers of Iowa, gave to me the name of William Frederick. I was the fourth child in the family. Martha and Julia, my sisters, and Samuel my brother, had preceded me, and the children who came after me were Eliza, Nellie, Mary, and Charles, born in the order named.[2]

At the time of my birth the family resided on a farm which they called "Napsinekee Place,"—an Indian name—and here the first six or seven years of my childhood were spent. When I was about seven years old my father moved the family to the little town of LeClair, located on the bank of the Mississippi, fifteen miles above the city of Davenport. Even at that early age my adventurous spirit led me into all sorts of mischief and danger, and when I look back upon my childhood's days I often wonder that I did not get drowned while swimming or sailing, or my neck broken while I was stealing apples in the neighboring orchards.

I well remember one day that I went sailing with two other boys; in a few minutes we found ourselves in the middle of the Mississippi; becoming frightened at the situation we lost our presence of mind, as well as our oars. We at once set up a chorus of pitiful yells, when a man, who fortunately heard us, came to our rescue with a canoe and towed us ashore. We had stolen the boat, and our trouble did not end until we had each received a merited whipping, which impressed the incident vividly upon my mind. I recollect several occasions when I was nearly eaten up by a large and savage dog, which acted as custodian of an orchard and also of a melon patch, which I frequently visited. Once, as I was climbing over the fence with a hatful of apples, this dog, which had started for me, caught me by the seat of the pantaloons, and while I clung to the top of the fence he literally tore them from my legs, but fortunately did not touch my flesh. I got away with the apples, however, by tumbling over to the opposite side of the fence with them.

It was at LeClair that I acquired my first experience as an equestrian. Somehow or other I had managed to corner a horse near a fence, and had climbed upon his back. The next moment the horse got his back up and hoisted me into the air, I fell violently to the ground, striking upon my side in such a way as to severely wrench and strain my arm, from the effects of which I did not recover for some time. I abandoned the art of horsemanship for a while, and was induced after considerable persuasion to turn my attention to letters—my A, B, C's—which were taught me at the village school.

My father at this time was running a stage line, between Chicago and Davenport, no railroads then having been built west of Chicago. In 1849 he got the California fever[3] and made up his mind to cross the great plains—which were then and for years afterwards called the American Desert—to the Pacific coast. He got ready a complete outfit and started with quite a party. After proceeding a few miles, all but my father, and greatly to his disappointment, changed their minds for some reason and abandoned the enterprise. They all returned home, and soon afterwards father moved his family out to Walnut Grove Farm, in Scott county.

While living there I was sent to school, more for the purpose of being kept out of mischief than to learn anything. Much of my time was spent in trapping quails, which were very plentiful. I greatly enjoyed studying the habits of the little birds, and in devising traps to take them in. I was most successful with the common figure "4" trap[4] which I could build myself. Thus I think it was that I acquired my love for hunting. I visited the quail traps twice a day, morning and evening, and as I had now become quite a good rider I was allowed to have one of the farm horses to carry me over my route. Many a jolly ride I had and many a boyish prank was perpetrated after getting well away from and out of the sight of home with the horse.

There was one event which occurred in my childhood, which I cannot recall without a feeling of sadness. It was the death of my brother Samuel, who was accidentally killed in his twelfth year.

My father at the time, being considerable of a politician as well as a farmer, was attending a political convention; for he was well known in those days as an old line Whig.[5] He had been a member of the Iowa legislature, was a Justice of the Peace, and had held other offices. He was

7. Youthful Adventures

an excellent stump speaker and was often called upon to canvass the country round about for different candidates. The convention which he was attending at the time of the accident was being held at a cross-road tavern called "Sherman's," about a mile away.

Samuel and I had gone out together on horseback for the cows. He rode a vicious mare, which mother had told him time and again not to ride, as it had an ugly disposition. We were passing the school house just as the children were being dismissed, when Samuel undertook to give an exhibition of his horsemanship, he being a good rider for a boy. The mare, Betsy, became unmanageable, reared and fell backward upon him, injuring him internally. He was picked up and carried amid great excitement to the house of a neighbor.

I at once set out with my horse at the top of his speed for my father, and informed him of Samuel's mishap. He took the horse and returned immediately. When I arrived at Mr. Burns' house, where my brother was, I found my father, mother and sisters there, all weeping bitterly at Samuel's bedside. A physician, after examining him, pronounced his injuries to be of a fatal character. He died the next morning.

My brother was a great favorite with everybody, and his death cast a gloom upon the whole neighborhood. It was a great blow to all of the family, and especially to father who seemed to be almost heart broken over it.

Father had been greatly disappointed at the failure of his California expedition, and still desired to move to some new country. The death of Samuel no doubt increased this desire, and he determined to emigrate. Accordingly, early

8. Samuel's Fatal Accident

in the spring of 1852, he disposed of his farm, and late in March we took our departure for Kansas, which was then an unsettled territory. Our outfit consisted of one carriage, three wagons and some fine blooded horses. The carriage was occupied by my mother and sisters. Thus we left our Iowa home.

Father had a brother, Elijah Cody, living at Weston, Platte county, Missouri. He was the leading merchant of the place. As the town was located near the Kansas line father determined to visit him, and thither our journey was directed. Our route lay across Iowa and Missouri, and the trip proved of interest to all of us, and especially to me. There was something new to be seen at nearly every turn of the road. At night the family generally "put up" at hotels or cross-road taverns along the way.

One day as we were proceeding on our way, we were met by a horseman who wanted to sell his horse, or trade him for another. He said the horse had been captured wild in California; that he was a runner and a racer; that he had been sold by his different owners on account of his great desire to run away when taking part in a race.

The stranger seemed to be very frank in his statements, and appeared to be very anxious to get rid of the animal, and as we were going to Kansas where there would be plenty of room for the horse to run as far as he pleased, father concluded to make a trade for him; so an exchange of animals was easily and satisfactorily effected.

The new horse being a small gray, we named him "Little Gray."

An opportunity of testing the racing qualities of the horse was soon afforded. One day we drove into a small Missouri town or hamlet which lay on our route, where the farmers from the surrounding country were congregated for the purpose of having a holiday—the principal amusement being horse-racing. Father had no trouble in arranging a race for Little Gray, and selected one of his teamsters to ride him.

The Missourians matched their fastest horse against him and were confident of cleaning out "the emigrant," as they called father. They were a hard looking crowd. They wore their pantaloons in their boots; their hair was long, bushy and untrimmed; their faces had evidently never made the acquaintance of a razor. They seemed determined to win the race by fair means or foul. They did a great deal of swearing, and swaggered about in rather a ruffianly style.

All these incidents attracted my attention—everything being new to me—and became firmly impressed upon my memory. My father, being unaccustomed to the ways of such rough people, acted very cautiously; and as they were all very anxious to bet on their own horse, he could not be induced to wager a very large sum on Little Gray, as he was afraid of foul play.

"Wa-al, now, stranger," exclaimed one of the crowd, "what kind o' critter have you got anyhow, as how you're afraid to back him up very heavy?"

"I'll bet five to one agin the emergrant's gray," said another.

"I'm betting the same way. I'll go yer five hundred dollars agin a hundred that the gray nag gits left behind. Do I hear any man who wants to come agin me on them yer terms?" shouted still another.

"Hi! yer boys, give the stranger a chance. Don't scare him out of his boots," said a man who evidently was afraid that my father might back out.

Father had but little to say, however, and would not venture more than fifty dollars on the result of the race.

"Gentlemen, I am only racing my horse for sport," said he, "and am only betting enough to make it interesting. I have never seen Little Gray run, and therefore don't know what he can do"; at the same time he was confident that his horse would come in the winner, as he had chosen an excellent rider for him.

Finally all the preliminaries of the contest were arranged. The judges were chosen and the money was deposited in the hands of a stake-holder. The race was to be a single dash of a mile. The horses were brought side by side and mounted by their riders.

At the signal—"One, two, three, go!"—off they started like a flash. The Missouri horse took the lead for the first quarter of a mile; at the half-mile, however, he began to weaken. The Missourians shouted themselves hoarse in urging their horse, but all to no avail. The Little Gray passed him and continued to leave him farther and farther behind, easily winning the race.

The affair created a great deal of enthusiasm; but the race was conducted with honor and fairness, which was quite an agreeable surprise to my father, who soon found the Missourians to be at heart very clever men—thus showing that outside appearances are sometimes very deceptive; they nearly all came up and congratulated him on his success, asked him why he had not bet more money on the race, and wanted to buy Little Gray.

"Gentlemen," said he, "when I drove up here and arranged for this race, I felt confident that my horse would win it. I was among entire strangers, and therefore I only bet a small amount. I was afraid that you would cheat me in some way or other. I see now that I was mistaken, as I have found you to be honorable men."

"Wa-all, you could have broke *me*," said the man who wanted to bet the five hundred dollars to one hundred, "for that there nag o' yourn looks no more like a runner nor I do."

During our stay in the place they treated us very kindly, and continued to try to purchase Little Gray. My father, however, remained firm in his determination not to part with him.

The next place of interest which we reached, after re-suming our journey, was within twenty miles of Weston. We had been stopping at farm houses along the road, and could not get anything to eat in the shape of bread, except corn bread, of which all had become heartily tired. As we were driving along, we saw in the distance a large and handsome brick residence. Father said: "They probably have white bread there."

We drove up to the house and learned that it was owned and occupied by Mrs. Burns; mother of a well-known lawyer of that name, who is now living in Leavenworth. She was a wealthy lady, and gave us to understand in a pleasant way, that she did not entertain travelers. My father, in the course of the conversation with her, said: "Do you know Elijah Cody?"

"Indeed, I do," said she; "he frequently visits us, and we visit him; we are the best of friends."

"He is a brother of mine," said father.

"Is it possible!" she exclaimed; "Why, you must remain here all night. Have your family come into the house at once. You must not go another step today."

The kind invitation was accepted, and we remained there over night. As father had predicted, we found plenty of white bread at this house, and it proved quite a luxuri-ous treat.

My curiosity was considerably aroused by the many negroes which I saw about the premises, as I had scarcely ever seen any colored people, the few, being on the steam-boats as they passed up and down the Mississippi river.

The next day my father and mother drove over to Weston in a carriage, and returned with my Uncle Elijah.

We then all proceeded to his house, and as Kansas was not yet open for settlement as a territory,[6] we remained there a few days, while father crossed over into Kansas on a prospecting tour. He visited the Kickapoo Agency[7]—five miles above Weston—on the Kansas side of the Missouri river. He became acquainted with the agent, and made arrangements to establish himself there as an Indian trader. He then returned to Weston and located the family on one of Elijah Cody's farms, three miles from town, where we were to remain until Kansas should be thrown open for settlement. After completing these arrangements, he established a trading post at Salt Creek Valley, in Kansas, four miles from the Kickapoo Agency.

One day, after he had been absent some little time, he came home and said that he had bought two ponies for me, and that next morning he would take me over into Kansas. This was pleasant news, as I had been very anxious to go there with him, and the fact that I was now the owner of two ponies made me feel very proud. That night I could not sleep a wink. In the morning I was up long before the sun, and after an early breakfast, father and I started out on our trip. Crossing the Missouri river at the Rialto Ferry, we landed in Kansas and passed along to Fort Leavenworth,[8] four miles distant.

CHAPTER II

Early Influences

General Harney[1] was in command at Fort Leavenworth at the time of our visit, and a regiment of cavalry was stationed there. They were having a dress parade when we rode up, and as this was the first time that I had ever seen any soldiers, I thought it was a grand sight. I shall never forget it, especially the manoeuvres on horseback.

After witnessing the parade we resumed our journey. On the way to my father's trading camp we had to cross over a high hill known as Salt Creek Hill, from the top of which we looked down upon the most beautiful valley I have ever seen. It was about twelve miles long and five miles wide. The different tributaries of Salt Creek came down from the range of hills at the southwest. At the foot of the valley another small river—Plum Creek, also flowed. The bluffs fringed with trees, clad in their full foliage, added greatly to the picturesqueness of the scene.

While this beautiful valley greatly interested me, yet the most novel sight, of an entirely different character, which met my enraptured gaze, was the vast number of white-covered wagons, or "prairie-schooners," which were encamped along the different streams. I asked my father what they were and where they were going; he explained to me that they were emigrant wagons bound for Utah and California.

At that time the Mormon and California trails[2] ran through this valley, which was always selected as a camping place. There were at least one thousand wagons in the valley, and their white covers lent a pleasing contrast to the green grass. The cattle were quietly grazing near the wagons, while the emigrants were either resting or attending to camp duties.

A large number of the wagons, as I learned from my father, belonged to Majors & Russell,[3] the great government freighters. They had several trains there, each consisting of twenty-five wagons, heavily loaded with government supplies. They were all camped and corraled in a circle.

While we were viewing this scene, a long wagon train came pulling up the hill, bound out from Fort Leavenworth to some distant frontier post. The cattle were wild and the men were whipping them fearfully, the loud reports of the bull-whips sounding like gun-shots. They were "doubling-up," and some of the wagons were being drawn by fifteen yokes of oxen. I remember asking my father a great many questions, and he explained to me all about the freighting business across the great plains, and told me about the different government posts.[4]

Pointing over to the army of wagons camped below us, he showed me which were the Mormons'[5] and which were the Californians', and said that we must steer clear of the former as the cholera[6] was raging among them. Five hundred had died that spring—1853—and the grave-yard was daily increasing its dimensions. The unfortunate people had been overtaken by the dreadful disease, and had been compelled to halt on their journey until it abated.

While we were looking at the Mormons they were

holding a funeral service over the remains of some of their number who had died. Their old cemetery is yet indicated by various land-marks, which, however, with the few remaining head-boards, are fast disappearing.

We passed on through this "Valley of Death," as it might then have been very appropriately called, and after riding for some time, my father pointed out a large hill and showed me his camp, which afterwards became our home.

There was another trading-post near by, which was conducted by Mr. M. P. Rively, who had a store built, partly frame, and partly of logs. We stopped at this establishment for a while, and found perhaps a hundred men, women and children gathered there, engaged in trading and gossiping. The men had huge pistols and knives in their belts; their pantaloons were tucked in their boots; and they wore large broad-rimmed hats.

To me they appeared like a lot of cut-throat pirates who had come ashore for a lark.[7] It was the first time I had ever seen men carrying pistols and knives, and they looked like a very dangerous crowd. Some were buying articles of merchandise; others were talking about the cholera, the various camps, and matters of interest; while others were drinking whisky freely and becoming intoxicated. It was a busy and an exciting scene, and Rively appeared to be doing a rushing trade.

At some little distance from the store I noticed a small party of dark-skinned and rather fantastically dressed people, whom I ascertained were Indians, and as I had never before seen a real live Indian, I was much interested in them. I went over and endeavored to talk to them, but our conversation was very limited.

That evening we reached our camp, which was located two miles west of Rively's. The first thing I did was to hunt up my ponies, and from my father's description of them, I had no difficulty in finding them. They were lariated[8] in the grass and I immediately ran up to them supposing them to be gentle animals. I was greatly mistaken, however, as they snorted and jumped away from me, and would not allow me to come near them.

My father, who was standing not far distant, informed me that the ponies were not yet broken. I was somewhat disappointed at this; and thereupon he and one of his men caught one of the animals and bridled her, then putting me on her back, led her around, greatly to my delight. I kept petting her so much that she soon allowed me to approach her. She was a beautiful bay, and I named her "Dolly;" the other pony was a sorrel, and I called him "Prince."

In the evening some Indians visited the camp—which as yet consisted only of tents, though some logs had been cut preparatory to building houses—and exchanged their furs for clothing, sugar and tobacco. Father had not learned their language, and therefore communicated with them by means of signs. We had our supper by the camp-fire, and that night was the first time I ever camped out and slept upon the ground.

The day had been an eventful one to me, for all the incidents were full of excitement and romance to my youthful mind, and I think no apology is needed for mentioning so many of the little circumstances, which so greatly interested me in my childhood's days, and which no doubt had a great influence in shaping my course in after years. My love of hunting and scouting, and life on the plains generally, was the result of my early surroundings.

The next morning father visited the Kickapoo Agency, taking me along. He rode a horse, and putting me on my pony "Dolly," led the animal all the way. He seemed anxious to break me in, as well as the pony, and I greatly enjoyed this, my first day's ride on a Kansas prairie.

At the Kickapoo village I saw hundreds of Indians, some of whom were living in lodges,[9] but the majority occupied log cabins. The agent resided in a double-hewed log house,[10] one of the apartments of which was used as a school for the Indians. The agency store was opposite this structure.

All the buildings were whitewashed, and looked neat and clean. The Kickapoos[11] were very friendly Indians, and we spent much of our time among them, looking about and studying their habits.

After a while we returned to our own camp, and just as we arrived there, we saw a drove of horses—there were three or four hundred in all—approaching from the west, over the California trail. They were being driven by seven or eight mounted men, wearing sombreros, and dressed in buckskin, with their lariats dangling from their saddles, and they were followed by two or three pack-mules or horses. They went into camp a little below us on the bank of the stream.

Presently one of the men walked out towards our camp, and my father called to me to come and see a genuine Western man; he was about six feet two inches tall, was well built, and had a light, springy and wiry step. He wore a broad-brimmed California hat, and was dressed in a complete suit of buckskin, beautifully trimmed and beaded. He saluted us, and father invited him to sit down, which

9. Billings as a Bocarro

he did. After a few moments conversation, he turned to me and said:

"Little one, I see you are working with your ponies. They are wild yet."

I had been petting Dolly and trying to break her, when my father called me to come and look at the Californian.

"Yes," I replied, "and one of them never has been ridden."

"Well, I'll ride him for you;" and springing lightly to his feet, he continued: "Come on. Where is the animal?"

Accordingly we all went to the place where Prince was lariated. The stranger untied the rope from the picket pin, and taking a half-loop around the pony's nose, he jumped on his back.

In a moment he was flying over the prairie, the untamed steed rearing and pitching every once in a while in his efforts to throw his rider; but the man was not unseated. He was evidently an experienced horseman. I watched his every movement. I was unconsciously taking another lesson in the practical education which has served me so well through my life.

The Californian rode the pony until it was completely mastered, then coming up to me, jumped to the ground, handed me the rope, and said:

"Here's your pony. He's all right now."

I led Prince away, while father and the stranger sat down in the shade of a tent, and began talking about the latter's horsemanship, which father considered very remarkable.

"Oh, that's nothing; I was raised on horseback," said the Californian; "I ran away from home when a boy, went to sea, and finally landed in the Sandwich Islands, where I fell in with a circus, with which I remained two years. During that time I became a celebrated bare-back rider. I then went to California, being attracted there by the gold excitement, the news of which had reached the Islands. I did not go to mining, however, but went to work as a *bo-carro*[12]—catching and breaking wild horses, great numbers of which were roaming through California.

Last summer we caught this herd that we have brought with us across the plains, and are taking it to the States to sell. I came with the outfit, as it gave me a good opportunity to visit my relatives, who live at Cleveland, Ohio. I also had an uncle over at Weston, across the river, when I ran away, and to-morrow I am going to visit the town to see if he is there yet."

"I am acquainted in Weston," said father, "and perhaps I can tell you about your uncle. What is his name?"

10. Billings Riding Little Gray

"Elijah Cody," said the Californian.

"Elijah Cody!" exclaimed father, in great surprise; "Why Elijah Cody is my brother. I am Isaac Cody. Who are you?"

"My name is Horace Billings," was the reply.

"And you are my nephew. You are the son of my sister Sophia."

Both men sprang to their feet and began shaking hands in the heartiest manner possible.

The next moment father called me, and said: "Come here, my son. Here is some one you want to know."

As I approached he introduced us. "Horace, this is my only son. We call him little Billy;" and turning to me said: "Billy, my boy, this is a cousin of yours, Horace Billings, whom you've often heard me speak of."

Horace Billings had never been heard of from the day he ran away from home, and his relatives had frequently wondered what had become of him. His appearance, therefore, in our camp in the guise of a Californian was somewhat of a mystery to me, and I could hardly comprehend it until I had heard his adventurous story and learned the accidental manner in which he and father had made themselves known to each other.

Neither father nor myself would be satisfied until he had given us a full account of his wanderings and adventures, which were very exciting to me.

Late in the afternoon and just before the sun sank to rest, the conversation again turned upon horses and horsemanship. Father told Billings all about Little Gray, and his great fault of running away. Billings laughed and said Little Gray could not run away with him.

After supper he went out to look at the horse, which was picketed in the grass. Surveying the animal carefully, he untied the lariat and slipped a running noose over his nose; then giving a light bound, he was on his back in a second, and away went the horse and his rider, circling round and round on the prairie. Billings managed him by the rope alone, and convinced him that he was his master. When half a mile away, the horse started for camp at the top of his speed. Billings stood straight up on his back, and thus rode him into camp. As he passed us he jumped to the ground, allowed the horse to run to the full length of the lariat, when he threw him a complete somersault.

"That's a pretty good horse," said Billings.

"Yes, he's a California horse; he was captured there wild," replied father.

11. Exciting Sport

The exhibition of horsemanship given by Billings on this occasion was really wonderful, and was the most skillful and daring feat of the kind that I ever witnessed. The remainder of the evening was spent around the camp, and Horace, who remained there, entertained us with several interesting chapters of his experiences.

Next morning he walked over to his own camp, but soon returned, mounted on a beautiful horse, with a handsome saddle, bridle and lariat. I thought he was a magnificent looking man. I envied his appearance, and my ambition just then was to become as skillful a horseman as he was. He had rigged himself out in his best style in order to make a good impression on his uncle at Weston, whither father and I accompanied him on horseback.

He was cordially received by Uncle Elijah, who paid him every possible attention, and gave me a handsome saddle and bridle for my pony, and in the evening when we rode out to the farm to see my mother and sisters, I started ahead to show them my present, as well as to tell them who was coming. They were delighted to see the long-lost Horace, and invited him to remain with us. When we returned to camp next day, Horace settled up with the proprietor of the horses, having concluded to make his home with us for that summer at least.

Father employed him in cutting house logs and building houses, but this work not being adapted to his tastes, he soon gave it up, and obtained government employment in catching United States horses. During the previous spring the government herd had stampeded from Fort Leavenworth, and between two and three hundred of the horses were running at large over the Kansas prairies, and had become quite wild. A reward of ten dollars was offered for every one of the horses that was captured and delivered to the quartermaster at Fort Leavenworth. This kind of work of course just suited the roaming disposition of Billings, especially as it was similar to that in which he had been engaged in California. The horses had to be caught with a lasso, with which he was very expert. He borrowed Little Gray, who was fleet enough for the wildest of the runaways, and then he at once began his horse hunting.

Everything that he did, I wanted to do. He was a sort of hero in my eyes, and I wished to follow in his footsteps. At my request and with father's consent, he took me with him, and many a wild and perilous chase he led me over the prairie. I made rapid advances in the art of horsemanship, for I could have had no better teacher than Horace Billings. He also taught me how to throw the lasso, which, though it was a difficult thing to learn, I finally became quite skillful in.

Whenever Horace caught one of the horses which acted obstinately, and would not be led, he immediately threw him to the ground, put a saddle and bridle on him, and gave me Little Gray to take care of. He would then mount the captive horse and ride him into Fort Leavenworth. I spent two months with Horace in this way, until at last no more of the horses were to be found. By this time I had become a remarkably good rider for a youth, and had brought both of my ponies under easy control.

Horace returned to assist father in hauling logs, which were being used in building a dwelling for the family who had moved over from Missouri. One day a team did not work to suit him, and he gave the horses a cruel beating. This greatly displeased father, who took him to task for it. Horace's anger flew up in a moment; throwing down the lines he hurried to the house, and began packing up his traps. That same day he hired out to a Mormon train, and bidding us all good-bye started for Salt Lake, driving six yokes of oxen.

CHAPTER III

Boy Days in Kansas

During the summer of 1853 we lived in our little log house, and father continued to trade with the Indians, who became very friendly; hardly a day passed without a social visit from them. I spent a great deal of time with the Indian boys, who taught me how to shoot with the bow and arrow, at which I became quite expert. I also took part in all their sports, and learned to talk the Kickapoo language to some extent.

Father desired to express his friendship for these Indians, and accordingly arranged a grand barbecue for them. He invited them all to be present on a certain day, which they were; he then presented them with two fat beeves,[1] to be killed and cooked in the various Indian styles. Mother made several large boilers full of coffee, which she gave to them, together with sugar and bread. There were about two hundred Indians in attendance at the feast, and they all enjoyed and appreciated it. In the evening they had one of their grand fantastic war dances, which greatly amused me, it being the first sight of the kind I had ever witnessed.

My Uncle Elijah and quite a large number of gentlemen and ladies came over from Weston to attend the entertainment. The Indians returned to their homes well satisfied.

My uncle at that time owned a trading post at Silver

Lake, in the Pottawattamie country,[2] on the Kansas river, and he arranged an excursion to that place. Among the party were several ladies from Weston, and father, mother and myself. Mr. McMeekan, my uncle's superintendent, who had come to Weston for supplies, conducted the party to the post.

The trip across the prairies was a delightful one, and we remained at the post several days. Father and one or two of the men went on to Fort Riley[3] to view the country, and upon their return my uncle entertained the Pottawattamie Indians with a barbecue similar to the one given by father to the Kickapoos.

During the latter part of the summer father filled a hay contract at Fort Leavenworth. I passed much of my time among the campers, and spent days and days in riding over the country with Mr. William Russell, who was engaged in the freighting business and who seemed to take a considerable interest in me. In this way I became acquainted with many wagon-masters, hunters and teamsters, and learned a great deal about the business of handling cattle and mules.

It was an excellent school for me, and I acquired a great deal of practical knowledge, which afterwards I found to be of invaluable service, for it was not long before I became employed by Majors & Russell, remaining with them in different capacities, for several years.

The winter of 1853–54 was spent by father at our little prairie home in cutting house logs and fence rails, which he intended to use on his farm, as soon as the bill for the opening of the territory for settlement should pass. This bill, which was called the "Enabling act of Kansas territory," was passed in April, 1854,[4] and father immediately pre-empted the claim on which we were living.

The summer of that year was an exciting period in the history of the new territory. Thousands and thousands of people, seeking new homes, flocked thither, a large number of the emigrants coming over from adjoining states. The Missourians, some of them, would come laden with bottles of whisky, and after drinking the liquor would drive the bottles into the ground to mark their land claims, not waiting to put up any buildings.

The Missourians, mostly, were pro-slavery men, and held enthusiastic meetings at which they expressed their desire that Kansas should be a slave state and did not hesitate to declare their determination to make it so. Rively's store was the headquarters for these men, and there they held their meetings.

At first they thought father would coincide with them on account of his brother Elijah being a Missourian, but in this they were greatly mistaken. At one of their gatherings, when there were about one hundred of the reckless men present, my father, who happened also to be there, was called upon for a speech. After considerable urging, he mounted the box and began speaking, as nearly as I can recollect, as follows:

"Gentlemen and Fellow-citizens: You have called upon me for a speech, and I have accepted your invitation rather against my will, as my views may not accord with the sentiments of the rest of this assembly. My remarks, at this time, will be brief and to the point. The question before us to-day is, shall the territory of Kansas be a free or a slave state. The question of slavery in itself is a broad

12. Staking Out Lots

one, and one which I do not care at this time and place to discuss at length. I apprehend that your motive in calling upon me is to have me express my sentiments in regard to the introduction of slavery into Kansas. I shall gratify your wishes in that respect. I was one of the pioneers of the State of Iowa, and aided in its settlement when it was a territory, and helped to organize it as a state.

"Gentlemen, I voted that it should be a *white* state—that negroes, whether free or slave, should never be allowed to locate within its limits; and, gentlemen, I say to you now, and I say it boldly, that I propose to exert all my power in making Kansas the same kind of a state as Iowa. I believe in letting slavery remain as it now exists, and I shall always oppose its further extension. These are my sentiments, gentlemen and let me tell you—"

He never finished this sentence, or his speech. His expressions were anything but acceptable to the rough-looking crowd, whose ire had been gradually rising to fever heat, and at this point they hooted and hissed him, and shouted, "You black abolitionist, shut up!" "Get down from that box!" "Kill him!" "Shoot him!" and so on. Father, however, maintained his position on the dry-goods box, notwithstanding the excitement and the numerous invitations to step down, until a hot-headed pro-slavery man, who was in the employ of my Uncle Elijah, crowded up and said: "Get off that box, you black abolitionist, or I'll pull you off."

Father paid but little attention to him, and attempted to resume his speech, intending doubtless to explain his position and endeavor to somewhat pacify the angry crowd. But the fellow jumped up on the box, and pulling out a huge bowie knife, stabbed father twice, who reeled and

13. My Father Stabbed

fell to the ground. The man sprang after him, and would have ended his life then and there, had not some of the better men in the crowd interfered in time to prevent him from carrying out his murderous intention.

The excitement was intense, and another assault would probably have been made on my father, had not Rively hurriedly carried him to his home. There was no doctor within any reasonable distance, and father at once requested that he be conveyed in the carriage to his brother Elijah's house in Weston. My mother and a driver accordingly went there with him, where his wounds were dressed. He remained in Weston several weeks before he was able to stir about again, but he never fully recovered from the wounds, which eventually proved the cause of his death.

14. My Father's Escape

My uncle of course at once discharged the ruffian from his employ. The man afterwards became a noted desperado, and was quite conspicuous in the Kansas war.[5]

My father's indiscreet speech at Rively's brought upon our family all of the misfortunes and difficulties which from that time on befell us. As soon as he was able to attend to his business again, the Missourians began to harass him in every possible way, and kept it up with hardly a moment's cessation. Kickapoo City, as it was called, a small town that had sprung into existence seven miles up the river from Fort Leavenworth, became the hot-bed of the pro-slavery doctrine and the headquarters of its advocates. Here was really the beginning of the Kansas troubles. My father, who had shed the first blood in the cause of the freedom of Kansas, was notified, upon his return to his trading post, to leave the territory, and he was threatened with death by hanging or shooting, if he dared to remain.

One night a body of armed men, mounted on horses, rode up to our house and surrounded it. Knowing what they had come for, and seeing that there would be but little chance for him in an encounter with them, father determined to make his escape by a little stratagem. Hastily disguising himself in mother's bonnet and shawl, he boldly walked out of the house and proceeded towards the corn-field. The darkness proved a great protection, as the horsemen, between whom he passed, were unable to detect him in his disguise; supposing him to be a woman, they neither halted him nor followed him, and he passed safely on into the corn-field, where he concealed himself.

The horsemen soon dismounted and inquired for father; mother very truthfully told them that he was away. They were not satisfied with her statement, however, and they at once made a thorough search of the house. They raved and swore when they could not find him, and threatened him with death whenever they should catch him. I am sure if they had captured him that night, they would have killed him. They carried off nearly everything of value in the house and about the premises; then going to the pasture, they drove off all the horses; my pony Prince afterward succeeding in breaking away from them and came back home. Father lay secreted in the corn-field for three days, as there were men in the vicinity who were watching for him all the time; he finally made his escape, and reached Fort Leavenworth in safety, whither the pro-slavery men did not dare to follow him.

While he was staying at Fort Leavenworth, he heard that Jim Lane,[6] Captain Cleveland and Captain Chandler were on their way from Indiana to Kansas with a body of Free State men, between two and three hundred strong. They were to cross the Missouri river near Doniphan, between Leavenworth and Nebraska City; their destination being Lawrence.[7] Father determined to join them, and took passage on a steamboat which was going up the river. Having reached the place of crossing, he made himself known to the leaders of the party, by whom he was most cordially received.

The pro-slavery men, hearing of the approach of the Free State party,[8] resolved to drive them out of the territory. The two parties met at Hickory Point, where a severe battle was fought, several being killed; the victory resulted in favor of the Free State men, who passed on to Lawrence without much further opposition. My father finally left them, and seeing that he could no longer live at home, went to Grasshopper Falls, thirty-five miles west of Leavenworth; there he began the erection of a saw-mill.

While he was thus engaged we learned from one of our hired workmen at home, that the pro-slavery men had laid another plan to kill him, and were on their way to Grasshopper Falls to carry out their intention. Mother at once started me off on Prince to warn father of the coming danger. When I had gone about seven miles I suddenly came upon a party of men, who were camped at the crossing of Stranger Creek. As I passed along I heard one of them, who recognized me, say, "That's the son of the old abolitionist we are after;" and the next moment I was commanded to halt.

15. Life or Death

Instead of stopping I instantly started my pony on a run, and on looking back I saw that I was being pursued by three or four of the party, who had mounted their horses, no doubt supposing that they could easily capture me. It was very fortunate that I had heard the remark about my being "the son of the abolitionist," for then I knew in an instant that they were *en route* to Grasshopper Falls to murder my father. I at once saw the importance of my escaping and warning father in time. It was a matter of life or death to him. So I urged Prince to his utmost speed, feeling that upon him and myself depended a human life—a life that was dearer to me than that of any other man in the world. I led my pursuers a lively chase for four or five miles; finally, when they saw they could not catch me, they returned to their camp. I kept straight on to Grasshopper Falls, arriving there in ample time to inform him of the approach of his old enemies.

That same night father and I rode to Lawrence, which had become the headquarters of the Free State men. There he met Jim Lane and several other leading characters, who were then organizing what was known as the Lecompton Legislature.[9]

Father was elected as a member of that body, and took an active part in organizing the first legislature of Kansas, under Governor Reeder[10] who, by the way, was a Free State man and a great friend of father's.

About this time agents were being sent to the East to induce emigrants to locate in Kansas, and father was sent as one of these agents to Ohio. After the legislature had been organized at Lawrence, he departed for Ohio and was absent several months.

A few days after he had gone, I started for home by the way of Fort Leavenworth, accompanied by two men, who were going to the fort on business. As we were crossing a stream called Little Stranger, we were fired upon by some unknown party; one of my companions, whose name has escaped my memory, was killed. The other man and myself put spurs to our horses and made a dash for our lives. We succeeded in making our escape, though a farewell shot or two was sent after us. At Fort Leavenworth I parted company with my companion, and reached home without any further adventure.

My mother and sisters, who had not heard of my father or myself since I had been sent to warn him of his danger, had become very anxious and uneasy about us, and were uncertain as to whether we were dead or alive. I received a warm welcome home, and as I entered the house, mother seemed to read from the expression of my countenance that father was safe; of course the very first question she asked was as to his whereabouts, and in reply I handed her a long letter from him which explained everything. Mother blessed me again and again for having saved his life.

While father was absent in Ohio, we were almost daily visited by some of the pro-slavery men, who helped themselves to anything they saw fit, and frequently compelled my mother and sisters to cook for them, and to otherwise submit to a great deal of bad treatment. Hardly a day passed without some of them inquiring "where the old man was," saying they would kill him on sight. Thus we passed the summer of 1854, remaining at our home notwithstanding the unpleasant surroundings, as mother had made up her mind not to be driven out of the country. My uncle and other friends advised her to leave Kansas and move to Missouri, because they did not consider our lives safe, as we lived so near the headquarters of the pro-slavery men, who had sworn vengeance upon father.

Nothing, however, could persuade mother to change her determination. She said that the pro-slavery men had taken everything except the land and the little home, and she proposed to remain there as long as she lived, happen what might. Our only friends in Salt Creek valley were two families; one named Lawrence, the other Hathaway, and the peaceable Indians, who occasionally visited us. My uncle, living in Missouri and being somewhat in fear of the pro-slavery men, could not assist us much, beyond expressing his sympathy and sending us provisions.

In the winter of 1854–55 father returned from Ohio, but as soon as his old enemies learned that he was with us, they again compelled him to leave. He proceeded to Lawrence, and there spent the winter in attending the Lecompton Legislature. The remainder of the year he passed mostly at Grasshopper Falls, where he completed his saw-mill. He occasionally visited home under cover of the night, and in the most secret manner; virtually carrying his life in his hand.

In the spring of this year (1855) a pro-slavery party came to our house to search for father; not finding him, they departed, taking with them my pony, Prince. I shall never forget the man who stole that pony. He afterwards rose from the low level of a horse thief to the high dignity of a justice of the peace, and I think still lives at Kickapoo. The loss of my faithful pony nearly broke my heart and bankrupted me in business, as I had nothing to ride.

One day, soon afterwards, I met my old friend, Mr. Russell, to whom I related all my troubles, and his generous heart was touched by my story. "Billy, my boy," said he, "cheer up, and come to Leavenworth, and I'll employ you. I'll give you twenty-five dollars a month to herd cattle."

I accepted the offer, and heartily thanking him, hurried home to obtain mother's consent. She refused to let me go, and all my pleading was in vain. Young as I was—being then only in my tenth year, my ideas and knowledge of the world, however, being far in advance of my age—I determined to run away from home. Mr. Russell's offer of twenty-five dollars a month was a temptation which I could not resist. The remuneration for my services seemed very large to me, and I accordingly stole away and walked to Leavenworth.

Mr. Badger, one of Mr. Russell's superintendents, immediately sent me out, mounted on a little gray mule, to herd cattle. I worked at this for two months, and then came into Leavenworth. I had not been home during all this time, but mother had learned from Mr. Russell where I was, and she no longer felt uneasy, as he had advised her to let me remain in his employ. He assured her that I was all right, and said that when the herd came in he would allow me to make a visit home.

Upon my arrival in Leavenworth with the herd of cattle, Mr. Russell instructed his book-keeper, Mr. Byers, to pay me my wages, amounting to fifty dollars. Byers gave me the sum all in half-dollar pieces. I put the bright silver coins into a sack, which I tied to my mule, and started home, thinking myself a *millionaire*. This money I gave to mother, who had already forgiven me for running away.

Thus began my service for the firm of Russell & Majors, afterwards Russell, Majors & Waddell, with whom I spent seven years of my life in different capacities—such as cavallard-driver,[11] wagon-master, pony express rider and driver. I continued to work for Mr. Russell during the rest of the summer of 1855, and in the winter of 1855–56 I attended school.

Father, who still continued to secretly visit home, was anxious to have his children receive as much of an education as possible, under the adverse circumstances surrounding us, and he employed a teacher, Miss Jennie Lyons, to come to our house and teach. My mother was well educated—more so than my father—and it used to worry her a great deal because her children could not receive better educational advantages. However, the little school at home got along exceedingly well, and we all made rapid advances in our studies, as Miss Lyons was an excellent teacher. She afterwards married a gentleman named Hook, who became the first mayor of Cheyenne, where she now lives.

The Kansas troubles reached their highest pitch in the spring of 1856, and our family continued to be harassed as much as ever by our old enemies. I cannot now recollect one-half of the serious difficulties that we had to encounter; but I very distinctly remember one incident well worth relating. I came home one night on a visit from Leavenworth, being accompanied by a fellow-herder—a young man. During the night we heard a noise outside of the house, and soon the dogs began barking loudly. We looked out to ascertain the cause of the disturbance, and saw that the house was surrounded by a party of men. Mother had become accustomed to such occurrences, and on this occasion she seemed to be master of the situation from the start. Opening a window, she coolly sang out, in a firm tone of voice: "Who are you? What do you want here?"

"We are after that old abolition husband of yours," was the answer from one of the crowd.

"He is not in this house, and has not been here for a long time," said my mother.

"That's a lie! We know he is in the house, and we are bound to have him," said the spokesman of the party.

I afterwards learned they had mistaken the herder,

who had ridden home with me, for my father for whom they had been watching.

"My husband is not at home," emphatically repeated my heroic mother—for if there ever was a heroine she certainly was one—"but the house is full of armed men," continued she, "and I'll give you just two minutes to get out of the yard; if you are not out by the end of that time I shall order them to fire on you."

She withdrew from the window for a few moments and hurriedly instructed the herder to call aloud certain names—any that he might think of—just as if the house was full of men to whom he was giving orders. He followed her directions to the very letter. He could not have done it any better had he rehearsed the act a dozen times.

The party outside heard him, as it was intended they should, and they supposed that my mother really had quite a force at her command. While this little by play was being enacted, she stepped to the open window again and said:

"John Green, you and your friends had better go away or the men will surely fire on you."

At this, point the herder, myself and my sisters commenced stamping on the floor in imitation of a squad of soldiers, and the herder issued his orders in a loud voice to his imaginary troops, who were apparently approaching the window preparatory to firing a volley at the enemy. This little stratagem proved eminently successful. The cowardly villains began retreating, and then my mother fired an old gun into the air which greatly accelerated their speed, causing them to break and run. They soon disappeared from view in the darkness.

The next morning we accidentally discovered that they

had intended to blow up the house. Upon going into the cellar which had been left open on one side, we found two kegs of powder together with a fuse secreted there. It only required a lighted match to have sent us into eternity. My mother's presence of mind, which had never yet deserted her in any trying situation, had saved our lives.

Shortly after this affair, I came home again on a visit and found father there sick with fever, and confined to his bed. One day my old enemy rode up to the house on my pony Prince, which he had stolen from me.

"What is your business here to-day?" asked mother.

"I am looking for the old man," he replied. "I am going to search the house, and if I find him I am going to kill him. Here, you girls," said he, addressing my sisters, "get me some dinner, and get it quick, too, for I am as hungry as a wolf."

"Very well; pray be seated, and we'll get you something to eat," said one of my sisters, without exhibiting the least sign of fear.

He sat down, and while they were preparing a dinner for him, he took out a big knife and sharpened it on a whetstone, repeating his threat of searching the house and killing my father.

I had witnessed the whole proceeding, and heard the threats, and I determined that the man should never go up stairs where father was lying in bed, unable to rise. Taking a double-barreled pistol which I had recently bought, I went to the head of the stairs, cocked the weapon, and waited for the ruffian to come up, determined, that the moment he set foot on the steps I would kill him. I was relieved, however, from the stern necessity, as he did not make his appearance.

The brute was considerably intoxicated when he came to the house, and the longer he sat still the more his brain became muddled with liquor, and he actually forgot what he had come there for. After he had eaten his dinner, he mounted his horse and rode off, and it was a fortunate thing for him that he did.

Father soon recovered and returned to Grasshopper Falls, while I resumed my cattle herding.

CHAPTER IV

Youthful Experiences

In July, 1856, the people living in the vicinity of our home—feeling the necessity of more extensive educational facilities for their children than they had yet had—started a subscription school in a little log cabin on the bank of the creek, which for a while proved quite a success. My mother being very anxious to have me attend this school, I acceded to her oft-repeated wishes, and returning home, I became a pupil of the institution. I made considerable progress in my studies—such as they were—and was getting along very well in every other respect, until I became involved in my first love affair.

Like all school-boys, I had a sweetheart with whom I was "dead in love"—in a juvenile way. Her name was Mary Hyatt. Of course I had a rival, Stephen Gobel, a boy about three years my senior—the "bully" of the school. He was terribly jealous, and sought in every way to revenge himself upon me for having won the childish affections of sweet little Mary.

The boys of the school used to build play-houses or arbors among the trees and bushes for their sweethearts. I had built a play-house for Mary, when Steve, as we called him, leveled it to the ground. We immediately had a very lively fight, in which I got badly beaten. The teacher heard

17. Two to One

of our quarrel and whipped us both. This made matters worse than ever, as I had received two thrashings to Steve's one; I smothered my angry feelings as much as possible under the humiliating circumstances, and during the afternoon recess built another play-house, thinking that Gobel would not dare to destroy a second one; but I was mistaken, for he pushed the whole structure over at the first opportunity. I came up to him just as he finished the job, and said:

"Steve Gobel, the next time you do that, I'll hurt you." And I meant it, too; but he laughed and called me names.

At recess, next morning, I began the construction of still another playhouse, and when I had it about two-thirds finished, Steve slyly sneaked up to the spot and tipped the whole thing over. I jumped for him with the quickness of a cat, and clutching him by the throat for a moment I had the advantage of him. But he was too strong for me, and soon had me on the ground and was beating me severely. While away from home I had someway come into possession of a very small pocket dagger, which I had carried about with me in its sheath, using it in place of a knife. During the struggle this fell from my pocket, and my hand by accident rested upon it as it lay upon the ground. Exasperated beyond measure at Steve's persistence in destroying my play-houses, and smarting under his blows, I forgot myself for the moment, grasped the dagger and unthinkingly thrust it into Steve's thigh. Had it been larger it would probably have injured him severely; as it was, it made a small wound, sufficient to cause the blood to flow freely and Steve to cry out in affright:

"I am killed! O, I am killed!"

The school children all rushed to the spot and were terrified at the scene.

"What's the matter?" asked one.

"Bill Cody has killed Steve Gobel," replied another.

The uproar reached the teacher's ear, and I now saw him approaching, with vengeance in his eye and a big club in his hand. I knew that he was coming to interview *me*. I was dreadfully frightened at what I had done, and undecided whether to run away or to remain and take the consequences; but the sight of that flag-staff in the school teacher's hand was too much for me. I no longer hesitated, but started off like a deer. The teacher followed in hot pursuit, but soon became convinced that he could not catch me, and gave up the chase. I kept on running, until I reached one of Russell, Major & Waddell's freight trains which I had noticed going over the hill for the west. Fortunately for me I knew the wagon-master, John Willis, and as soon as I recovered my breath I told him what had happened.

"Served him right, Billy," said he, "and what's more, we'll go over and clean out the teacher."

"Oh, no; don't do that," said I, for I was afraid that I might fall into the hands of the wounded boy's friends, who I knew would soon be looking for me.

"Well, Billy, come along with me; I am bound for Fort Kearney;[1] the trip will take me forty days. I want you for a cavallard driver."

"All right," I replied, "but I must go home and tell mother about it, and get some clothes."

"Well then, to-night after we make our camp, I'll go back with you."

The affray broke up the school for the rest of the day as the excitement was too much for the children. Late in the afternoon, after the train had moved on some considerable distance, I saw Steve's father, his brother Frank, and one of the neighbors rapidly approaching.

"Mr. Willis, there comes old Gobel, with Frank and somebody else, and they are after me—what am I going to do?" I asked.

"Let 'em come," said he, "they can't take you if I've got anything to say about it, and I rather think I have. Get into one of the wagons—keep quiet and lay low. I'll manage this little job. Don't you fret a bit about it."

I obeyed his orders and felt much easier.

Old Gobel, Frank and the neighbor soon came up and inquired for me.

"He's around here somewhere," said Mr. Willis.

"We want him," said Gobel; "he stabbed my son a little while ago, and I want to arrest him."

"Well, you can't get him; that settles it; so you needn't waste any of your time around here," said Willis.

Gobel continued to talk for a few minutes, but getting no greater satisfaction, the trio returned home.

When night came, Willis accompanied me on horseback to my home. Mother, who had anxiously searched for me everywhere—being afraid that something had befallen me at the hands of the Gobels—was delighted to see me, notwithstanding the difficulty in which I had become involved. I at once told her that at present I was afraid to remain at home, and had accordingly made up my mind to absent myself for a few weeks or months—at least until the excitement should die out. Mr. Willis said to her that he would take me to Fort Kearney with him, and see that I was properly cared for, and would bring me back safely in forty days.

Mother at first seriously objected to my going on this trip fearing I would fall into the hands of Indians. Her fears, however, were soon overcome, and she concluded to let me go. She fixed me up a big bundle of clothing and gave me a quilt. Kissing her and my sisters a fond farewell, I started off on my first trip across the plains, and with a light heart too, notwithstanding my trouble of a few hours before.

The trip proved a most enjoyable one to me, although no incidents worthy of note occurred on the way. On my return from Fort Kearney I was paid off the same as the rest of the employees. The remainder of the summer and fall I spent in herding cattle and working for Russell, Majors & Waddell.

I finally ventured home—not without some fear, however, of the Gobel family—and was delighted to learn that during my absence mother had had an interview with Mr. Gobel, and having settled the difficulty with him, the two families had become friends again, and I may state, incidentally, that they ever after remained so. I have since often met Stephen Gobel, and we have had many a laugh together over our love affair and the affray at the school-house. Mary Hyatt, the innocent cause of the whole difficulty, is now married and living in Chicago. Thus ended my first love scrape.

In the winter of 1856–57 my father, in company with a man named J. C. Boles, went to Cleveland, Ohio, and organized a colony of about thirty families, whom they brought to Kansas and located on the Grasshopper. Several of these families still reside there.

It was during this winter that father, after his return from Cleveland, caught a severe cold. This, in connection with the wound he had received at Rively's—from which he had never entirely recovered—affected him seriously, and in April, 1857, he died at home from kidney disease.

This sad event left my mother and the family in poor circumstances, and I determined to follow the plains for a livelihood for them and myself. I had no difficulty in obtaining work under my old employers, and in May, 1857, I started for Salt Lake City with a herd of beef cattle, in charge of Frank and Bill McCarthy, for General Albert Sidney Johnston's army, which was then being sent across the plains to fight the Mormons.[2]

Nothing occurred to interrupt our journey until we reached Plum Creek, on the South Platte river, thirty-five miles west of Old Fort Kearney. We had made a morning drive and had camped for dinner. The wagon-masters and a majority of the men had gone to sleep under the mess wagons; the cattle were being guarded by three men, and the cook was preparing dinner. No one had any idea that Indians were anywhere near us. The first warning we had that they were infesting that part of the country was the firing of shots and the whoops and yells from a party of them, who, catching us napping, gave us a most unwelcome surprise. All the men jumped to their feet and seized their guns. They saw with astonishment the cattle running in every direction, they having been stampeded by the Indians, who had shot and killed the three men who were on day-herd duty, and the red devils were now charging down upon the rest of us.

I then thought of mother's fears of my falling into the

18. Killing My First Indian

hands of the Indians, and I had about made up my mind that such was to be my fate; but when I saw how coolly and determinedly the McCarthy brothers were conducting themselves and giving orders to the little band, I became convinced that we would "stand the Indians off," as the saying is. Our men were all well armed with Colt's revolvers and Mississippi yagers,[3] which last, carried a bullet, and two buckshots.

The McCarthy boys, at the proper moment, gave orders to fire upon the advancing enemy. The volley checked them, although they returned the compliment, and shot one of our party through the leg. Frank McCarthy then sang out, "Boys, make a break for the slough yonder, and we can then have the bank for a breast-work."

We made a run for the slough which was only a short distance off, and succeeded in safely reaching it, bringing with us the wounded man. The bank proved to be a very effective breast-work, affording us good protection. We had been there but a short time when Frank McCarthy, seeing that the longer we were corraled the worse it would be for us, said:

"Well, boys, we'll try to make our way back to Fort Kearney by wading in the river and keeping the bank for a breast-work."

We all agreed that this was the best plan, and we accordingly proceeded down the river several miles in this way, managing to keep the Indians at a safe distance with our guns, until the slough made a junction with the main Platte river. From there down we found the river at times quite deep, and in order to carry the wounded man along with us we constructed a raft of poles for his accommodation, and in this way he was transported.

Occasionally the water would be too deep for us to wade, and we were obliged to put our weapons on the raft and swim. The Indians followed us pretty close, and were continually watching for an opportunity to get a good range and give us a raking fire. Covering ourselves by keeping well under the bank, we pushed ahead as rapidly as possible, and made pretty good progress, the night finding us still on the way and our enemies still on our track.

I being the youngest and smallest of the party, became somewhat tired, and without noticing it I had fallen behind the others for some little distance. It was about ten o'clock and we were keeping very quiet and hugging close to the bank, when I happened to look up to the moon-lit sky and saw the plumed head of an Indian peeping over the bank. Instead of hurrying ahead and alarming the men in a quiet way, I instantly aimed my gun at the head and fired. The report rang out sharp and loud on the night air, and was immediately followed by an Indian whoop, and the next moment about six feet of dead Indian came tumbling into the river. I was not only overcome with astonishment, but was badly scared, as I could hardly realize what I had done. I expected to see the whole force of Indians come down upon us. While I was standing thus bewildered, the men, who had heard the shot and the war-whoop and had seen the Indian take a tumble, came rushing back.

"Who fired that shot?" cried Frank McCarthy.

"I did," replied I, rather proudly, as my confidence returned and I saw the men coming up.

"Yes, and little Billy has killed an Indian stone-dead— too dead to skin," said one of the men, who had approached nearer than the rest, and had almost stumbled upon the corpse. From that time forward I became a hero and an Indian killer. This was, of course, the first Indian I had ever shot, and as I was not then more than eleven years of age, my exploit created quite a sensation.

The other Indians, upon learning what had happened to their "advance guard," set up a terrible howling, and fired several volleys at us, but without doing any injury, as we were so well protected by the bank. We resumed our journey down the river, and traveled all night long. Just before daylight, Frank McCarthy crawled out over the bank and discovered that we were only five miles from Fort Kearney, which post we reached in safety in about two hours,—shortly after *reveille*[4]—bringing the wounded man with us. It was indeed a relief to us all to feel that once more we were safe.

Frank McCarthy immediately reported to the commanding officer and informed him of all that had happened. The commandant at once ordered a company of cavalry and one of infantry to proceed to Plum Creek on a forced march—taking a howitzer[5] with them—to endeavor to recapture the cattle from the Indians.

The firm of Russell, Majors & Waddell had a division agent at Kearney, and this agent mounted us on mules so that we could accompany the troops. On reaching the place where the Indians had surprised us, we found the bodies of the three men whom they had killed and scalped, and literally cut into pieces. We of course buried the remains. We caught but few of the cattle; the most of them having been driven off and stampeded with the buffaloes, there being numerous immense herds of the latter in that section of the country at that time. The Indians' trail was discovered running south towards the Republican river,[6] and the troops followed it to the head of Plum Creek, and there abandoned it, returning to Fort Kearney without having seen a single red-skin.

The company's agent, seeing that there was no further use for us in that vicinity—as we had lost our cattle and mules—sent us back to Fort Leavenworth. The company, it is proper to state, did not have to stand the loss of the expedition, as the government held itself responsible for such depredations by the Indians.

On the day that I got into Leavenworth, sometime in July, I was interviewed for the first time in my life by a newspaper reporter, and the next morning I found my name in print as "the youngest Indian slayer on the plains." I am candid enough to admit that I felt very much elated over this notoriety. Again and again I read with eager interest the long and sensational account of our adventure. My exploit was related in a very graphic manner, and for a long time afterwards I was considerable of a hero. The reporter who had thus set me up, as I then thought, on the highest pinnacle of fame, was John Hutchinson, and I felt very grateful to him. He now lives in Wichita, Kansas.

CHAPTER V

In Business

In the summer of 1857, Russell, Majors & Waddell were sending a great many trains across the plains to Salt Lake with supplies for General Johnston's army. Men were in great demand, and the company was paying teamsters forty dollars per month in gold. An old and reliable wagon-master named Lewis Simpson—who had taken a great fancy to me, and who, by the way, was one of the best wagon-masters that ever ran a bull train—was loading a train for the company, and was about to start out with it for Salt Lake. He asked me to go along as an "extra hand." The high wages that were being paid were a great inducement to me, and the position of an "extra hand" was a pleasant one. All that I would have to do would be to take the place of any man who became sick, and drive his wagon until he recovered. I would have my own mule to ride, and to a certain extent I would be a minor boss.

My mother was very much opposed to my taking this long trip, as I would be absent nearly a year, and there was a possibility that something might arise to prevent me from ever coming back, as we could not often tell how the Mormon difficulty would terminate. Then again, owing to the Indians, a journey over the plains in those days was a perilous undertaking. She said that as I had recently returned from the plains, and had had a narrow escape from death at the hands of the Indians, she did not want me to risk my life a second time. I told her that inasmuch as I had determined to follow the plains for an occupation, nothing could now stop me from going on this trip, and if it became necessary I would run away.

Seeing that it was impossible to keep me at home, she reluctantly gave her consent, but not until she had called upon Mr. Russell and Mr. Simpson in regard to the matter, and had obtained from the latter gentleman his promise that I should be well taken care of, if we had to winter in the mountains. She did not like the appearance of Simpson, and upon inquiry she learned, to her dismay, that he was a desperate character, and that on nearly every trip he had made across the plains he had killed some one. Such a man, she thought, was not a fit master or companion for her son, and she was very anxious to have me go with some other wagon-master; but I still insisted upon remaining with Simpson.

"Madam, I can assure you that Lew. Simpson is one of the most reliable wagon-masters on the plains," said Mr. Russell, "and he has taken a great fancy to Billy. If your boy is bound to go, he can go with no better man. No one will dare to impose on him while he is with Lew. Simpson, whom I will instruct to take good care of the boy. Upon reaching Fort Laramie, Billy can, if he wishes, exchange places with some fresh man coming back on a returning train, and thus come home without making the whole trip."

This seemed to satisfy mother, and then she had a long talk with Simpson himself, imploring him not to forget his promise to take good care of her precious boy.

He promised everything that she asked. Thus, after much trouble, I became one of the members of Simpson's train. Before taking our departure, I arranged with Russell, Majors & Waddell that when my pay should fall due it should be paid over to mother.

As a matter of interest to the general reader, it may be well in this connection to give a brief description of a freight train. The wagons used in those days by Russell, Majors & Waddell were known as the "J. Murphy wagons," made at St. Louis specially for the plains business. They were very large and were strongly built, being capable of carrying seven thousand pounds of freight each. The wagon-boxes were very commodious—being as large as the rooms of an ordinary house—and were covered with two heavy canvas sheets to protect the merchandise from the rain. These wagons were generally sent out from Leavenworth, each loaded with six thousand pounds of freight, and each drawn by several yokes of oxen in charge of one driver. A train consisted of twenty-five wagons, all in charge of one man, who was known as the wagon-master. The second man in command was the assistant wagon-master; then came the "extra hand"; next the night herder; and lastly, the cavallard driver, whose duty it was to drive the lame and loose cattle. There were thirty-one men all told in a train. The men did their own cooking, being divided into messes of seven. One man cooked, another brought wood and water, another stood guard, and so on, each having some duty to perform while getting meals. All were heavily armed with Colt's pistols and Mississippi yagers, and every one always had his weapons handy so as to be prepared for any emergency.

19. A Prairie Schooner

The wagon-master, in the language of the plains, was called the "bull-wagon boss"; the teamsters were known as "bull-whackers"; and the whole train was denominated a "bull-outfit." Everything at that time was called an "outfit." The men of the plains were always full of droll humor and exciting stories of their own experiences, and many an hour I spent in listening to the recitals of thrilling adventures and hair-breadth escapes.

Russell, Majors & Waddell had in their employ two hundred and fifty trains, composed of 6,250 wagons, 75,000 oxen, and about eight thousand men; their business reaching to all the government frontier posts in the north and west, to which they transported supplies, and they also carried freight as far south as New Mexico.

The trail to Salt Lake ran through Kansas to the northwest, crossing the Big Blue river, then over the Big and Little Sandy, coming into Nebraska near the Big Sandy. The next stream of any importance was the Little Blue, along which the trail ran for sixty miles; then crossed a range of sand-hills and struck the Platte river ten miles below Old Fort Kearney; thence the course lay up the South Platte to the old Ash Hollow Crossing, thence eighteen miles across to the North Platte—near the mouth of the Blue Water, where General Harney had his great battle in 1855 with the Sioux and Cheyenne Indians.[1] From this point the North Platte was followed, passing Court House Rock, Chimney Rock and Scott's Bluffs, and then on to Fort Laramie, where the Laramie River was crossed. Still following the North Platte for some considerable distance, the trail crossed this river at old Richard's Bridge, and followed it up to the celebrated Red Buttes—crossing the Willow creeks to the Sweet Water, passing the great Independence Rock and the Devil's gate, up to the Three Crossings of the Sweet Water, thence past the Cold Springs, where, three feet under the sod, on the hottest day of summer, ice can be found; thence to the Hot Springs and the Rocky Ridge, and through the Rocky Mountains and Echo Cañon, and thence on to the Great Salt Lake valley.

We had started on our trip with everything in good shape, following the above described trail. During the first week or two out, I became well acquainted with most of the train men, and with one in particular, who became a life-long and intimate friend of mine. His real name was James B. Hickok; he afterwards became famous as "Wild Bill, the Scout of the Plains"—though why he was so called I never could ascertain—and from this time forward I shall refer to him by his popular nickname.[2]

He was ten years my senior—a tall, handsome,

magnificently built and powerful young fellow, who could out-run, out-jump and out-fight any man in the train. He was generally admitted to be the best man physically, in the employ of Russell, Majors & Waddell; and of his bravery there was not a doubt. General Custer,[3] in his "Life on the Plains," thus speaks of Wild Bill:

"Among the white scouts were numbered some of the most noted of their class. The most prominent man among them was 'Wild Bill,' whose highly varied career was made the subject of an illustrated sketch in one of the popular monthly periodicals a few years ago. 'Wild Bill' was a strange character, just the one which a novelist might gloat over. He was a plains-man in every sense of the word, yet unlike any other of his class. In person he was about six feet and one inch in height, straight as the straightest of the warriors whose implacable foe he was. He had broad shoulders, well-formed chest and limbs, and a face strikingly handsome; a sharp, clear blue eye, which stared you straight in the face when in conversation; a finely shaped nose, inclined to be aquiline; a well-turned mouth, with lips only partially concealed by a handsome moustache. His hair and complexion were those of the perfect blonde. The former was worn in uncut ringlets, falling carelessly over his powerfully formed shoulders. Add to this figure a costume blending the immaculate neatness of the dandy with the extravagant taste and style of the frontiersman, and you have Wild Bill. Whether on foot or on horseback, he was one of the most perfect types of physical manhood I ever saw.

"Of his courage there could be no question; it had been brought to the test on too many occasions to admit of a doubt. His skill in the use of the pistol and rifle was unerring; while his deportment was exactly the opposite of what might be expected from a man of his surroundings. It was entirely free from all bluster or bravado. He seldom spoke himself unless requested to do so. His conversation, strange to say, never bordered either on the vulgar or blasphemous. His influence among the frontiersmen was unbounded, his word was law; and many are the personal quarrels and disturbances which he has checked among his comrades by his simple announcement that 'This has gone far enough,'—if need be followed by the ominous warning that when persisted in or renewed the quarreler 'must settle it with me.'

"Wild Bill was anything but a quarrelsome man; yet no one but him could enumerate the many conflicts in which he had been engaged, and which had almost always resulted in the death of his adversary. I have a personal knowledge of at least half a dozen men whom he had at various times killed, one of these being at the time a member of my command. Others had been severely wounded, yet he always escaped unhurt.

"On the plains every man openly carries his belt with its invariable appendages, knife and revolver—often two of the latter. Wild Bill always carried two handsome ivory-handled revolvers of the large size; he was never seen without them. Yet in all the many affairs of this kind in which Wild Bill has performed a part, and which have come to my knowledge, there was not a single instance in which the verdict of twelve fair-minded men would not have been pronounced in his favor."[4]

Such is the faithful picture of Wild Bill as drawn by

20. Wild Bill

General Custer, who was a close observer and student of personal character, and under whom Wild Bill served as a scout.

The circumstances under which I first made his acquaintance and learned to know him well and to appreciate his manly character and kind-heartedness, were these. One of the teamsters in Lew. Simpson's train was a surly, overbearing fellow, and took particular delight in bullying and tyrannizing over me, and one day while we were at dinner he asked me to do something for him. I did not start at once, and he gave me a slap in the face with the back of his hand,—knocking me off an ox-yoke on which

I was sitting, and sending me sprawling on the ground. Jumping to my feet I picked up a camp kettle full of boiling coffee which was setting on the fire, and threw it at him. I hit him in the face, and the hot coffee gave him a severe scalding. He sprang for me with the ferocity of a tiger, and would undoubtedly have torn me to pieces, had it not been for the timely interference of my new-found friend, Wild Bill, who knocked the man down. As soon as he recovered himself, he demanded of Wild Bill what business it was of his that he should "put in his oar." "It's my business to protect that boy, or anybody else, from being unmercifully abused, kicked and cuffed, and I'll whip any man who tries it on," said Wild Bill; "and if you ever again lay a hand on that boy—little Billy there—I'll give you such a pounding that you won't get over it for a month of Sundays." From that time forward Wild Bill was my protector and intimate friend, and the friendship thus begun continued until his death.

Nothing transpired on the trip to delay or give us any trouble whatever, until the train struck the South Platte river. One day we camped on the same ground where the Indians had surprised the cattle herd, in charge of the Mc-Carthy brothers. It was with difficulty that we discovered any traces of anybody ever having camped there before, the only landmark being the single grave, now covered with grass, in which we had buried the three men who had been killed. The country was alive with buffaloes. Vast herds of these monarchs of the plains were roaming all around us, and we laid over one day for a grand hunt. Besides killing quite a number of buffaloes, and having a day of rare sport, we captured ten or twelve head of cattle, they being a portion of the herd which had been stampeded by the Indians, two months before. The next day we pulled out of camp, and the train was strung out to a considerable length along the road which ran near the foot of the sand-hills, two miles from the river. Between the road and the river we saw a large herd of buffaloes grazing quietly, they having been down to the stream for a drink.

Just at this time we observed a party of returning Californians coming from the West. They, too, noticed the buffalo herd, and in another moment they were dashing down upon them, urging their steeds to the greatest speed. The buffalo herd stampeded at once, and broke for the hills; so hotly were they pursued by the hunters that about five hundred of them rushed through our train pell-mell, frightening both men and oxen. Some of the wagons were turned clear round, and many of the terrified oxen attempted to run to the hills, with the heavy wagons attached to them. Others turned around so short that they broke the wagon tongues off. Nearly all the teams got entangled in their gearing, and became wild and unruly, so that the perplexed drivers were unable to manage them.

The buffaloes, the cattle, and the drivers, were soon running in every direction, and the excitement upset nearly everybody and everything. Many of the cattle broke their yokes and stampeded. One big buffalo bull became entangled in one of the heavy wagon-chains, and it is a fact that in his desperate efforts to free himself, he not only actually snapped the strong chain in two, but broke the ox-yoke to which it was attached, and the last seen of him he was running towards the hills with it hanging from his horns. A dozen other equally remarkable incidents happened during the short time that the frantic buffaloes were playing havoc with our train, and when they had got through and left us, our outfit was very badly crippled and scattered. This caused us to go into camp and spend a day in replacing the broken tongues, and repairing other damages, and gathering up our scattered ox-teams.

The next day we rolled out of camp, and proceeded on our way towards the setting sun. Everything ran along smoothly with us from that point until we came within about eighteen miles of Green river, in the Rocky mountains—where we camped at noon. At this place we had to drive our cattle about a mile and a half to a creek to water them. Simpson, his assistant, George Woods and myself, accompanied by the usual number of guards, drove the cattle over to the creek, and while on our way back to camp, we suddenly observed a party of twenty horsemen rapidly approaching us. We were not yet in view of our wagons, as a rise of ground intervened, and therefore we could not signal the train-men in case of any unexpected danger befalling us. We had no suspicion, however, that we were about to be trapped, as the strangers were white men. When they had come up to us, one of the party, who evidently was the leader, rode out in front and said:

"How are you, Mr. Simpson?"

"You've got the best of me, sir," said Simpson, who did not know him.

"Well, I rather think I have," coolly replied the stranger, whose words conveyed a double meaning, as we soon learned. We had all come to a halt by this time, and the strange horsemen had surrounded us. They were all armed with double-barreled shot guns, rifles and revolvers. We also were armed with revolvers, but we had had no idea of danger, and these men, much to our surprise, had "got the drop" on us, and had covered us with their weapons, so that we were completely at their mercy. The whole movement of corraling us was done so quietly and quickly that it was accomplished before we knew it.

"I'll trouble you for your six shooters, gentlemen," now said the leader.

"I'll give 'em to you in a way you don't want," replied Simpson.

The next moment three guns were leveled at Simpson. "If you make a move you're a dead man," said the leader.

Simpson saw that he was taken at a great disadvantage, and thinking it advisable not to risk the lives of the party by any rash act on his part, he said: "I see now that you have the best of me, but who are you, anyhow?"

"I am Joe Smith," was the reply.[5]

"What! the leader of the Danites?"[6] asked Simpson.

"You are correct," said Smith, for he it was.

"Yes," said Simpson, "I know you now; you are a spying scoundrel."

Simpson had good reason for calling him this and applying to him a much more opprobrious epithet, for only a short time before this, Joe Smith had visited our train in the disguise of a teamster, and had remained with us two days. He suddenly disappeared, no one knowing where he had gone or why he had come among us. But it was all explained to us now that he had returned with his Mormon Danites. After they had disarmed us, Simpson asked, "Well, Smith, what are you going to do with us?"

"Ride back with us and I'll soon show you," said Smith.

We had no idea of the surprise which awaited us. As we came upon the top of the ridge, from which we could view our camp, we were astonished to see the remainder of the train men disarmed and stationed in a group and surrounded by another squad of Danites, while other Mormons were searching our wagons for such articles as they wanted.

"How is this?" inquired Simpson. "How did you surprise my camp without a struggle? I can't understand it."

"Easily enough," said Smith; "your men were all asleep under the wagons, except the cooks, who saw us coming and took us for returning Californians or emigrants, and paid no attention to us until we rode up and surrounded your train. With our arms covering the men, we woke them up, and told them that all they had to do was to walk out and drop their pistols—which they saw was the best thing they could do under circumstances over which they had no control—and you can just bet they did it."

"And what do you propose to do with us now?" asked Simpson.

"I intend to burn your train," said he; "you are loaded with supplies and ammunition for Sidney Johnston, and as I have no way to convey the stuff to my own people, I'll see that it does not reach the United States troops."

"Are you going to turn us adrift here?" asked Simpson, who was anxious to learn what was to become of himself and his men.

"No; I hardly am as bad as that. I'll give you enough provisions to last you until you can reach Fort Bridger," replied Smith; "and as soon as your cooks can get the stuff out of the wagons, you can start."

"On foot?" was the laconic inquiry of Simpson.

"Yes sir," was the equally short reply.

"Smith, that's too rough on us men. Put yourself in our place and see how you would like it," said Simpson; "you can well afford to give us at least one wagon and six yokes of oxen to convey us and our clothing and provisions to Fort Bridger. You're a brute if you don't do this."

"Well," said Smith, after consulting a minute or two with some of his company, "I'll do that much for you."

The cattle and the wagon were brought up according to his orders, and the clothing and provisions were loaded on.

"Now you can go," said Smith, after everything had been arranged.

"Joe Smith, I think you are a mean coward to set us afloat in a hostile country, without giving us our arms," said Simpson, who had once before asked for the weapons, and had had his request denied.

Smith, after further consultation with his comrades, said: "Simpson, you are too brave a man to be turned adrift here without any means of defense. You shall have your revolvers and guns." Our weapons were accordingly handed over to Simpson, and we at once started for Fort Bridger, knowing that it would be useless to attempt the recapture of our train.

When we had traveled about two miles we saw the smoke arising from our old camp. The Mormons after taking what goods they wanted and could carry off, had set fire to the wagons, many of which were loaded with bacon, lard, hard-tack, and other provisions, which made a very hot, fierce fire, and the smoke to roll up in dense clouds. Some of the wagons were loaded with ammunition, and it was not long before loud explosions followed in rapid succession. We waited and witnessed the burning of the train, and then pushed on to Fort Bridger. Arriving at this post, we learned that two other trains had been captured and destroyed in the same way, by the Mormons. This made seventy-five wagon loads, or 450,000 pounds of supplies, mostly provisions, which never reached General Johnston's command, to which they had been consigned.

CHAPTER VI

Hard Times

As it was getting very late in the fall, we were compelled to winter at Fort Bridger; and a long, tedious winter it was. There were a great many troops there, and about four hundred of Russell, Majors & Waddell's employees. These men were all organized into militia companies, which were officered by the wagon-masters. Some lived in tents, others in cabins. It was known that our supplies would run short during the winter, and so all the men at the post were put on three-quarter rations to begin with; before long they were reduced to one-half rations, and finally to one-quarter rations. We were forced to kill our poor worn-out cattle for beef. They were actually so poor that we had to prop them up to shoot them down. At last we fell back on the mules, which were killed and served up in good style. Many a poor, unsuspecting government mule passed in his chips that winter in order to keep the soldiers and bull-whackers from starvation.

It was really a serious state of affairs. The wood for the post was obtained from the mountains, but having no longer any cattle or mules to transport it, the men were obliged to haul it themselves. Long lariats were tied to the wagons, and twenty men manning each, they were pulled to and from the mountains. Notwithstanding all these hardships, the men seemed to be contented and to enjoy themselves.

The winter finally passed away, and early in the spring, as soon as we could travel, the civil employees of the government, with the teamsters and freighters, started for the Missouri river; the Johnston expedition having been abandoned.

On the way down we stopped at Fort Laramie,[1] and there met a supply train bound westward. Of course we all had a square meal once more, consisting of hard tack, bacon, coffee and beans. I can honestly say that I thought it was the best meal I had ever eaten; at least I relished it more than any other, and I think the rest of the party did the same.

On leaving Fort Laramie, Simpson was made brigade wagon-master, and was put in charge of two large trains, with about four hundred extra men, who were bound for Fort Leavenworth. When we came to Ash Hollow, instead of taking the usual trail over to the South Platte, Simpson concluded to follow the North Platte down to its junction with the South Platte. The two trains were traveling about fifteen miles apart, when one morning while Simpson was with the rear train, he told his assistant wagon-master, George Woods and myself to saddle up our mules, as he wanted us to go with him and overtake the head train.

We started off at about eleven o'clock, and had ridden about seven miles when—while we were on a big plateau, back of Cedar Bluffs—we suddenly discovered a band of Indians coming out of the head of a ravine, half a mile distant, and charging down upon us at full speed. I thought that our end had come this time, sure. Simpson, however, took in the situation in a moment, and knowing that it would be impossible to escape by running our played-out mules, he adopted a bolder and much better plan. He jumped from his own mule, and told us to dismount also. He then shot the three animals, and as they fell to the ground he cut their throats to stop their kicking. He then jerked them into the shape of a triangle, and ordered us inside of the barricade.

All this was but the work of a few moments, yet it was not done any too soon, for the Indians had got within three hundred yards of us, and were still advancing, and uttering their demoniacal yells or war-whoops. There were forty of the red-skins and only three of us. We were each armed with a Mississippi yager and two Colt's revolvers.

"Get ready for them with your guns, and when they come within fifty yards, aim low, blaze away and bring down your man!"

Such was the quick command of Simpson. The words had hardly escaped from his mouth, when the three yagers almost simultaneously belched forth their contents. We then seized our revolvers and opened a lively fire on the enemy, at short range, which checked their advance. Then we looked over our little barricade to ascertain what effect our fire had produced, and were much gratified at seeing three dead Indians and one horse lying on the ground. Only two or three of the Indians, it seemed, had fire-arms. It must be remembered that in those days every Indian did not own a needle gun[2] or a Winchester rifle, as they now do.

Seeing that they could not take our little fortification, or drive us from it, they circled around us several times,

21. Holding the Fort

shooting their arrows at us. One of the arrows struck George Wood in the left shoulder, inflicting only a slight wound, however, and several lodged in the bodies of the dead mules; otherwise they did us no harm.

The Indians finally galloped off to a safe distance, where our bullets could not reach them, and seemed to be holding a council. This was a lucky move for us, for it gave us an opportunity to reload our guns and pistols, and prepare for the next charge of the enemy. During the brief cessation of hostilities, Simpson extracted the arrow from Wood's shoulder, and put an immense quid of tobacco on the wound. Wood was then ready for business again.

The Indians did not give us a very long rest, for with another desperate charge, as if to ride over us, they came dashing towards the mule barricade. We gave them a hot reception from our yagers and revolvers. They could not stand, or understand, the rapidly repeating fire of the revolvers, and we again checked them. They circled around us once more and gave us a few parting shots as they rode off, leaving behind them another dead Indian and a horse.

For two hours afterwards they did not seem to be doing anything but holding a council. We made good use of this time by digging up the ground inside the barricade with our knives and throwing the loose earth around and over the mules, and we soon had a very respectable fortification. We were not troubled any more that day, but during the night the cunning rascals tried to burn us out by setting fire to the prairie. The buffalo grass was so short that the fire did not trouble us much, but the smoke concealed the Indians from our view, and they thought that they could approach close to us without being seen. We were aware of this, and kept a sharp look-out, being prepared all the time to receive them. They finally abandoned the idea of surprising us.

Next morning, bright and early, they gave us one more grand charge, and again we "stood them off." They then rode away half a mile or so, and formed a circle around us. Each man dismounted and sat down, as if to wait and starve us out. They had evidently seen the advance train pass on the morning of the previous day, and believed that we belonged to that outfit and were trying to overtake it; they had no idea that another train was on its way after us.

Our hopes of escape from this unpleasant and perilous situation now depended upon the arrival of the rear train, and when we saw that the Indians were going to besiege us instead of renewing their attacks, we felt rather confident of receiving timely assistance. We had expected that the train would be along late in the afternoon of the previous day, and as the morning wore away we were somewhat anxious and uneasy, at its non-arrival.

At last, about ten o'clock, we began to hear in the distance the loud and sharp reports of the big bull-whips, which were handled with great dexterity by the teamsters, and cracked like rifle shots. These were as welcome sounds to us as were the notes of the bag-pipes to the besieged garrison at Lucknow, when the reinforcements were coming up and the pipers were heard playing, "The Campbells are Coming."[3] In a few moments we saw the lead or head wagon coming slowly over the ridge, which had concealed the train from our view, and soon the whole outfit made its appearance. The Indians observed the approaching train, and assembling in a group they held a short consultation.

They then charged upon us once more, for the last time, and as they turned and dashed away over the prairie, we sent our farewell shots rattling after them. The teamsters, seeing the Indians and hearing the shots, came rushing forward to our assistance, but by the time they reached us the red-skins had almost disappeared from view. The teamsters eagerly asked us a hundred questions concerning our fight, admired our fort and praised our pluck. Simpson's remarkable presence of mind in planning the defense was the general topic of conversation among all the men.

When the teams came up we obtained some water and bandages with which to dress Wood's wound, which had become quite inflamed and painful, and we then put him into one of the wagons. Simpson and myself obtained a remount, bade good-bye to our dead mules which had served us so well, and after collecting the ornaments and other plunder from the dead Indians, we left their bodies and bones to bleach on the prairie. The train moved on again and we had no other adventures, except several exciting buffalo hunts on the South Platte, near Plum Creek.

We arrived at Fort Leavenworth about the middle of July, 1858, when I immediately visited home. I found mother in very poor health, as she was suffering from asthma. My oldest sister, Martha, had, during my absence, been married to John Crane, and was living at Leavenworth.

During the winter at Fort Bridger I had frequently talked with Wild Bill about my family, and as I had become greatly attached to him I asked him to come and make a visit at our house, which he promised to do. So one day, shortly after our return from Fort Bridger, he accompanied me home from Leavenworth. My mother and sisters, who had heard so much about him from me, were delighted to see him and he spent several weeks at our place. They did everything possible to repay him for his kindness to me. Ever afterwards, when he was at or near Leavenworth, Wild Bill came out to our house to see the family, whether I was at home or not, and he always received a most cordial reception. His mother and sisters lived in Illinois, and he used to call our house his home, as he did not have one of his own.

I had been home only about a month, after returning from Fort Bridger, when I again started out with another train, going this time as assistant wagon-master under Buck Bomer. We went safely through to Fort Laramie, which was our destination, and from there we were ordered to take a load of supplies to a new post called Fort Wallace, which was being established at Cheyenne Pass. We made this trip and got back to Fort Laramie about November 1st. I then quit the employ of Russell, Majors & Waddell, and joined a party of trappers who were sent out by the post trader, Mr. Ward, to trap on the streams of the Chugwater and Laramie for beaver, otter, and other fur animals, and also to poison wolves for their pelts. We were out two months, but as the expedition did not prove very profitable, and was rather dangerous on account of the Indians, we abandoned the enterprise and came into Fort Laramie in the latter part of December.

Being anxious to return to the Missouri river, I joined with two others, named Scott and Charley, who were also desirous of going East on a visit, bought three ponies and a pack-mule, and we started out together. We made rapid progress on our journey, and nothing worthy of note happened until one afternoon, along the banks of the Little Blue River, we spied a band of Indians hunting on the opposite side of the stream, three miles away. We did not escape their notice, and they gave us a lively chase for two hours, but they could find no good crossing, and as evening came on we finally got away from them.

We traveled until late in the night; when upon discovering a low, deep ravine which we thought would make a comfortable and safe camping-place, we stopped for a rest. In searching for a good place to make our beds, I found a hole, and I called to my companions that I had found a fine place for a nest. One of the party was to stand guard while the others slept. Scott took the first watch, while Charley and I made a bed in the hole.

While clearing out the place we felt something rough, but as it was dark we could not make out what it was. At any rate we concluded that it was bones or sticks of wood; we thought perhaps it might be the bones of some animal which had fallen in there and died. These bones, for such they really proved to be, we pushed one side and then we lay down. But Charley, being an inveterate smoker, could not resist the temptation of indulging in a smoke before going to sleep. So he sat up and struck a match to light his old pipe. Our subterranean bed-chamber was thus illuminated for a moment or two; I sprang to my feet in an instant for a ghastly and horrifying sight was revealed to us. Eight or ten human skeletons lay scattered upon the ground.

The light of the match died out, but we had seen enough to convince us that we were in a large grave, into which, perhaps, some unfortunate emigrants, who had

22. Camping in a Sepulchre

been killed by the Indians, had been thrown; or, perhaps, seeking refuge there, they had been corraled and then killed on the spot. If such was the case, they had met the fate of thousands of others, whose friends have never heard of them since they left their eastern homes to seek their fortunes in the Far West. However, we did not care to investigate this mystery any further, but we hustled out of that chamber of death and informed Scott of our discovery. Most of the plains-men are very superstitious, and we were no exception to the general rule. We surely thought that this incident was an evil omen, and that we would be killed if we remained there any longer.

"Let us dig out of here quicker than we can say Jack Robinson," said Scott; and we began to "dig out" at once. We saddled our animals and hurriedly pushed forward through the darkness, traveling several miles before we again went into camp. Next morning it was snowing fiercely, but we proceeded as best we could, and that night we succeeded in reaching Oak Grove ranch, which had been built during the summer. We here obtained comfortable accommodations and plenty to eat and drink—especially the latter.

Scott and Charley were great lovers and consumers of "tanglefoot,"[4] and they soon got gloriously drunk, keeping it up for three days, during which time they gambled with the ranchmen, who got away with all their money; but little they cared for that, as they had their spree. They finally sobered up, and we resumed our journey, urging our jaded animals as much as they could stand, until we struck Marysville, on the Big Blue.[5] From this place to Leavenworth we secured first-rate accommodations along

23. Rafting on the Platte

the road, as the country had become pretty well settled.

It was in February, 1859, that I got home. As there was now a good school in the neighborhood, taught by Mr. Divinny, my mother wished me to attend it, and I did so for two months and a half—the longest period of schooling that I ever received at any one time in my life. As soon as the spring came and the grass began growing, I became uneasy and discontented, and again longed for the free and open life of the plains.

The Pike's Peak gold excitement was then at its height, and everybody was rushing to the new gold diggings.[6] I caught the gold-fever myself, and joined a party bound for the new town of Auraria, on Cherry Creek, afterwards called Denver, in honor of the then governor of Kansas.

On arriving at Auraria we pushed on to the gold streams in the mountains, passing up through Golden Gate, and over Guy Hill, and thence on to Black Hawk. We prospected for two months, but as none of us knew anything about mining we met with very poor success, and we finally concluded that prospecting for gold was not our forte. We accordingly abandoned the enterprise and turned our faces eastward once more.

When we struck the Platte River, the happy thought of constructing a small raft—which would float us clear to the Missouri and thence down to Leavenworth—entered our heads, and we accordingly carried out the plan. Upon the completion of the raft we stocked it with provisions, and "set sail" down the stream. It was a light craft and a jolly crew, and all was smooth sailing for four or five days.

When we got near old Julesburg, we met with a serious mishap. Our raft ran into an eddy, and quick as lightning went to pieces, throwing us all into the stream, which was so deep that we had to swim ashore. We lost everything we had, which greatly discouraged us, and we thereupon abandoned the idea of rafting it any farther. We then walked over to Julesburg, which was only a few miles distant. This ranch, which became a somewhat famous spot, had been established by "Old Jules,"[7] a Frenchman, who was afterwards killed by the notorious Alf. Slade.[8]

The great pony express,[9] about which so much has been said and written, was at that time just being started. The line was being stocked with horses and put into good running condition. At Julesburg I met Mr. George Chrisman, the leading wagon-master of Russell, Majors & Waddell, who had always been a good friend to me. He

had bought out "Old Jules," and was then the owner of Julesburg ranch, and the agent of the pony express line. He hired me at once as a pony express rider, but as I was so young he thought I would not be able to stand the fierce riding which was required of the messengers. He knew, however, that I had been raised in the saddle—that I felt more at home there than in any other place—and as he saw that I was confident that I could stand the racket, and could ride as far and endure it as well as some of the older riders, he gave me a short route of forty-five miles, with the stations fifteen miles apart, and three changes of horses. I was required to make fifteen miles an hour, including the changes of horses. I was fortunate in getting well-broken animals, and being so light, I easily made my forty-five miles on time on my first trip out, and ever afterwards.

I wrote to mother and told her how well I liked the exciting life of a pony express rider. She replied, and begged of me to give it up, as it would surely kill me. She was right about this, as fifteen miles an hour on horseback would, in a short time, shake any man "all to pieces"; and there were but very few, if any, riders who could stand it for any great length of time. Nevertheless, I stuck to it for two months, and then, upon receiving a letter informing me that my mother was very sick, I gave it up and went back to the old home in Salt Creek Valley.

CHAPTER VII

Accidents and Escapes

My restless, roaming spirit would not allow me to remain at home very long, and in November, after the recovery of my mother, I went up the Republican River and its tributaries on a trapping expedition in company with Dave Harrington. Our outfit consisted of one wagon and a yoke of oxen for the transportation of provisions, traps, and other necessaries. We began trapping near Junction City, Kansas, and then proceeded up the Republican River to the mouth of Prairie Dog Creek, where we found plenty of beavers.

Having seen no signs of Indians thus far, we felt comparatively safe. We were catching a large number of beavers and were prospering finely, when one of our oxen, having become rather poor, slipped and fell upon the ice, dislocating his hip, so that we had to shoot him to end his misery. This left us without a team; but we cared little for that, however, as we had made up our minds to remain there till spring, when, and it was decided, that one of us should go to the nearest settlement and get a yoke of oxen with which to haul our wagon into some place of safety where we could leave it.

We would probably have pulled through the winter all right had it not been for a very serious accident which befell me just at that time. Spying a herd of elk, we started in pursuit of them, and creeping up towards them as slyly as possible, while going around the bend of a sharp bluff or bank of the creek I slipped and broke my leg just above the ankle. Notwithstanding the great pain I was suffering, Harrington could not help laughing when I urged him to shoot me, as he had the ox, and thus end my misery. He told me to "brace up," and that he would bring me out "all right."

"I am not much of a surgeon," said he, "but I can fix that leg of yours, even if I haven't got a diploma."

He succeeded in getting me back to camp, which was only a few yards from the creek, and then he set the fracture as well as he knew how, and made me as comfortable as was possible under the circumstances. We then discussed the situation, which to say the least, looked pretty blue. Knowing that, owing to our mishaps, we could not do anything more that winter, and as I dreaded the idea of lying there on my back with a broken leg for weeks, and perhaps months, I prevailed upon Harrington to go the nearest settlement—about 125 miles distant—to obtain a yoke of cattle, and then come back for me.

This he consented to do; but before leaving he gathered plenty of wood, and as the ground was covered with snow, I would have no difficulty in getting water if I had a fire. There was plenty of fresh meat and other provisions in the "dug-out," so that I had no fears of starvation. The "dugout," which we had built immediately after we had determined to remain there all winter, was a very cosy hole in the ground, covered with poles, grass and sod, with a fireplace in one end.

Harrington thought it would take him twenty days or more to make the round trip; but being well provided for--for this length of time—I urged him to go at once. Bidding me good-bye he started on foot. After his departure, each day, as it came and went, seemed to grow longer to me as I lay there helpless and alone. I made a note of each day, so as to know the time when I might expect him back.

On the twelfth day after Harrington left me, I was awakened from a sound sleep by some one touching me upon the shoulder. I looked up and was astonished to see an Indian warrior standing at my side. His face was hideously daubed with paint, which told me more forcibly than words could have done that he was on the war-path. He spoke to me in broken English and Sioux mixed, and I understood him to ask what I was doing there, and how many there were with me.

By this time the little dug-out was nearly filled with other Indians, who had been peeping in at the door, and I could hear voices of still more outside as well as the stamping of horses. I began to think that my time had come, as the saying is, when into the cabin stepped an elderly Indian, whom I readily recognized as old Rain-in-the-Face,[1] a Sioux chief from the vicinity of Fort Laramie. I rose up as well as I could and showed him my broken leg. I told him where I had seen him, and asked him if he remembered me. He replied that he knew me well, and that I used to come to his lodge at Fort Laramie to visit him. I then managed to make him understand that I was there alone and having broken my leg, I had sent my partner off for a team to take me away. I asked him if his young men intended to kill me, and he answered,

25. Saved by Chief Rain-In-The-Face

that was what they had proposed to do, but he would see what they had to say.

The Indians then talked among themselves for a few minutes, and upon the conclusion of the consultation, old Rain-in-the-Face turned to me and gave me to understand that as I was yet a "papoose," or a very young man, they would not take my life. But one of his men, who had no fire-arms, wanted my gun and pistol. I implored old Rain-in-the-Face to be allowed to keep the weapons, or at least one of them, as I needed something with which to keep the wolves away. He replied that as his young men were out on the war path, he had induced them to spare my life; but he could not prevent them from taking what ever else they wanted.

They unsaddled their horses as if to remain there for some time, and sure enough they stayed the remainder of the day and all night. They built a fire in the dug-out and cooked a lot of my provisions, helping themselves to everything as if they owned it. However, they were polite enough to give me some of the food after they had cooked it. It was a sumptuous feast that they had, and they seemed to relish it as if it was the best lay-out they had had for many a long day. They took all my sugar and coffee, and left me only some meat and a small quantity of flour, a little salt and some baking powder. They also robbed me of such cooking utensils as they wished; then bidding me good-bye, early in the morning, they mounted their ponies and rode off to the south, evidently bent on some murdering and thieving expedition.

I was glad enough to see them leave, as my life had undoubtedly hung by a thread during their presence. I am confident that had it not been for my youth and the timely recognition and interference of old Rain-in-the-Face they would have killed me without any hesitation or ceremony.

The second day after they had gone it began snowing, and for three long and weary days the snow continued to fall thick and fast. It blocked the door-way and covered the dug-out to the depth of several feet, so that I became a snowbound prisoner. My wood was mostly under the snow, and it was with great difficulty that I could get enough to start a fire with. My prospects were gloomy indeed. I had just faced death at the hands of the Indians, and now I was in danger of losing my life from starvation and cold. I knew that the heavy snow would surely delay Harrington on his return; and I feared that he might have perished in the storm, or that some other accident might have befallen him. Perhaps some wandering band of Indians had run across him and killed him.

I was continually thinking of all these possibilities, and I must say that my outlook seemed desperate. At last the twentieth day arrived—the day on which Harrington was to return—and I counted the hours from morning till night, but the day passed away with no signs of Harrington. The wolves made the night hideous with their howls; they gathered around the dug-out; ran over the roof; and pawed and scratched as if trying to get in.

Several days and nights thus wore away, the monotony all the time becoming greater, until at last it became almost unendurable. Some days I would go without any fire at all, and eat raw frozen meat and melt snow in my mouth for water. I became almost convinced that Harrington had been caught in the storm and had been buried under the snow, or was lost. Many a time during that dreary period of uncertainty, I made up my mind that if I ever got out of that place alive, I would abandon the plains and the life of a trapper forever. I had nearly given up all hopes of leaving the dug-out alive.

It was on the twenty-ninth day, while I was lying thus despondently thinking and wondering, that I heard the cheerful sound of Harrington's voice as he came slowly up the creek, yelling, "Whoa! Haw!" to his cattle. A criminal on the scaffold, with the noose around his neck, the trap about to be sprung, and receiving a pardon just at the last moment, thus giving him a new lease of life, could not have been more grateful than I was at that time. It was useless for me to try to force the door open, as the snow had completely blockaded it, and I therefore anxiously awaited Harrington's arrival.

"Hello! Billy!" he sang out in a loud voice as he came up, he evidently being uncertain as to my being alive.

"All right, Dave," was my reply.

"Well, old boy, you're alive, are you?" said he.

"Yes; and that's about all. I've had a tough siege of it since you've been away, and I came pretty nearly passing in my chips. I began to think you never would get here, as I was afraid you had been snowed under," said I.

He soon cleared away the snow from the entrance, and opening the door he came in. I don't think there ever was a more welcome visitor than he was. I remember that I was so glad to see him that I put my arms around his neck and hugged him for five minutes; never shall I forget faithful Dave Harrington.

"Well, Billy, my boy, I hardly expected to see you alive

again," said Harrington, as soon as I had given him an opportunity to draw his breath; "I had a terrible trip of it, and I didn't think I ever would get through. I was caught in the snow-storm, and was laid up for three days. The cattle wandered away, and I came within an ace of losing them altogether. When I got started again the snow was so deep that it prevented me from making much headway. But as I had left you here I was bound to come through, or die in the attempt."

Again I flung my arms around Dave's neck and gave him a hug that would have done honor to a grizzly bear. My gratitude was thus much more forcibly expressed than it could have been by words. Harrington understood this, and seemed to appreciate it. The tears of joy rolled down my cheeks, and it was impossible for me to restrain them. When my life had been threatened by the Indians I had not felt half so miserable as when I lay in the dug-out thinking I was destined to die a slow death by starvation and cold. The Indians would have made short work of it, and would have given me little or no time to think of my fate.

I questioned Harrington as to his trip, and learned all the details. He had passed through hardships which but few men could have endured. Noble fellow, that he was. He had risked his own life to save mine.

After he had finished his story, every word of which I had listened to with eager interest, I related to him my own experiences, in which he became no less interested. He expressed great astonishment that the Indians had not killed me, and he considered it one of the luckiest and most remarkable escapes he had ever heard of. It amused me, however, to see him get very angry when I told him that they had taken my gun and pistol and had used up our provisions. "But never mind, Billy," said he, "we can stand it till the snow goes off, which will not be long, and then we will pull our wagon back to the settlements."

A few days afterwards Harrington gathered up our traps, and cleaned the snow out of the wagon. Covering it with the sheet which we had used in the dug-out, he made a comfortable bed inside, and helped me into it. We had been quite successful in trapping, having caught three hundred beavers and one hundred otters, the skins of which Harrington loaded on the wagon. We then pulled out for the settlements, making good headway, as the snow had nearly disappeared, having been blown or melted away, so that we had no difficulty in finding a road. On the eighth day out we came to a farmer's house, or ranch, on the Republican River, where we stopped and rested for two days, and then went on to the ranch where Harrington had obtained the yoke of cattle. We gave the owner of the team twenty-five beaver skins, equal to $60, for the use of the cattle, and he let us have them until we reached Junction City, sending his boy with us to bring them back.

At Junction City we sold our wagon and furs and went with a government mule train to Leavenworth—arriving there in March, 1860. I was just able to get around on crutches when I got into Leavenworth, and it was several months after that before I entirely recovered the use of my leg.

During the winter I had often talked to Harrington about my mother and sisters, and had invited him to go home with me in the spring. I now renewed the invitation, which he accepted, and accompanied me home.

When I related to mother my adventures and told her how Harrington had saved my life, she thanked him again and again. I never saw a more grateful woman than she was. She asked him to always make his home with us, as she never could reward him sufficiently for what he had done for her darling boy, as she called me. Harrington concluded to remain with us through the summer and farm mother's land. But alas! the uncertainty of life. The coming of death when least expected was strikingly illustrated in his case. During the latter part of April he went to a nursery for some trees, and while coming home late at night he caught a severe cold and was taken seriously sick, with lung fever.[2] Mother did everything in her power for him. She could not have done more had he been her own son, but notwithstanding her motherly care and attention, and the skill of a physician from Leavenworth, he rapidly grew worse. It seemed hard, indeed, to think that a great strong man like Harrington, who had braved the storms, and endured the other hardships of the plains all winter long, should, during the warm and beautiful days of spring, when surrounded by friends and the comforts of a good home, be fatally stricken down. But such was his fate. He died one week from the day on which he was taken sick. We all mourned his loss as we would that of a loved son or brother, as he was one of the truest, bravest, and best of friends. Amid sorrow and tears we laid him away to rest in a picturesque spot on Pilot Knob. His death cast a gloom over our household, and it was a long time before it was entirely dispelled. I felt very lonely without Harrington, and I soon wished for a change of scene again.

CHAPTER VIII

Adventures on the Overland Road

As the warm days of summer approached I longed for the cool air of the mountains; and to the mountains I determined to go. After engaging a man to take care of the farm, I proceeded to Leavenworth and there met my old wagon-master and friend, Lewis Simpson, who was fitting out a train at Atchison and loading it with supplies for the Overland Stage Company,[1] of which Mr. Russell, my old employer, was one of the proprietors. Simpson was going with this train to Fort Laramie and points further west.

"Come along with me, Billy," said he, "I'll give you a good lay-out. I want you with me."

"I don't know that I would like to go as far west as that again," replied I, "but I do want to ride the pony express once more; there's some life in that."

"Yes, that's so; but it will soon shake the life out of you," said he. "However, if that's what you've got your mind set on, you had better come to Atchison with me and see Mr. Russell, who I'm pretty certain, will give you a situation."

I replied that I would do that. I then went home and informed mother of my intention, and as her health was very poor I had great difficulty in obtaining her consent. I finally convinced her that as I was of no use on the farm, it would be better and more profitable for me to return to the plains. So after giving her all the money I had earned by trapping, I bade her good-bye and set out for Atchison.

I met Mr. Russell there and asked him for employment as a pony express-rider; he gave me a letter to Mr. Slade, who was then the stage agent for the division extending from Julesburg to Rocky Ridge. Slade had his headquarters at Horseshoe Station, thirty-six miles west of Fort Laramie and I made the trip thither in company with Simpson and his train.

Almost the very first person I saw after dismounting from my horse was Slade. I walked up to him and presented Mr. Russell's letter, which he hastily opened and read. With a sweeping glance of his eye he took my measure from head to foot, and then said:

"My boy, you are too young for a pony express-rider. It takes men for that business."

"I rode two months last year on Bill Trotter's division, sir, and filled the bill then; and I think I am better able to ride now," said I.

"What! are you the boy that was riding there, and was called the youngest rider on the road?"

"I am the same boy," I replied, confident that everything was now all right for me.

"I have heard of you before. You are a year or so older now, and I think you can stand it. I'll give you a trial anyhow and if you weaken you can come back to Horseshoe Station and tend stock."

That ended our first interview. The next day he assigned me to duty on the road from Red Buttes on the North Platte, to the Three Crossings of the Sweetwater—a distance of seventy-six miles—and I began riding at once. It was a long piece of road, but I was equal to the undertaking; and soon afterwards had an opportunity to exhibit my power of endurance as a pony express rider.

One day when I galloped into Three Crossings, my home station, I found that the rider who was expected to take the trip out on my arrival, had got into a drunken row the night before and had been killed; and that there was no one to fill his place. I did not hesitate for a moment to undertake an extra ride of eighty-five miles to Rocky Ridge, and I arrived at the latter place on time. I then turned back and rode to Red Buttes, my starting place, accomplishing on the round trip a distance of 322 miles.

Slade heard of this feat of mine, and one day as he was passing on a coach he sang out to me, "My boy, you're a brick, and no mistake. That was a good run you made when you rode your own and Miller's routes, and I'll see that you get extra pay for it."

Slade, although rough at times and always a dangerous character—having killed many a man—was always kind to me. During the two years that I worked for him as pony express-rider and stage-driver, he never spoke an angry word to me.

As I was leaving Horse Creek one day, a party of fifteen Indians "jumped me" in a sand ravine about a mile west of the station. They fired at me repeatedly, but missed their mark. I was mounted on a roan California horse—the fleetest steed I had. Putting spurs and whip to him, and lying flat on his back, I kept straight on for Sweetwater Bridge—eleven miles distant—instead of trying to turn back to Horse Creek. The Indians came on in hot pursuit, but my horse soon got away from them, and ran into the

26. I Immediately Changed Horses

station two miles ahead of them. The stock-tender had been killed there that morning, and all the stock had been driven off by the Indians, and as I was therefore unable to change horses, I continued on to Plant's Station—twelve miles further—thus making twenty-four miles straight run with one horse. I told the people at Plant's what had happened at Sweetwater Bridge, and with a fresh horse went on and finished the trip without any further adventure.

About the middle of September the Indians became very troublesome on the line of the stage road along the Sweetwater. Between Split Rock and Three Crossings they robbed a stage, killed the driver and two passengers, and badly wounded Lieut. Flowers, the assistant division agent. The red-skinned thieves also drove off the stock from the different stations, and were continually lying in wait for the passing stages and pony express-riders, so that we had to take many desperate chances in running the gauntlet.

The Indians had now become so bad and had stolen so

much stock that it was decided to stop the pony express for at least six weeks, and to run the stages but occasionally during that period; in fact, it would have been almost impossible to have run the enterprise much longer without restocking the line.

While we were thus nearly all lying idle, a party was organized to go out and search for stolen stock. This party was composed of stage-drivers, express-riders, stock-tenders, and ranchmen—forty of them altogether—and they were well-armed and well-mounted. They were mostly men who had undergone all kinds of hardships and braved every danger, and they were ready and anxious to "tackle" any number of Indians. Wild Bill (who had been driving stage on the road and had recently come down to our division) was elected captain of the company.

It was supposed that the stolen stock had been taken to the head of Powder River and vicinity, and the party, of which I was a member, started out for that section in high hopes of success.

Twenty miles out from Sweetwater Bridge, at the head of Horse Creek, we found an Indian trail running north towards Powder River, and we could see by the tracks that most of the horses had been recently shod and were undoubtedly our stolen stage stock. Pushing rapidly forward, we followed this trail to Powder River; thence down this stream to within about forty miles of the spot where old Fort Reno now stands. Here the trail took a more westerly course along the foot of the mountains, leading eventually to Crazy Woman's Fork—a tributary of Powder River. At this point we discovered that the party whom we were trailing had been joined by another band of Indians, and,

27. Attack on Stage Coach

judging from the fresh appearance of the trail, the united body could not have left this spot more than twenty-four hours before.

Being aware that we were now in the heart of the hostile country and that we might at any moment find more Indians than we had "lost," we advanced with more caution than usual, and kept a sharp lookout. As we were approaching Clear Creek, another tributary of Powder River, we discovered Indians on the opposite side of the creek, some three miles distant; at least we saw horses grazing, which was a sure sign that there were Indians there.

The Indians thinking themselves in comparative safety—never before having been followed so far into their own country by white men—had neglected to put out any scouts. They had no idea that there were any white men in that part of the country. We got the lay of their camp, and then held a council to consider and mature a plan for capturing it. We knew full well that the Indians would outnumber us at least three to one, and perhaps more. Upon the advice and suggestion of Wild Bill, it was finally decided that we should wait until it was nearly dark, and then, after creeping as close to them as possible, make a dash through their camp, open a general fire on them, and stampede the horses.

This plan, at the proper time, was most successfully executed. The dash upon the enemy was a complete surprise to them. They were so overcome with astonishment that they did not know what to make of it. We could not have astonished them any more if we had dropped down into their camp from the clouds. They did not recover from the surprise of this sudden charge until after we had ridden pell-mell through their camp and got away with our own horses as well as theirs. We at once circled the horses around towards the south, and after getting them on the south side of Clear Creek, some twenty of our men—just as the darkness was coming on—rode back and gave the Indians a few parting shots. We then took up our line of march for Sweetwater Bridge, where we arrived four days afterwards with all of our own horses and about one hundred captured Indian ponies.

The expedition had proved a grand success, and the event was celebrated in the usual manner—by a grand spree. The only store at Sweetwater Bridge did a rushing business for several days. The returned stock-hunters drank,

28. Alf. Slade Killing the Driver

and gambled and fought. The Indian ponies, which had
been distributed among the captors, passed from hand to
hand at almost every deal of the cards. There seemed to
be no limit to the rioting, and carousing; revelry reigned
supreme. On the third day of the orgy, Slade, who had
heard the news, came up to the bridge and took a hand
in the "fun," as it was called. To add some variation and
excitement to the occasion, Slade got in to a quarrel with
a stage-driver and shot him, killing him almost instantly.

The "boys" became so elated as well as "elevated" over
their success against the Indians, that most of them were
in favor of going back and cleaning out the whole Indian
race. One old driver especially, Dan Smith, was eager to

open a war on all the hostile nations, and had the drinking been continued another week he certainly would have undertaken the job, single-handed and alone. The spree finally came to an end; the men sobered down and abandoned the idea of again invading the hostile country. The recovered horses were replaced on the road, and the stages and pony express were again running on time.

Slade, having taken a great fancy to me, said: "Billy, I want you to come down to my headquarters, and I'll make you a sort of supernumerary rider, and send you out only when it is necessary."

I accepted the offer, and went with him down to Horseshoe, where I had a comparatively easy time of it. I had always been fond of hunting, and I now had a good opportunity to gratify my ambition in that direction, as I had plenty of spare time on my hands. In this connection I will relate one of my bear-hunting adventures. One day, when I had nothing else to do, I saddled up an extra pony express horse, and arming myself with a good rifle and pair of revolvers, struck out for the foot hills of Laramie Peak for a bear-hunt. Riding carelessly along, and breathing the cool and bracing autumn air which came down from the mountains, I felt as only a man can feel who is roaming over the prairies of the far West, well armed, and mounted on a fleet and gallant steed. The perfect freedom which he enjoys is in itself a refreshing stimulant to the mind as well as to the body. Such indeed were my feelings on this beautiful day, as I rode up the valley of the Horseshoe. Occasionally I scared up a flock of sage-hens or a jack-rabbit. Antelopes and deer were almost always in sight in any direction, but as they were not the kind of game I was after, on that day, I passed them by, and kept on towards the higher mountains. The further I rode the rougher and wilder became the country, and I knew that I was approaching the haunts of the bear. I did not discover any, however, although I saw plenty of tracks in the snow.

About two o'clock in the afternoon, my horse having become tired, and myself being rather weary, I shot a sage-hen, and dismounting, I unsaddled my horse and tied him to a small tree, where he could easily feed on the mountain grass. I then built a little fire, and broiling the chicken and seasoning it with salt and pepper, which I had obtained from my saddle-bags, I soon sat down to a "genuine square meal," which I greatly relished.

After resting for a couple of hours, I remounted and resumed my upward trip to the mountains, having made up my mind to camp out that night rather than go back without a bear, which my friends knew I had gone out for. As the days were growing short, night soon came on, and I looked around for a suitable camping place. While thus engaged, I scared up a flock of sage-hens, two of which I shot, intending to have one for supper and the other for breakfast.

By this time it was becoming quite dark, and I rode down to one of the little mountain streams, where I found an open place in the timber suitable for a camp. I dismounted, and after unsaddling my horse and hitching him to a tree, I prepared to start a fire. Just then I was startled by hearing a horse whinnying further up the stream. It was quite a surprise to me, and I immediately ran to my animal to keep him from answering, as horses usually do in such cases. I thought that the strange horse might belong to some roaming band of Indians, as I knew of no white men being in that portion of the country at that time. I was certain that the owner of the strange horse could not be far distant, and I was very anxious to find out who my neighbor was, before letting him know that I was in his vicinity. I therefore re-saddled my horse, and leaving him tied so that I could easily reach him I took my gun and started out on a scouting expedition up the stream. I had gone about four hundred yards when, in a bend of the stream, I discovered ten or fifteen horses grazing.

On the opposite side of the creek a light was shining high up the mountain bank. Approaching the mysterious spot as cautiously as possible, and when within a few yards of the light—which I discovered came from a dug-out in the mountain side—I heard voices, and soon I was able to distinguish the words, as they proved to be in my own language. Then I knew that the occupants of the dug-out, whence the voices proceeded, were white men. Thinking that they might be a party of trappers, I boldly walked up to the door and knocked for admission. The voices instantly ceased, and for a moment a deathlike silence reigned inside. Then there seemed to follow a kind of hurried whispering—a sort of consultation—and then some one called out:

"Who's there?"

"A friend and a white man," I replied.

The door opened, and a big, ugly-looking fellow stepped forth and said:

"Come in."

I accepted the invitation with some degree of fear and hesitation, which I endeavored to conceal, as I saw that it was too late to back out, and that it would never do to

29. The Horse Thieves' Den

weaken at that point, whether they were friends or foes. Upon entering the dug-out my eyes fell upon eight as rough and villainous looking men as I ever saw in my life. Two of them I instantly recognized as teamsters who had been driving in Lew Simpson's train, a few months before, and had been discharged.

They were charged with the murdering and robbing of a ranchman; and having stolen his horses it was supposed that they had left the country. I gave them no signs of recognition however, deeming it advisable to let them remain in ignorance as to who I was. It was a hard crowd, and I concluded that the sooner I could get away from them the better it would be for me. I felt confident that they were a band of horse-thieves.

"Where are you going, young man; and who's with you?" asked one of the men who appeared to be the leader of the gang.

"I am entirely alone. I left Horseshoe station this morning for a bear hunt, and not finding any bears, I had determined to camp out for the night and wait till morning," said I; "and just as I was going into camp, a few hundred yards down the creek, I heard one of your horses whinnying, and then I came up to your camp."

I was thus explicit in my statement in order, if possible to satisfy the cut-throats that I was not spying upon them, but that my intrusion was entirely accidental.

"Where's your horse?" demanded the boss thief.

"I left him down the creek," I answered.

They proposed going after the horse, but I thought that that would never do, as it would leave me without any means of escape, and I accordingly said, in hopes to throw them off the track, "Captain, I'll leave my gun here and go down and get my horse, and come back and stay all night."

I said this in as cheerful and as careless a manner as possible, so as not to arouse their suspicions in any way, or lead them to think that I was aware of their true character. I hated to part with my gun, but my suggestion of leaving it was a part of the plan of escape which I had arranged. If they have the gun, thought I, they would surely believe that I intended to come back. But this little game did not work at all, as one of the desperadoes spoke up and said:

"Jim and I will go down with you after your horse, and you can leave your gun here all the same, as you'll not need it."

"All right," I replied, for I could certainly have said nothing else. It became evident to me that it would be better to trust myself with two men than with the whole party. It

30. My Escape from the Horse Thieves

was apparent that from this time on, I would have to be on the alert for some good opportunity to give them the slip.

"Come along," said one of them, and together we went down the creek, and soon came to the spot where my horse was tied. One of the men unhitched the animal and said: "I'll lead the horse."

"Very well," said I, "I've got a couple of sage-hens here. Lead on."

I picked up the sage-hens, which I had killed a few hours before, and followed the man who was leading the horse, while his companion brought up the rear. The nearer we approached the dug-out the more I dreaded the idea of going back among the villainous cut-throats.

My first plan of escape having failed, I now determined upon another.

I had both of my revolvers with me, the thieves not having thought it necessary to search me. It was now quite dark, and I purposely dropped one of the sage-hens, and asked the man behind me to pick it up. While he was hunting for it on the ground, I quickly pulled out one of my Colt's revolvers and struck him a tremendous blow on the back of the head, knocking him senseless to the ground. I then instantly wheeled around, and saw that the man ahead who was only a few feet distant, had heard the blow and had turned to see what was the matter, his hand upon his revolver. We faced each other at about the same instant, but before he could fire, as he tried to do, I shot him dead in his tracks. Then jumping on my horse, I rode down the creek as fast as possible, through the darkness and over the rough ground and rocks.

The other outlaws in the dug-out, having heard the shot which I had fired, knew there was trouble, and they all came rushing down the creek. I suppose, by the time they reached the man whom I had knocked down, that he had recovered and hurriedly told them of what had happened. They did not stay with the man whom I had shot, but came on in hot pursuit of me. They were not mounted, and were making better time down the rough cañon than I was on horseback. From time to time I heard them gradually gaining on me.

At last they had come so near that I saw that I must abandon my horse. So I jumped to the ground, and gave him a hard slap with the butt of one of my revolvers, which started him on down the valley, while I scrambled up the mountain side. I had not ascended more than forty feet when I heard my pursuers coming closer and closer; I quickly hid behind a large pine tree, and in a few moments they all rushed by me, being led on by the rattling footsteps of my horse, which they heard ahead of them. Soon I heard them firing at random at the horse, as they no doubt supposed I was still seated on his back. As soon as they had passed me I climbed further up the steep mountain, and knowing that I had given them the slip, and feeling certain that I could keep out of their way, I at once struck out for Horseshoe station, which was twenty-five miles distant. I had hard traveling at first, but upon reaching lower and better ground, I made good headway, walking all night and getting into the station just before daylight,—foot-sore, weary, and generally played out.

I immediately waked up the men of the station and told them of my adventure. Slade himself happened to be there, and he at once organized a party to go out and hunt up the horse-thieves. Shortly after daylight twenty well-armed stage-drivers, stock-tenders and ranchmen were galloping in the direction of the dug-out. Of course I went along with the party, notwithstanding I was very tired and had had hardly any rest at all. We had a brisk ride, and arrived in the immediate vicinity of the thieves' rendezvous at about ten o'clock in the morning. We approached the dug-out cautiously, but upon getting in close proximity to it we could discover no horses in sight. We could see the door of the dug-out standing wide open, and we then marched up to the place. No one was inside, and the general appearance of everything indicated that the place had been deserted—that the birds had flown. Such, indeed, proved to be the case.

We found a new-made grave, where they had evidently buried the man whom I had shot. We made a thorough search of the whole vicinity, and finally found their trail going southeast in the direction of Denver. As it would have been useless to follow them, we rode back to the station; and thus ended my eventful bear-hunt. We had no more trouble for some time from horse-thieves after that.

During the winter of 1860 and the spring of 1861 I remained at Horseshoe, occasionally riding pony express and taking care of stock.

CHAPTER IX

Fast Driving

It was in the spring of 1861, while I was at Horseshoe, that the eastern-bound coach came in one day loaded down with passengers and baggage, and stopped for dinner; Horseshoe being a regular dinner station as well as a home station. The passengers consisted of six Englishmen, and they had been continually grumbling about the slow time that was being made by the stages, saying that the farther they got East the slower they went.

"These blarsted 'eathens don't know hanything habout staging, hany-'ow," remarked one of them.

"Blarst me bloody heyes! they cawn't stage in this country as we do in Hingland, you know," said another.

Their remarks were overheard by Bob Scott, who was to drive the coach from Horseshoe to Fort Laramie, and he determined to give them satisfaction before they got over his route. Scott was known to be the best reinsman and the most expert driver on the whole line of the road. He was a very gentlemanly fellow in his general appearance and conduct, but at times he would become a reckless dare-devil, and would take more desperate chances than any other driver. He delighted in driving wild teams on the darkest nights, over a mountain road, and had thus become the hero of many a thrilling adventure.

It happened on this day he was to drive a team of six pony express horses, which had been only partially broken in as a stage team. As the stock-tenders were hitching them up, Bob, who was standing by, said, "I'll show them Englishmen that we 'blarsted heathens' do know something about staging in this country." We all knew from Bob's looks that something was up.

It required several men to hitch up this frisky team, as a man had to hold on to each one of the horses by the bits, while they were stringing them out. The Englishmen came out from dinner, and were delighted to see the horses prancing and pawing as if anxious to start.

"Ha! my deah fellah, now we will 'ave a fine ride this hafternoon," said one of them.

"By Jove! those are the kind of 'orses they hought to 'ave on hall the teams," remarked another.

"Are you the lad who is going to drive to-day?" asked another of Bob.

"Yes, gentlemen," answered Bob, "I'll show you how we stage it in this country."

Bob mounted the box, gathered the lines, and pulling the horses strongly by the bits, he sang out to the Englishmen, "All aboard!" Bob's companion on the box was Capt. Cricket; a little fellow who was the messenger of the coach. After everybody was seated, Bob told the stock-tenders to "turn 'em loose."

We, who were standing around to see the stage start out, expected it would go off at a lively rate. We were considerably surprised, therefore, when, after the horses had made a few lively jumps, Bob put on the big California brakes and brought them down to a walk. The road, for a distance of four miles, gradually rose to the top of a hill, and all the way up this ascent, Bob held the impatient team in check.

"Blarst your heyes, driver, why don't you let them go?" exclaimed one of the passengers, who had all along been expecting a very brisk ride. Every once in a while they would ask him some such question, but he paid no attention to them. At last he reached the top of the hill, and then he suddenly flung three of the lines on the left side of the team, and the other three on the right side. He then began "playing the silk to them,"—that is to say, he began to lash them unmercifully. The team started off like a streak of lightning, so to speak, without a single rein being held by the driver. Bob cried out to the Englishmen, saying, "Hold on, gentlemen, and I'll give you a lively ride, and show you how to stage it in the Rocky Mountains."

His next movement was to pull the lamps out of the sockets and throw them at the leaders. The glass broke upon their backs and nearly set them wild, but being so accustomed to running the road, they never once left the track, and went flying on down the grade towards the next station, eight miles distant, the coach bouncing over the loose stones and small obstacles, and surging from side to side, as an eggshell would in the rapids of Niagara. Not satisfied with the break-neck rate at which they were traveling, Bob pulled out his revolver and fired in rapid succession, at the same time yelling in a demoniacal manner.

By this time the Englishmen had become thoroughly frightened, as they saw the lines flying wildly in every direction and the team running away. They did not know whether to jump out or remain in the coach. Bob would

31. Bob Scott's Famous Coach Ride

occasionally look down from his seat, and, seeing their frightened faces, would ask, "Well, how do you like staging in this country now?" The Englishmen stuck to the coach, probably thinking it would be better to do so than to take the chances of breaking their necks by jumping.

As the flying team was nearing the station, the stock tender saw that they were running away and that the driver had no control over them whatever. Being aware that the pony express horses were accustomed to running right into the stable on arriving at the station, he threw open the large folding doors, which would just allow the passage of the team and coach into the stable. The horses, sure enough, made for the open doorway. Capt. Cricket, the messenger, and Scott got down in the boot of the coach to save themselves from colliding with the top of the stable door. The coach would probably have passed through into the stable without any serious damage had it not been for the bar or threshold that was stretched across the ground to fasten the doors to. This bar was a small log, and the front wheels struck it with such force that the coach was thrown up high enough to strike the upper portion of the door frame. The top of the coach was completely torn off, and one of the passenger's arms was broken. This was the only serious injury that was done; though it was a matter of surprise to all, that any of the travelers escaped.

The coach was backed out, when the running gear was found to be as good as ever. The top was soon patched up, a change of team was made, and Bob Scott, mounting the box as if nothing had happened, took the reins in hand, and shouted, "All aboard!" The Englishmen, however, had had enough of Bob Scott, and not one of the party was willing to risk his life with him again. They said that he was drunk, or crazy or both, and that they would report him and have him discharged for what he had already done.

Bob waited a few minutes to give them an opportunity to take their seats in the coach, but they told him most emphatically that he could drive on without them, as they intended to wait there for the next stage. Their traps were taken off, and Bob drove away without a single passenger. He made his usual time into Fort Laramie, which was the end of his run. The Englishmen came through on the next day's coach, and proceeded on to Atchison, where they reported Bob to the superintendent of the line, who, however, paid little or no attention to the matter, as Bob remained on the road. Such is the story of the liveliest and most reckless piece of stage-driving that ever occurred on the Overland stage road.

CHAPTER X

Questionable Proceedings

Having been away from home nearly a year, and having occasionally heard of my mother's poor health, I determined to make her a visit; so procuring a pass over the road, I went to Leavenworth, arriving there about June 1st, 1861, going from there home. The civil war had broken out, and excitement ran high in that part of the country. My mother, of course, was a strong Union woman, and had such great confidence in the government that she believed the war would not last over six months.

Leavenworth at that time was quite an important outfitting post for the West and Southwest, and the fort there was garrisoned by a large number of troops. While in the city one day I met several of the old, as well as the young men, who had been members of the Free State party all through the Kansas troubles, and who had, like our family, lost everything at the hands of the Missourians. They now thought a good opportunity offered to retaliate and get even with their persecutors, as they were all considered to be secessionists. That they were all secessionists, however, was not true, as all of them did not sympathize with the South. But the Free State men, myself among them, took it for granted that as Missouri was a slave state the inhabitants must all be secessionists, and therefore our

32. Nearly Every Man Had Two Horses

enemies. A man by the name of Chandler proposed that we organize an independent company for the purpose of invading Missouri and making war on its people on our own responsibility. He at once went about it in a very quiet way, and succeeded in inducing twenty-five men to join him in the hazardous enterprise. Having a longing and revengeful desire to retaliate upon the Missourians for the brutal manner in which they had treated and robbed my family, I became a member of Chandler's company. His plan was that we should leave our homes in parties of not more than two or three together, and meet at a certain point near Westport, Missouri, on a fixed day. His instructions were carried out to the letter, and we met at the rendezvous at the appointed time. Chandler had been there some days before us, and, thoroughly disguised, had been looking around the country for the whereabouts of all the best horses. He directed us to secretly visit certain farms and collect all the horses possible, and bring them together the next night. This we did, and upon reassembling it was found that nearly every man had two horses. We immediately struck out for the Kansas line, which we crossed at an Indian ferry on the Kansas river, above Wyandotte, and as soon as we had set foot upon Kansas soil we separated with the understanding that we were to meet one week from that day at Leavenworth.

Some of the parties boldly took their confiscated horses into Leavenworth, while others rode them to their homes. This action may look to the reader like horse-stealing, and some people might not hesitate to call it by that name; but Chandler plausibly maintained that we were only getting back our own, or the equivalent, from the Missourians, and as the government was waging war against the South, it was perfectly square and honest, and we had a good right to do it. So we didn't let our consciences trouble us very much.

We continued to make similar raids upon the Missourians off and on during the summer, and occasionally we had running fights with them; none of the skirmishes, however, amounting to much.

The government officials hearing of our operations, put detectives upon our track, and several of the party were arrested. My mother, upon learning that I was engaged in this business, told me it was neither honorable nor right, and she would not for a moment countenance any such proceedings. Consequently I abandoned the jay-hawking enterprise, for such it really was.[1]

About this time the government bought from Jones and Cartwright[2] several ox-trains, which were sent to Rolla, Missouri, all being put in charge of my old and gallant friend, Wild Bill, who had just become the hero of the day, on account of a terrible fight which he had had with a gang of desperadoes and outlaws, who infested the border under the leadership of the then notorious Jake McCandless. In this fight he had killed McCandless and three of his men.[3]

The affair occurred while Wild Bill was riding the pony express in western Kansas.

The custom with the express riders, when within half a mile of a station, was either to begin shouting or blowing a horn in order to notify the stock tender of his approach, and to have a fresh horse already saddled for him on his arrival, so that he could go right on without a moment's delay.

One day, as Wild Bill neared Rock Creek station, where he was to change horses, he began shouting as usual at the proper distance; but the stock-tender, who had been married only a short time and had his wife living with him at the station, did not make his accustomed appearance. Wild Bill galloped up and instead of finding the stock-tender ready for him with a fresh horse, he discovered him lying across the stable door with the blood oozing from a bullet-hole in his head. The man was dead, and it was evident that he had been killed only a few moments before.

In a second Wild Bill jumped from his horse, and looking in the direction of the house he saw a man coming towards him. The approaching man fired on him at once, but missed his aim. Quick as lightning Wild Bill pulled his revolver and returned the fire. The stranger fell dead, shot through the brain.

"Bill, Bill! Help! Help! save me!" Such was the cry that Bill now heard. It was the shrill and pitiful voice of the dead stock-tender's wife, and it came from a window of the house. She had heard the exchange of shots, and knew that Wild Bill had arrived.

He dashed over the dead body of the villain whom he had killed, and just as he sprang into the door of the house, he saw two powerful men assaulting the woman. One of the desperadoes was in the act of striking her with the butt end of a revolver, and while his arm was still raised, Bill sent a ball crashing through his skull, killing him instantly. Two other men now came rushing from an adjoining room, and Bill, seeing that the odds were three to one against him, jumped into a corner, and then firing, he killed another of the villains. Before he could shoot again the remaining two men closed in upon him, one of whom had drawn a large bowie knife. Bill wrenched the knife from his grasp and drove it through the heart of the outlaw.

The fifth and last man now grabbed Bill by the throat, and held him at arm's length, but it was only for a moment, as Bill raised his own powerful right arm and struck his antagonist's left arm such a terrible blow that he broke it.

33. Wild Bill and the Outlaws

The disabled desperado, seeing that he was no longer a match for Bill, jumped through the door, and mounting a horse he succeeded in making his escape—being the sole survivor of the Jake McCandless gang.

Wild Bill remained at the station with the terrified woman until the stage came along, and he then consigned her to the care of the driver. Mounting his horse he at once galloped off, and soon disappeared in the distance, making up for lost time.

This was the exploit that was on everybody's tongue and in every newspaper. It was one of the most remarkable and desperate hand to hand encounters that has ever taken place on the border.

I happened to meet Wild Bill at Leavenworth as he was about to depart for Rolla; he wished me to take charge of the government trains as a sort of assistant under him, and I gladly accepted the offer. Arriving at Rolla, we loaded the trains with freight and took them to Springfield, Missouri.

On our return to Rolla we heard a great deal of talk about the approaching fall races at St. Louis, and Wild Bill having brought a fast running horse from the mountains, determined to take him to that city and match him against some of the high-flyers there; and down to St. Louis we went with this running horse, placing our hopes very high on him.

Wild Bill had no difficulty in making up a race for him. All the money that he and I had we put up on the mountain runner, and as we thought we had a sure thing, we also bet the horse against $250. I rode the horse myself, but nevertheless, our sure thing, like many another sure thing, proved a total failure, and we came out of that race minus the horse and every dollar we had in the world.

Before the race it had been "make or break" with us, and we got "broke." We were "busted" in the largest city we had ever been in, and it is no exaggeration to say that we felt mighty blue.

On the morning after the race we went to the military headquarters, where Bill succeeded in securing an engagement for himself as a government scout, but I being so young failed in obtaining similar employment. Wild Bill, however, raised some money, by borrowing it from a friend, and then buying me a steamboat ticket he sent me back to Leavenworth, while he went to Springfield, which place he made his headquarters while scouting in southeastern Missouri.

One night, after he had returned from a scouting expedition, he took a hand in a game of poker, and in the course of the game he became involved in a quarrel with Dave Tutt, a professional gambler, about a watch which he had won from Tutt, who would not give it up.

Bill told him he had won it fairly, and that he proposed to have it; furthermore, he declared his intention of carrying the watch across the street next morning to military headquarters, at which place he had to report at nine o'clock.

Tutt replied that he would himself carry the watch across the street at nine o'clock, and no other man would do it.

Bill then said to Tutt that if he attempted anything of the kind, he would kill him.

A challenge to a duel had virtually been given and accepted, and everybody knew that the two men meant business. At nine o'clock the next morning, Tutt started to cross the street. Wild Bill, who was standing on the opposite side, told him to stop. At that moment Tutt, who was carrying his revolver in his hand, fired at Bill but missed him. Bill quickly pulled out his revolver and returned the fire, hitting Tutt squarely in the forehead and killing him instantly.

Quite a number of Tutt's friends were standing in the vicinity, having assembled to witness the duel, and Bill, as soon as Tutt fell to the ground, turned to them and asked if any one of them wanted to take it up for Tutt; if so, he would accommodate any of them then and there. But none of them cared to stand in front of Wild Bill to be shot at by him.

Nothing of course was ever done to Bill for the killing of Tutt.[4]

CHAPTER XI

A Soldier

In the fall of 1861 I made a trip to Fort Larned, Kansas, carrying military dispatches, and in the winter I accompanied George Long through the country, and assisted him in buying horses for the government.

The next spring, 1862, an expedition against the Indians was organized, consisting of a volunteer regiment, the Ninth Kansas, under Colonel Clark. This expedition, which I had joined in the capacity of guide and scout, proceeded to the Kiowa and Comanche country,[1] on the Arkansas river,[2] along which stream we scouted all summer between Fort Lyon and Fort Larned, on the old Santa Fe trail. We had several engagements with the Indians, but they were of no great importance.

In the winter of 1862, I became one of the "Red Legged Scouts,"—a company of scouts commanded by Captain Tuff.[3] Among its members were some of the most noted Kansas Rangers, such as Red Clark, the St. Clair brothers, Jack Harvey, an old pony express-rider named Johnny Fry,[4] and many other well known frontiersmen. Our field of operations was confined mostly to the Arkansas country and southwestern Missouri. We had many a lively skirmish with the bushwhackers[5] and Younger brothers,[6] and when we were not hunting them, we were generally employed in carrying dispatches between Forts Dodge, Gibson, Leavenworth, and other posts. Whenever we were in Leavenworth we had a very festive time. We usually attended all the balls in full force, and "ran things" to suit ourselves. Thus I passed the winter of 1862 and the spring of 1863.

Subsequently I engaged to conduct a small train to Denver for some merchants, and on reaching that place in September, I received a letter stating that my mother was not expected to live. I hastened home, and found her dangerously ill. She grew gradually worse, and at last, on the 22d of November, 1863, she died. Thus passed away a loving and affectionate mother and a noble, brave, good and loyal woman. That I loved her above all other persons, no one who has read these reminiscences can for a moment doubt.

Previous to this sad event my sister Julia had been married to a gentleman named J. A. Goodman, and they now came to reside at our house and take charge of the children, as my mother had desired that they should not be separated. Mr. Goodman became the guardian of the minor children.

I soon left the home now rendered gloomy by the absence of her whom I had so tenderly loved, and going to Leavenworth I entered upon a dissolute and reckless life—to my shame be it said—and associated with gamblers, drunkards, and bad characters generally. I continued my dissipation about two months, and was becoming a very "hard case." About this time the Seventh Kansas regiment, known as "Jennison's Jay-hawkers," returned from the war, and re-enlisted and re- organized as veterans.

Among them I met quite a number of my old comrades and neighbors, who tried to induce me to enlist and go south with them. I had no idea of doing anything of the kind; but one day, after having been under the influence of bad whisky, I awoke to find myself a soldier in the Seventh Kansas. I did not remember how or when I had enlisted, but I saw I was in for it, and that it would not do for me to endeavor to back out.

In the spring of 1864 the regiment was ordered to Tennessee, and we got into Memphis just about the time that General Sturgis was so badly whipped by General Forrest.[7] General A. J. Smith re-organized the army to operate against Forrest, and after marching to Tupalo, Mississippi, we had an engagement with him and defeated him. This kind of fighting was all new to me, being entirely different from any in which I had ever before engaged. I soon became a non-commissioned officer, and was put on detached service as a scout.

After skirmishing around the country with the rest of the army for some little time, our regiment returned to Memphis, but was immediately ordered to Cape Girardeau, in Missouri, as a confederate force under General Price was then raiding that state.[8] The command of which my regiment was a part hurried to the front to intercept Price, and our first fight with him occurred at Pilot Knob. From that time for nearly six weeks we fought or skirmished every day.

I was still acting as a scout, when one day I rode ahead of the command, some considerable distance, to pick up all possible information concerning Price's movements. I was dressed in gray clothes, or Missouri jeans, and on riding up to a farm-house and entering, I saw a man, also dressed in gray costume, sitting at a table eating bread and milk. He looked up as I entered, and startled me by saying:

"You little rascal, what are you doing in those 'secesh'[9] clothes?" Judge of my surprise when I recognized in the stranger my old friend and partner, Wild Bill, disguised as a Confederate officer.

"I ask you the same question, sir," said I without the least hesitation.

"Hush! sit down and have some bread and milk, and we'll talk it all over afterwards," said he.

I accepted the invitation and partook of the refreshments. Wild Bill paid the woman of the house, and we went out to the gate where my horse was standing.

"Billy, my boy," said he, "I am mighty glad to see you. I haven't seen or heard of you since we got busted on that St. Louis' horse-race."

"What are you doing out here?" I asked.

"I am a scout under General McNeil. For the last few days I have been with General Marmaduke's division of Price's army, in disguise as a southern officer from Texas, as you see me now," said he.[10]

"That's exactly the kind of business that I am out on to-day," said I; "and I want to get some information concerning Price's movements."

"I'll give you all that I have;" and he then went on and told me all that he knew regarding Price's intentions, and the number and condition of his men. He then asked about my mother, and when he learned that she was dead he was greatly surprised and grieved; he thought a great deal of her, for she had treated him almost as one of her own children. He finally took out a package, which he had concealed about his person, and handing it to me he said:

"Here are some letters which I want you to give to General McNeil."

"All right," said I as I took them, "but where will I meet you again?"

"Never mind that," he replied; "I am getting so much valuable information that I propose to stay a little while longer in this disguise." Thereupon we shook hands and parted.

It is not necessary to say much concerning Price's raid in general, as that event is a matter of recorded history. I am only relating the incidents in which I was personally interested either as one of the actors or as an observer.

Another interesting and I may say exciting episode happened to me a day or two after my unexpected meeting with Wild Bill. I was riding with the advance guard of our army, and wishing a drink of water, I stopped at a farmhouse. There were no men about the premises, and no one excepting a very fine and intellectual looking lady and her two daughters. They seemed to be almost frightened to death at seeing me—a "yank"—appear before them. I quieted their fears somewhat, and the mother then asked me how far back the army was. When I told her it would be along shortly, she expressed her fears that they would take everything on the premises. They set me out a lunch and treated me rather kindly, so that I really began to sympathize with them; for I knew that the soldiers would ransack their house and confiscate everything they could lay their hands on. At last I resolved to do what I could to protect them.

After the generals and the staff officers had passed by, I took it upon myself to be a sentry over the house. When the command came along some of the men rushed up with the intention of entering the place and carrying off all the desirable plunder possible, and then tearing and breaking everything to pieces, as they usually did along the line of march.

"Halt!" I shouted; "I have been placed here by the commanding officer as a guard over this house, and no man must enter it."

This stopped the first squad; and seeing that my plan was a success, I remained at my post during the passage of the entire command and kept out all intruders.

It seemed as if the ladies could not thank me sufficiently for the protection I had afforded them. They were perfectly aware of the fact that I had acted without orders and entirely on my own responsibility, and therefore they felt the more grateful. They urgently invited me to remain a little while longer and partake of an excellent dinner which they said they were preparing for me. I was pretty hungry about that time, as our rations had been rather slim of late, and a good dinner was a temptation I could not withstand, especially as it was to be served up by such elegant ladies. While I was eating the meal, I was most agreeably entertained by the young ladies, and before I had finished it the last of the rear-guard must have been at least two miles from the house.

Suddenly three men entered the room, and I looked up and saw three double-barreled shot-guns leveled straight at me. Before I could speak, however, the mother and her daughters sprang between the men and me.

"Father! Boys! Lower your guns! You must not shoot this man," and similar exclamations, were the cry of all three.

The guns were lowered, and then the men, who were the father and brothers of the young ladies, were informed of what I had done for them. It appeared that they had been concealed in the woods near by while the army was passing, and on coming into the house and finding a Yankee there, they determined to shoot him. Upon learning the facts, the old man extended his hand to me, saying:

"I would not harm a hair of your head for the world; but it is best that you stay here no longer, as your command is some distance from here now, and you might be cut off by bushwhackers before reaching it."

Bidding them all good-bye, and with many thanks from the mother and daughters, I mounted my horse and soon overtook the column, happy in the thought that I had done a good deed, and with no regrets that I had saved from pillage and destruction the home and property of a confederate and his family.

Our command kept crowding against Price and his army until they were pushed into the vicinity of Kansas City, where their further advance was checked by United States troops from Kansas; and then was begun their memorable and extraordinary retreat back into Kansas.

While both armies were drawn up in [a] skirmish line near Fort Scott, Kansas, two men on horseback were seen rapidly leaving the Confederate lines, and suddenly they made a dash towards us. Instantly quick volleys were discharged from the Confederates, who also began a pursuit, and some five hundred shots were fired at the flying men. It was evident that they were trying to reach our lines, but when within about a quarter of a mile of us, one of them fell from his horse to rise no more. He had been fatally shot. His companion galloped on unhurt, and seven companies of our regiment charged out and met him, and checked his pursuers. The fugitive was dressed in Confederate uniform, and as he rode into our lines I recognized him as Wild Bill, the Union scout. He immediately sought Generals Pleasonton[11] and McNeil, with whom he held a consultation. He told them that although Price made a bold showing on the front, by bringing all his men into view, yet he was really a great deal weaker than the appearance of his lines would indicate; and that he was then trying to cross a difficult stream four miles from Fort Scott.

It was late in the afternoon, but General Pleasonton immediately ordered an advance, and we charged in full force upon the rear of Price's army, and drove it before us for two hours.

If Wild Bill could have made his successful dash into our lines earlier in the day, the attack would have been made sooner, and greater results might have been expected. The Confederates had suspected him of being a spy for two or three days, and had watched him too closely to allow an opportunity to get away from them sooner. His unfortunate companion who had been shot, was a scout from Springfield, Missouri, whose name I cannot now remember.

From this time on, Wild Bill and myself continued to scout together until Price's army was driven south of the Arkansas River and the pursuit abandoned. We then returned to Springfield, Missouri, for a rest and for supplies, and Wild Bill and myself spent two weeks there in "having a jolly good time," as some people would express it.

CHAPTER XII

A Wedding

It was during the winter of 1864–65, while I was on detached service at military headquarters, at St. Louis, that I became acquainted with a young lady named Louisa Frederici, whom I greatly admired and in whose charming society I spent many a pleasant hour.

The war closing in 1865, I was discharged, and after a brief visit at Leavenworth I returned to St. Louis, having made up my mind to capture the heart of Miss Frederici, whom I now adored above any other young lady I had ever seen. Her lovely face, her gentle disposition and her graceful manners won my admiration and love; and I was not slow in declaring my sentiments to her. The result was that I obtained her consent to marry me in the near future, and when I bade her good-bye I considered myself one of the happiest of men.

Meantime I drove a string of horses from Leavenworth to Fort Kearney, where I met my old friend Bill Trotter, who was then division stage agent. He employed me at once to drive stage between Kearney and Plum Creek, the road running near the spot where I had my first Indian fight with the McCarthy brothers, and where I killed my first Indian, nearly nine years before. I drove stage over this route until February, 1866, and while bounding over the cold, dreary road day after day, my thoughts turned continually towards my promised bride, until I at last determined to abandon staging forever, and marry and settle down. Immediately after coming to this conclusion, I went to St. Louis, where I was most cordially received by my sweetheart; it was arranged between us that our wedding should take place on the 6th day of March, following.

At last the day arrived, and the wedding ceremony was performed at the residence of the bride's parents, in the presence of a large number of invited friends, whose hearty congratulations we received. I was certainly to be congratulated, for I had become possessed of a lovely and noble woman, and as I gazed upon her as she stood beside me arrayed in her wedding costume, I indeed felt proud of her; and from that time to this I have always thought that I made a most fortunate choice for a life partner.

An hour after the ceremony we—my bride and myself—were on board of a Missouri river steamboat, bound for our new home in Kansas. My wife's parents had accompanied us to the boat, and had bidden us a fond farewell and God-speed on our journey.

During the trip up the river several very amusing, yet awkward incidents occurred, some of which I cannot resist relating. There happened to be on board the boat an excursion party from Lexington, Missouri, and those comprising it seemed to shun me, for some reason which I could not then account for. They would point at me, and quietly talk among themselves, and eye me very closely. Their actions seemed very strange to me. After the boat had proceeded some little distance, I made the acquaintance of several families from Indiana, who were *en route* to Kansas. A gentleman, who seemed to be the leader of these colonists, said to me, "The people of this excursion party don't seem to have any great love for you."

"What does it mean?" I asked; "What are they saying? It's all a mystery to me."

"They say that you are one of the Kansas jay-hawkers, and one of Jennison's house burners," replied the gentleman.

"I am from Kansas—that's true; and was a soldier and a scout in the Union army," said I; "and I was in Kansas during the border ruffian war[1] of 1856. Perhaps these people know who I am, and that explains their hard looks." I had a lengthy conversation with this gentleman—for such he seemed to be—and entertained him with several chapters of the history of the early Kansas troubles, and told him the experiences of my own family.

In the evening the Lexington folks got up a dance, but neither the Indiana people, my wife or myself were invited to join them. My new-found friend thereupon came to me and said: "Mr. Cody, let us have a dance of our own."

"Very well," was my reply.

"We have some musicians along with us, so we can have plenty of music," remarked the gentleman.

"Good enough!" said I, "and I will hire the negro barber to play the violin for us. He is a good fiddler, as I heard him playing only a little while ago." The result was that we soon organized a good string band and had a splendid dance, keeping it up as long as the Lexington party did theirs.

The second day out from St. Louis, the boat stopped to wood up, at a wild-looking landing. Suddenly twenty horsemen were seen galloping up through the timber, and as they came nearer the boat they fired on the negro deckhands, against whom they seemed to have a special grudge, and who were engaged in throwing wood on board. The negroes all quickly jumped on the boat and pulled in the gang plank, and the captain had only just time to get the steamer out into the stream before the bushwhackers—for such they proved to be—appeared on the bank.

"Where is the black abolition jay-hawker?" shouted the leader.

"Show him to us, and we'll shoot him," yelled another. But as the boat had got well out in the river by this time, they could not board us, and the captain ordering a full head of steam, pulled out and left them.

I afterwards ascertained that some of the Missourians, who were with the excursion party, were bushwhackers themselves, and had telegraphed to their friends from some previous landing that I was on board, telling them to come to the landing which we had just left, and take me off. Had the villains captured me they would have undoubtedly put an end to my career, and the public would never have had the pleasure of being bored by this autobiography.

I noticed that my wife felt grieved over the manner in which these people had treated me. Just married, she was going into a new country, and seeing how her husband was regarded, how he had been shunned, and how his life had been threatened, I was afraid she might come to the conclusion too soon that she had wedded a "hard customer." So when the boat landed at Kansas City I telegraphed to some of my friends in Leavenworth that I would arrive there in the evening. My object was to have my acquaintances give me a reception, so that my wife could see that

I really did have some friends, and was not so bad a man as the bushwhackers tried to make out.

Just as I expected, when the boat reached Leavenworth, I found a general round-up of friends at the landing to receive us. There were about sixty gentlemen and ladies. They had a band of music with them, and we were given a fine serenade. Taking carriages, we all drove to South Leavenworth to the home of my sister Eliza, who had married George Myers, and there we were given a very handsome reception. All this cheered up my wife, who concluded that I was not a desperado after all.

Having promised my wife that I would abandon the plains, I rented a hotel in Salt Creek Valley—the same house by the way, which my mother had formerly kept, but which was then owned by Dr. J. J. Crook, late surgeon of the 7th Kansas. This hotel I called the Golden Rule House, and I kept it until the next September. People generally said I made a good landlord, and knew how to run a hotel—a business qualification which, it is said, is possessed by comparatively few men. But it proved too tame employment for me, and again I sighed for the freedom of the plains. Believing that I could make more money out West on the frontier than I could at Salt Creek Valley, I sold out the Golden Rule House, and started alone for Saline, Kansas, which was then the end of the track of the Kansas Pacific railway, which was at that time being built across the plains. On my way I stopped at Junction City, where I again met my old friend Wild Bill, who was scouting for the government; his headquarters being at Fort Ellsworth, afterwards called Fort Harker. He told me that they needed more scouts at this post, and I accordingly accompanied him to that fort, where I had no difficulty in obtaining employment.

During the winter of 1866–67, I scouted between Fort Ellsworth and Fort Fletcher. In the spring of 1867 I was at Fort Fletcher, when General Custer came out to go on an Indian expedition with General Hancock.[2] I remained at this post until it was drowned out by the heavy floods of Big Creek, on which it was located; the water rose about the fortifications and rendered the place unfit for occupancy; so the government abandoned the fort, and moved the troops and supplies to a new post—which had been named Fort Hays—located further west, on the south fork of Big Creek. It was while scouting in the vicinity of Fort Hays that I had my first ride with the dashing and gallant Custer, who had come up to the post from Fort Ellsworth with an escort of only ten men. He wanted a guide to pilot him to Fort Larned, a distance of sixty-five miles across the country.

I was ordered by the commanding officer to guide General Custer to his desired destination, and I soon received word from the General that he would start out in the morning with the intention of making the trip in one day. Early in the morning, after a good night's rest, I was on hand, mounted on my large mouse-colored mule—an animal of great endurance—and ready for the journey; when the General saw me, he said:

"Cody, I want to travel fast and go through as quickly as possible, and I don't think that mule of yours is fast enough to suit me."

"General, never mind the mule," said I, "he'll get there as soon as your horses. That mule is a good one," as I knew that the animal was better than most horses.

"Very well; go ahead, then," said he, though he looked as if he thought I would delay the party on the road.

For the first fifteen miles, until we came to the Smoky Hill River, which we were to cross, I could hardly keep the mule in advance of the General, who rode a frisky, impatient and ambitious thoroughbred steed; in fact, the whole party was finely mounted. The General repeatedly told me that the mule was "no good," and that I ought to have had a good horse. But after crossing the river and striking the sand-hills, I began letting my mule out a little, and putting the "persuaders" to him. He was soon out-traveling the horses, and by the time we had made about half the distance to Fort Larned, I occasionally had to wait for the General or some of his party, as their horses were beginning to show signs of fatigue.

"General, how about this mule, anyhow?" I asked, at last.

"Cody, you have a better vehicle than I thought you had," was his reply.

From that time on to Fort Larned I had no trouble in keeping ahead of the party. We rode into the fort at four o'clock in the afternoon with about half the escort only, the rest having lagged far behind.

General Custer thanked me for having brought him straight across the country without any trail, and said that if I were not engaged as post scout at Fort Hays he would like to have me accompany him as one of his scouts during the summer; and he added that whenever I was out of employment, if I would come to him he would find something for me to do. This was the beginning of my acquaintance with General Custer, whom I always admired as a man and as an officer.

35. General Custer

A few days after my return to Fort Hays, the Indians made a raid on the Kansas Pacific Railroad, killing five or six men and running off about one hundred horses and mules. The news was brought to the commanding officer, who immediately ordered Major Armes,[3] of the Tenth Cavalry—which, by the way, was a negro regiment,[4]—with his company and one mountain howitzer, to go in pursuit of the red-skins, and I was sent along with the expedition as scout and guide. On the second day out we suddenly discovered, on the opposite side of the Saline River, about a mile distant, a large body of Indians, who were charging down upon us. Major Armes, placing the cannon on a little knoll, limbered it up and left twenty men to guard it; and then, with the rest of the command, he crossed the river to meet the Indians.

Just as he had got the men over the stream, we heard a terrific yelling and shouting in our rear, and looking back to the knoll where the cannon had been stationed, we saw the negroes, who had been left there to guard the gun, flying towards us, being pursued by about one hundred Indians; while another large party of the latter were dancing around the captured cannon, as if they had got hold of an elephant and did not know what to do with it.

Major Armes turned his command back and drove the Indians from the gun. The troops then dismounted and took position there. Quite a severe fight ensued, lasting about two hours. Five or six of the soldiers, as well as Major Armes, were wounded, and several of the horses were shot. The Indians seemed to grow thicker and thicker, as if receiving reinforcements from some large party. The colored troops, who had been bragging all the way that if they could only see some Indians "dey would blow 'em off de farm,"—which was a favorite expression of theirs,—were now singing a different tune. Every time the Indians would make a charge at us, the darkeys would cry out:

"Heah dey cum;" "Dey must be ten thousand ob 'em;" "De whole country is alive wid 'em;" "Massa Bill, does you tink we is eber agoin' to get out o' heah?" and many other similar expressions.

Major Armes, who was wounded and lying under the cannon—which, by the way, had become useless,—called me up and asked if I thought there was any show of getting back to the fort. I replied that there was.

Orders were accordingly given by Major Armes for a retreat, the cannon being left behind. During the movement several of our men were killed, but as night came and dense darkness prevailed, we succeeded in making good headway, and got into Fort Hays just at daylight next morning, in a very played-out condition.

During our absence the cholera had broken out at the post, and five or six men were dying daily. It was difficult to tell which was the greater danger—fighting Indians on the prairie, or facing the cholera in camp; but the former was decidedly the more inviting.

CHAPTER XIII

A Millionaire

Soon after returning to Fort Hays, I was sent with dispatches to Fort Harker. After delivering the messages, I visited the town of Ellsworth, about three miles west of Fort Harker, and there I met a man named William Rose, a contractor on the Kansas Pacific Railroad,[1] who had a contract for grading[2] near Fort Hays. He had had his stock stolen by the Indians, and had come to Ellsworth to buy more.

During the course of our conversation, Mr. Rose incidentally remarked that he had some idea of laying out a town on the west side of Big Creek, about one mile from the fort, where the railroad was to cross. He asked my opinion of the contemplated enterprise, and I told him that I thought it was "a big thing." He then proposed taking me as a partner in the scheme, and suggested that after we got the town laid out and thrown open to the public, we should establish a store and saloon there.

Thinking it would be a grand thing to be half-owner of a town, I at once accepted his proposition. We bought a stock of such articles as are usually found in a frontier store, and transported them to the place on Big Creek, where we were to found our town. We hired a railroad engineer to survey the site and stake it off into lots; and we gave the new town the ancient and historical name of Rome. To a "starter," we donated lots to any one who would build on them, but reserved the corner lots and others which were best located for ourselves. These reserved lots we valued at fifty dollars each.

Our modern Rome, like all mushroom towns along the line of a new railroad, sprang up as if by magic, and in less than one month we had two hundred frame and log houses, three or four stores, several saloons, and one good hotel. Rome was looming up, and Rose and I already considered ourselves millionaires, and thought we "had the world by the tail." But one day a fine-looking gentleman, calling himself Dr. W. E. Webb, appeared in town, and dropping into our store introduced himself in a very pleasant way.

"Gentlemen, you've got a very flourishing little town here. Wouldn't you like to have a partner in your enterprise?"

"No, thank you," said I, "we have too good a thing here to whack up with anybody."

My partner agreed with me, but the conversation was continued, and at last the stranger said:

"Gentlemen, I am the agent or prospector of the Kansas Pacific Railroad, and my business is to locate towns for the company along the line."

"We think we have the only suitable town-site in this immediate locality," said Mr. Rose, "and as a town is already started, we have saved the company considerable expense."

"You know as well as I do," said Dr. Webb, "that the company expects to make money by selling lands and town lots; and as you are not disposed to give the company a show, or share with me, I shall probably have to start another town near you. Competition is the life of trade, you know."

"Start your town, if you want to. We've got the 'bulge' on you, and can hold it," said I, somewhat provoked at his threat.

But we acted too independently and too indiscreetly for our own good. Dr. Webb, the very next day after his interview with us, began hauling material to a spot about one mile east of us, where he staked out a new town, which he called Hays City. He took great pains to circulate in our town the story that the railroad company would locate their round-houses[3] and machine shops at Hays City, and that it was to be *the* town and a splendid business center. A ruinous stampede from our place was the result. People who had built in Rome came to the conclusion that they had built in the wrong place; they began pulling down their buildings and moving them over to Hays City, and in less than three days our once flourishing city had dwindled down to the little store which Rose and I had built.

It was on a bright summer morning that we sat on a pine box in front of our crib, moodily viewing the demolition of the last building. Three days before, we had considered ourselves millionaires; on that morning we looked around and saw that we were reduced to the ragged edge of poverty. Our sanguine expectations of realizing immense fortunes were dashed to the ground, and we felt pretty blue. The new town of Hays had swallowed Rome entirely. Mr. Rose facetiously remarked that he felt like "the last rose of summer," with all his lovely companions

36. Departing Riches

faded and gone, and *he* left blooming alone. I told him I was still there, staunch and true, but he replied that that didn't help the matter much. Thus ends the brief history of the "Rise, Decline and Fall" of Modern Rome.

It having become evident to me that there was very little hope of Rome ever regaining its former splendor and prosperity, I sent my wife and daughter Arta[4]—who had been born at Leavenworth in the latter part of December, 1866—to St. Louis on a visit. They had been living with me for some little time in the rear part of our "store."

At this time Mr. Rose and myself had a contract under Schumacher, Miller & Co., constructors of the Kansas Pacific, for grading five miles of track westward from Big Creek, and running through the site of Rome. Notwithstanding we had been deserted, we had some small hope that they would not be able to get water at the new town, and that the people would all soon move back to Rome, as we really had the best location. We determined, therefore, to go on with our grading contract, and wait for something better to turn up. It was indeed hard for us, who had been millionaires, to come down to the level of common railroad contractors—but we had to do it, all the same.

We visited the new town of Hays almost daily, to see how it was progressing, and in a short time we became much better acquainted with Dr. Webb, who had reduced us from our late independent to our present dependent position. We found him a perfect gentleman—a whole-souled, genial-hearted fellow, whom everybody liked and respected. Nearly every day, "Doc." and I would take a ride over the prairie together and hunt buffalo.

On one occasion, having ventured about ten miles

from the town, we spied a band of Indians not over two miles distant, who were endeavoring to get between us and the town, and thus cut us off. I was mounted on my celebrated horse Brigham, the fleetest steed I ever owned. On several subsequent occasions he saved my life, and he was the horse that I rode when I killed sixty-nine buffaloes in one day. Dr. Webb was riding a beautiful thoroughbred bay, which he had brought with him from the East. Having such splendid horses, we laughed at the idea of a band of Indians overtaking us on a square run, no matter how well they might be mounted; but not caring to be cut off by them, we ran our steeds about three miles towards home, thus getting between the braves and the town. The Indians were then about three-quarters of a mile distant, and we stopped and waved our hats at them, and fired some shots at long range. There were thirteen in the party, and as they were getting pretty close to us, we struck out for Hays. They came on in pursuit and sent several scattering shots after us, but we easily left them behind. They finally turned and rode off towards the Saline River.

The Doctor thought this glorious sport, and wanted to organize a party to go in pursuit of them, but I induced him to give up this idea, although he did so rather reluctantly. The Doctor soon became quite an expert hunter, and before he had remained on the prairie a year there were but few men in the country who could kill more buffaloes on a hunt than he.

Being aware that Rose and myself felt rather downhearted over our deserted village, the Doctor one day said that, as he had made the proprietors of Rome "howl," he would give us two lots each in Hays, and did so. We finally came to the conclusion that our old town was dead beyond redemption or revival, and we thereupon devoted our undivided attention to our railroad contract. One day we were pushed for horses to work on our scrapers[5]—so I hitched up Brigham, to see how he would work. He was not much used to that kind of labor, and I was about giving up the idea of making a work-horse of him, when one of the men called to me that there were some buffaloes coming over the hill. As there had been no buffaloes seen anywhere in the vicinity of the camp for several days, we had become rather short of meat. I immediately told one of our men to hitch his horses to a wagon and follow me, as I was going out after the herd, and we would bring back some fresh meat for supper. I had no saddle, as mine had been left at the camp a mile distant, so taking the harness from Brigham, I mounted him bareback and started out after the game, being armed with my celebrated buffalo-killer, "Lucretia Borgia,"[6]—a newly-improved breech-loading needle gun, which I had obtained from the government.

While I was riding toward the buffaloes I observed five horsemen coming out from the fort, who had evidently seen the buffaloes from the post, and were going out for a chase. They proved to be some newly-arrived officers in that part of the country, and when they came up closer, I could see by the shoulder straps that the senior officer was a captain, while the others were lieutenants.

"Hello! my friend," sang out the captain, "I see you are after the same game we are."

"Yes, sir; I saw those buffaloes coming over the hill, and as we were about out of fresh meat I thought I would go and get some," said I.

They scanned my cheap-looking outfit pretty closely, and as my horse was not very prepossessing in appearance, having on only a blind bridle, and otherwise looking like a work-horse they evidently considered me a green hand at hunting.

"Do you expect to catch those buffaloes on that Gothic steed?" laughingly asked the captain.

"I hope so, by pushing on the reins hard enough," was my reply.

"You'll never catch them in the world, my fine fellow," said the captain. "It requires a fast horse to overtake the animals on these prairies."

"Does it?" asked I as if I didn't know it.

"Yes; but come along with us as we are going to kill them more for pleasure than anything else. All we want are the tongues and a piece of tender loin, and you may have all that is left," said the generous man.

"I am much obliged to you, Captain, and will follow you," I replied.

There were eleven buffaloes in the herd and they were not more than a mile from us. The officers dashed ahead as if they had a sure thing on killing them all before I could come up with them; but I had noticed that the herd was making towards the creek for water, and as I knew buffalo nature, I was perfectly aware that it would be difficult to turn them from their direct course. Thereupon, I started towards the creek to head them off, while the officers came up in the rear and gave chase.

The buffaloes came rushing past me not a hundred yards distant, with the officers about three hundred yards in the rear. Now, thought I, is the time to "get my work in," as they say; and I pulled the blind-bridle from my horse, who knew as well as I did that we were out for buffaloes—as he was a trained hunter. The moment the bridle was off, he started at the top of his speed, running in ahead of the officers, and with a few jumps he brought me alongside of the rear buffalo. Raising old "Lucretia Borgia" to my shoulder, I fired, and killed the animal at the first shot. My horse then carried me alongside the next one, not ten feet away, and I dropped him at the next fire.

As soon as one buffalo would fall, Brigham would take me so close to the next, that I could almost touch it with my gun. In this manner I killed the eleven buffaloes with twelve shots; and, as the last animal dropped, my horse stopped. I jumped to the ground, knowing that he would not leave me—it must be remembered that I had been riding him without bridle, reins or saddle—and turning round as the party of astonished officers rode up, I said to them:

"Now, gentlemen, allow me to present to you all the tongues and tender-loins you wish from these buffaloes."

Captain Graham, for such I soon learned was his name, replied: "Well, I never saw the like before. Who under the sun are you, anyhow?"

"My name is Cody," said I.

One of the lieutenants, Thompson by name, who had met me at Fort Harker, then recognized me, and said: "Why, that is Bill Cody, our old scout." He then introduced me to the other officers, who were Captain Graham, of the Tenth Cavalry, and Lieutenants Reed, Emmick and Ezekiel.

Captain Graham, who was considerable of a horseman, greatly admired Brigham, and said: "That horse of yours has running points."

37. Tongues and Tender Loins

"Yes, sir; he has not only got the points, he is a runner and knows how to use the points," said I.

"So I noticed," said the captain.

They all finally dismounted, and we continued chatting for some little time upon the different subjects of horses, buffaloes, Indians and hunting. They felt a little sore at not getting a single shot at the buffaloes, but the way I had killed them had, they said, amply repaid them for their disappointment. They had read of such feats in books, but this was the first time they had ever seen anything of the kind with their own eyes. It was the first time, also, that they had ever witnessed or heard of a white man running buffaloes on horseback without a saddle or a bridle.

I told them that Brigham knew nearly as much about

the business as I did, and if I had had twenty bridles they would have been of no use to me, as he understood everything, and all that he expected of me was to do the shooting. It is a fact, that Brigham would stop if a buffalo did not fall at the first fire, so as to give me a second chance, but if I did not kill the buffalo then, he would go on, as if to say, "You are no good, and I will not fool away time by giving you more than two shots." Brigham was the best horse I ever owned or saw for buffalo chasing.

Our conversation was interrupted in a little while by the arrival of the wagon which I had ordered out; I loaded the hind-quarters of the youngest buffaloes on it, and then cut out the tongues and tender loins, and presented them to the officers, after which I rode towards the fort with them, while the wagon returned to camp.

Captain Graham told me that he expected to be stationed at Fort Hays during the summer, and would probably be sent out on a scouting expedition, and in case he was he would like to have me accompany him as scout and guide. I replied that notwithstanding I was very busy with my railroad contract I would go with him if he was ordered out. I then left the officers and returned to our camp.

That very night the Indians unexpectedly made a raid on the horses, and ran off five or six of our very best work-teams, leaving us in a very crippled condition. At daylight I jumped on old Brigham and rode to Fort Hays, when I reported the affair to the commanding officer; Captain Graham and Lieutenant Emmick were at once ordered out with their company of one hundred colored troops, to pursue the Indians and recover our stock if possible. In an hour we were under way. The darkies had never been

38. The Indian Horse Thieves

in an Indian fight and were anxious to catch the band we were after and "Sweep de red debels from off de face ob de earth." Captain Graham was a brave, dashing officer, eager to make a record for himself, and it was with difficulty that I could trail fast enough to keep out of the way of the impatient soldiers. Every few moments Captain Graham would ride up to see if the trail was freshening and how soon we should be likely to overtake the thieves.

At last we reached the Saline river, where we found the Indians had only stopped to feed and water the animals, and had then pushed on towards the Solomon. After crossing the Saline they made no effort to conceal their trail, thinking they would not be pursued beyond that point—consequently we were able to make excellent time. We reached the Solomon before sunset, and came to a halt; we surmised that if the Indians were camped on this river, that they had no suspicion of our being in the neighborhood. I advised Captain Graham to remain with the company where it was, while I went ahead on a scout to find the Indians, if they were in the vicinity.

After riding some distance down the ravine that led to the river, I left my horse at the foot of a hill; then, creeping to the top, I looked cautiously over the summit upon the Solomon, below. I at once discovered in plain view, not a mile away, a herd of horses grazing, our lost ones among them; very shortly I made out the Indian camp, noted its lay, and how we could best approach it. Reporting to Captain Graham, whose eyes fairly danced with delight at the prospect of surprising and whipping the redskins, we concluded to wait until the moon rose, then get into the timber so as to approach the Indians as closely as possible without being discovered, and finally to make a sudden dash into their camp, and clean them out. We had everything "cut and dried," as we thought, but, alas! just as we were nearing the point where we were to take the open ground and make our charge, one of the colored gentlemen became so excited that he fired off his gun. We immediately commenced the charge, but the firing of the gun and the noise of our rush through the crackling timber alarmed the Indians, who at once sprang to their horses and were away from us before we reached their late camp. Captain Graham called out "Follow me boys!" which we did for awhile, but in the darkness the Indians made good their escape. The bugle then gave the re-call, but some of the darkies did not get back until morning, having, in their fright, allowed their horses to run away with them whithersoever it suited the animal's pleasure to go.

We followed the trail the next day for awhile, but as it become evident that it would be a long chase to overtake the enemy, and as we had rations only for the day, we commenced the return. Captain Graham was bitterly disappointed in not being able to get the fight when it seemed so near at one time. He roundly cursed the "nigger" who fired the gun, and as a punishment for his carelessness, he was compelled to walk all the way back to Fort Hays.

CHAPTER XIV

Earning a Title

It was about this time that the end of the Kansas Pacific track was in the heart of the buffalo country, and the company was employing about twelve hundred men in the construction of the road. As the Indians were very troublesome, it was difficult to obtain fresh meat for the workmen, and the company therefore concluded to engage the services of hunters to kill buffaloes.

Having heard of my experience and success as a buffalo hunter, Messrs.[1] Goddard Brothers, who had the contract for boarding the employees of the road, met me in Hays City one day and made me a good offer to become their hunter, and I at once entered into a contract with them. They said that they would require about twelve buffaloes per day; that would be twenty-four hams, as we took only the hind-quarters and hump of each buffalo. As this was to be dangerous work, on account of the Indians, who were riding all over that section of the country, and as I would be obliged to go from five to ten miles from the road each day to hunt the buffaloes, accompanied by only one man with a light wagon for the transportation of the meat, I of course demanded a large salary. They could afford to remunerate me well, because the meat would not cost them anything. They agreed to give me five hundred

40. Buffalo Bill

dollars per month, provided I furnished them all the fresh meat required.

Leaving my partner, Rose, to complete our grading contract, I immediately began my career as a buffalo hunter for the Kansas Pacific Railroad, and it was not long before I acquired considerable notoriety. It was at this time that the very appropriate name of "Buffalo Bill," was conferred upon me by the road-hands. It has stuck to me ever since, and I have never been ashamed of it.

During my engagement as hunter for the company—a period of less than eighteen mouths—I killed 4,280 buffaloes; and I had many exciting adventures with the Indians, as well as hair-breadth escapes, some of which are well worth relating.

One day in the spring of 1868, I mounted Brigham and started for Smoky Hill River. After galloping about twenty miles I reached the top of a small hill overlooking the valley of that beautiful stream.

As I was gazing on the landscape, I suddenly saw a band of about thirty Indians nearly half a mile distant; I knew by the way they jumped on their horses that they had seen me as soon as I came into sight.

The only chance I had for my life was to make a run for it, and I immediately wheeled and started back towards the railroad. Brigham seemed to understand what was up, and he struck out as if he comprehended that it was to be a run for life. He crossed a ravine in a few jumps, and on reaching a ridge beyond, I drew rein, looked back and saw the Indians coming for me at full speed and evidently well-mounted. I would have had little or no fear of being overtaken if Brigham had been fresh; but as he was not, I felt uncertain as to how he would stand a long chase.

My pursuers seemed to be gaining on me a little, and I let Brigham shoot ahead again; when we had run about three miles farther, some eight or nine of the Indians were not over two hundred yards behind, and five or six of these seemed to be shortening the gap at every jump. Brigham now exerted himself more than ever, and for the next three or four miles he got "right down to business," and did some of the prettiest running I ever saw. But the Indians were about as well-mounted as I was, and one of their horses in particular—a spotted animal—was gaining on me all the time. Nearly all the other horses were strung out behind for a distance of two miles, but still chasing after me.

The Indian who was riding the spotted horse was armed with a rifle, and would occasionally send a bullet whistling

41. Down Went His Horse

along, sometimes striking the ground ahead of me. I saw that this fellow must be checked, or a stray bullet from his gun might hit me or my horse; so, suddenly stopping Brigham, and quickly wheeling him around, I raised old "Lucretia" to my shoulder, took deliberate aim at the Indian and his horse, hoping to hit one or the other, and fired. He was not over eighty yards from me at this time, and at the crack of my rifle down went his horse. Not waiting to see if he recovered, I turned Brigham, and in a moment we were again fairly flying towards our destination; we had urgent business about that time, and were in a hurry to get there.

The other Indians had gained on us while I was engaged in shooting at their leader, and they sent several shots whizzing past me, but fortunately none of them hit the intended mark. To return their compliment I occasionally wheeled myself in the saddle and fired back at them, and one of my shots broke the leg of one of their horses, which left its rider *hors(e) de combat*,[2] as the French would say.

Only seven or eight Indians now remained in dangerous proximity to me, and as their horses were beginning to lag somewhat, I checked my faithful old steed a little, to allow him an opportunity to draw an extra breath or two. I had determined, if it should come to the worst, to drop into a buffalo wallow, where I could stand the Indians off for a while; but I was not compelled to do this, as Brigham carried me through most nobly.

The chase was kept up until we came within three miles of the end of the railroad track, where two companies of soldiers were stationed for the purpose of protecting the workmen from the Indians. One of the outposts saw the Indians chasing me across the prairie, and gave the alarm. In a few minutes I saw, greatly to my delight, men coming on foot, and cavalrymen, too, came galloping to our rescue as soon as they could mount their horses. When the Indians observed this, they turned and ran in the direction from which they had come. In a very few minutes I was met by some of the infantrymen and trackmen, and jumping to the ground and pulling the blanket and saddle off of Brigham, I told them what he had done for me; they at once took him in charge, led him around, and rubbed him down so vigorously that I thought they would rub him to death.

Captain Nolan, of the Tenth Cavalry, now came up with forty of his men, and upon learning what had happened he determined to pursue the Indians. He kindly offered me one of the cavalry horses, and after putting my own saddle and bridle on the animal, we started out after the flying Indians, who only a few minutes before had been making it so uncomfortably lively for me. Our horses were all fresh and of excellent stock, and we soon began shortening the distance between ourselves and the redskins. Before they had gone five miles we overtook and killed eight of their number. The others succeeded in making their escape. On coming up to the place where I had killed the first horse—the spotted one—on my "home run," I found that my bullet had struck him in the forehead and killed him instantly. He was a noble animal, and ought to have been engaged in better business.

When we got back to camp I found old Brigham grazing quietly and contentedly on the grass. He looked up at me as if to ask if we had got away with any of those fellows who had chased us. I believe he read the answer in my eyes.

Another very exciting hunting adventure of mine which deserves a place in these reminiscences occurred near Saline river. My companion at the time was a man called Scotty, a butcher, who generally accompanied me on these hunting expeditions to cut up the buffaloes and load the meat into a light wagon which he brought to carry it in. He was a brave little fellow and a most excellent shot. I had killed some fifteen buffaloes, and we had started for home with a wagon-load of meat. When within about eight miles of our destination, we suddenly ran on to a party of at least thirty Indians who came riding out of the head of a ravine.

On this occasion I was mounted on a most excellent

horse belonging to the railroad company, and could easily have made my escape; but of course I could not leave Scotty who was driving a pair of mules hitched to the wagon. To think was to act, in those days; and as Scotty and I had often talked over a plan of defense in case we were ever surprised by Indians, we instantly proceeded to carry it out. We jumped to the ground, unhitched the mules quicker than it had ever been done before, and tied them and my horse to the wagon. We threw the buffalo hams upon the ground, and piled them around the wheels in such a shape as to form a breastwork. All this was done in a shorter time than it takes to tell it; and then, with our extra box of ammunition and three or four extra revolvers, which we always carried along with us, we crept under the wagon and were fully prepared to give our visitors the warmest kind of a reception.

The Indians came on pell-mell, but when they were within one hundred yards of us we opened such a sudden and galling fire upon them, that they held up and began to circle around the wagon instead of riding up to take tea with us. They however charged back and forth upon us several times, and their shots killed the two mules and my horse; but we gave it to them right and left, and had the satisfaction of seeing three of them fall to the ground not more than fifty yards away. On seeing how well we were fortified and protected by our breastwork of hams, they probably came to the conclusion that it would be a difficult undertaking to dislodge us, for they drew off and gave us a rest, but only a short one.

This was the kind of fighting we had been expecting for a long time, as we knew that sooner or later we would be

42. The Fire Signal

"jumped" by Indians while we were out buffalo hunting. I
had an understanding with the officers who commanded
the troops at the end of the track, that in case their pickets
should at any time notice a smoke in the direction of our
hunting ground, they were to give the alarm, so that assistance might be sent to us for the smoke was to indicate
that we were in danger.

I now resolved to signal to the troops in the manner
agreed on, and at the first opportunity set fire to the grass
on the windward side of the wagon. The fire spread over
the prairie at a rapid rate, causing a dense smoke which
I knew would be seen at the camp. The Indians did not
seem to understand this strategic movement. They got
off from their horses, and from behind a bank or knoll,

again peppered away at us; but we were well fortified, and whenever they showed their heads we let them know that we could shoot as well as they.

After we had been cooped up in our little fort, for about an hour, we discovered cavalry coming toward us at full gallop over the prairie. Our signal of distress had proved a success. The Indians saw the soldiers at about the same time that we did, and thinking that it would not be healthy for them to remain much longer in that vicinity, they mounted their horses and disappeared down the cañons of the creek. When the soldiers came up we had the satisfaction of showing them five *"good"* Indians, that is dead ones.

Two hours later we pulled into camp with our load of meat, which was found to be all right, except that it had a few bullets and arrows sticking in it.

While I was hunting for the Kansas Pacific railway, I had the pleasure, in the fall of 1867, of meeting the celebrated Kit Carson,[3] one of, if not the oldest and most noted scout, guide, and hunter that our western country has ever produced. He was on his way to Washington. I also met him on his return from the East, and invited him to be my guest for a few days at Hays City, which invitation he accepted. He then proceeded to Fort Lyon, Colorado, near which place his son-in-law, Mr. Boggs, and family, resided. At this time his health was failing, and shortly afterwards he died at Mr. Boggs' residence on the Picket Wire Creek.

43. Kit Carson

CHAPTER XV

Champion Buffalo Killer

Shortly after the adventures mentioned in the preceding chapter, I had my celebrated buffalo hunt with Billy Comstock,[1] a noted scout, guide and interpreter, who was then chief of scouts at Fort Wallace, Kansas. Comstock had the reputation, for a long time, of being a most successful buffalo hunter, and the officers in particular, who had seen him kill buffaloes, were very desirous of backing him in a match against me. It was accordingly arranged that I should shoot him a buffalo-killing match, and the preliminaries were easily and satisfactorily agreed upon. We were to hunt one day of eight hours, beginning at eight o'clock in the morning, and closing at four o'clock in the afternoon. The wager was five hundred dollars a side, and the man who should kill the greater number of buffaloes from on horseback was to be declared the winner.

The hunt took place about twenty miles east of Sheridan, and as it had been pretty well advertised and noised abroad, a large crowd witnessed the interesting and exciting scene. An excursion party, mostly from St. Louis, consisting of about a hundred gentlemen and ladies, came out on a special train to view the sport, and among the number was my wife, with little baby Arta, who had come to remain with me for a while.

The buffaloes were quite plenty, and it was agreed that we should go into the same herd at the same time and "make a run," as we called it, each one killing as many as possible. A referee was to follow each of us on horseback when we entered the herd, and count the buffaloes killed by each man. The St. Louis excursionists, as well as the other spectators, rode out to the vicinity of the hunting grounds in wagons and on horseback, keeping well out of sight of the buffaloes, so as not to frighten them, until the time came for us to dash into the herd; when they were to come up as near as they pleased and witness the chase.

We were fortunate in the first run in getting good ground. Comstock was mounted on one of his favorite horses, while I rode old Brigham. I felt confident that I had the advantage of Comstock in two things—first, I had the best buffalo horse that ever made a track; and second, I was using what was known at that time as the needle-gun, a breech-loading Springfield rifle—caliber 50,—it was my favorite old "Lucretia," which has already been introduced to the notice of the reader; while Comstock was armed with a Henry rifle,[2] and although he could fire a few shots quicker than I could, yet I was pretty certain that it did not carry powder and lead enough to do execution equal to my caliber 50.

At last the time came to begin the match. Comstock and I dashed into a herd, followed by the referees. The buffaloes separated; Comstock took the left bunch and I the right. My great *forte* in killing buffaloes from horseback was to get them circling by riding my horse at the head of the herd, shooting the leaders, thus crowding their followers to the left, till they would finally circle round and round.

On this morning the buffaloes were very accommo-dating, and I soon had them running in a beautiful circle, when I dropped them thick and fast, until I had killed thirty-eight; which finished my run.

Comstock began shooting at the rear of the herd, which he was chasing, and they kept straight on. He succeeded, however, in killing twenty-three, but they were scattered over a distance of three miles, while mine lay close together. I had "nursed" my buffaloes, as a billiard-player does the balls when he makes a big run.

After the result of the first run had been duly an-nounced, our St. Louis excursion friends—who had ap-proached to the place where we had stopped—set out a lot of champagne, which they had brought with them, and which proved a good drink on a Kansas prairie, and a buffalo hunter was a good man to get away with it.

While taking a short rest, we suddenly spied another herd of buffaloes coming toward us. It was only a small drove, and we at once prepared to give the animals a lively reception. They proved to be a herd of cows and calves—which, by the way, are quicker in their movements than the bulls. We charged in among them, and I concluded my run with a score of eighteen, while Comstock killed fourteen. The score now stood fifty-six to thirty-seven, in my favor.

Again the excursion party approached, and once more the champagne was tapped. After we had eaten a lunch which was spread for us, we resumed the hunt. Striking out for a distance of three miles, we came up close to an-other herd. As I was so far ahead of my competitor in the number killed, I thought I could afford to give an extra exhibition of my skill. I had told the ladies that I would, on the next run, ride my horse without saddle or bridle. This had raised the excitement to fever heat among the excursionists, and I remember one fair lady who endeavored to prevail upon me not to attempt it.

"That's nothing at all," said I; "I have done it many a time, and old Brigham knows as well as I what I am doing, and sometimes a great deal better."

So, leaving my saddle and bridle with the wagons, we rode to the windward of the buffaloes, as usual, and when within a few hundred yards of them we dashed into the herd. I soon had thirteen laid out on the ground, the last one of which I had driven down close to the wagons, where the ladies were. It frightened some of the tender creatures to see the buffalo coming at full speed directly toward them; but when he had got within fifty yards of one of the wagons, I shot him dead in his tracks. This made my sixty-ninth buffalo, and finished my third and last run, Comstock having killed forty-six.

As it was now late in the afternoon, Comstock and his backers gave up the idea that he could beat me, and thereupon the referees declared me the winner of the match, as well as the champion buffalo-hunter of the plains.[3]

On our way back to camp, we took with us some of the choice meat and finest heads. In this connection it will not be out of place to state that during the time I was hunting for the Kansas Pacific, I always brought into camp the best buffalo heads, and turned them over to the company, who found a very good use for them. They had them mounted in the best possible manner, and sent them to all the principal cities and railroad centers in the country, having them placed in prominent positions at the leading hotels, dépôts, and other public buildings, as a sort of trade-mark, or advertisement, of the Kansas Pacific Railroad; and to-day they attract the attention of the traveler almost everywhere. Whenever I am traveling over the country and see one of these trade-marks, I feel pretty certain that I was the cause of the death of the old fellow whose body it once ornamented, and many a wild and exciting hunt is thus called to mind.

The end of the track finally reached Sheridan, in the month of May, 1868, and as the road was not to be built any farther just then, my services as a hunter were not any longer required. At this time there was a general Indian war raging all along the western borders. General Sheridan had taken up his headquarters at Fort Hays, in order to be in the field to superintend the campaign in person. As scouts and guides were in great demand, I concluded once more to take up my old avocation of scouting and guiding for the army.

Having no suitable place in which to leave my old and faithful buffalo-hunter Brigham, and not wishing to kill him by scouting, I determined to dispose of him. I was very reluctant to part with him, but I consoled myself with the thought that he would not be likely to receive harder usage in other hands than he had in mine. I had several good offers to sell him; but at the suggestion of some gentlemen in Sheridan, all of whom were anxious to obtain possession of the horse, I put him up at a raffle, in order to give them all an equal chance of becoming the owner of the famous steed. There were ten chances at thirty dollars each, and they were all quickly taken.

Old Brigham was won by a gentleman—Mr. Ike

Bonham,—who took him to Wyandotte, Kansas, where he soon added new laurels to his already brilliant record. Although I am getting ahead of my story, I must now follow Brigham for a while. A grand tournament came off four miles from Wyandotte, and Brigham took part in it. As has already been stated, his appearance was not very prepossessing, and nobody suspected him of being anything but the most ordinary kind of a plug. The friends of the rider laughed at him for being mounted on such a dizzy-looking steed. When the exercises—which were of a very tame character, being more for style than speed—were over, and just as the crowd were about to return to the city, a purse of $250 was made up, to be given to the horse that could first reach Wyandotte, four miles distant. The arrangement was carried out, and Brigham was entered as one of the contestants for the purse. Everybody laughed at Mr. Bonham when it became known that he was to ride that pokylooking plug against the five thoroughbreds which were to take part in the race.

When all the preliminaries had been arranged, the signal was given, and off went the horses for Wyandotte. For the first half-mile several of the horses led Brigham, but on the second mile he began passing them one after the other, and on the third mile he was in advance of them all, and was showing them all the road at a lively rate. On the fourth mile his rider let him out, and arrived at the hotel—the home-station—in Wyandotte a long way ahead of his fastest competitor.

Everybody was surprised, as well as disgusted, that such a homely "critter" should be the winner. Brigham, of course, had already acquired a wide reputation, and his name and exploits had often appeared in the newspapers, and when it was learned that this "critter" was none other than the identical buffalo-hunting Brigham, nearly the whole crowd admitted that they had heard of him before, and had they known him in the first place they certainly would have ruled him out.

I finally lost track of Brigham, and for several years I did not know what had become of him. Three years ago, while I was at Memphis, Tennessee, I met a Mr. Wilcox, who had been one of the superintendents of construction of the Kansas Pacific Railroad, and he informed me that he owned Brigham, and that he was at that time on his farm, only a few miles out of town. The next day I rode out with Mr. Wilcox and took a look at the gallant old horse. He was comfortably cared for in Mr. Wilcox's stable, and looked the same clever pony that he always was. It seemed as if he almost remembered me, and I put my arms around his neck, as though he had been a long-lost child. Mr. Wilcox bought the horse at Wyandotte, from the gentleman who had won him at the raffle, and he intends to keep him as long as he lives. I am grateful that he is in such good hands, and whenever I again visit Memphis I shall surely go and see Brigham if he is still alive.

But to return to the thread of my narrative, from which I have wandered. Having received the appointment of guide and scout, and having been ordered to report at Fort Larned, then commanded by Captain Dangerfield Parker, I saw it was necessary to take my family—who had remained with me at Sheridan, after the buffalo-hunting match—to Leavenworth, and there leave them. This I did at once, and after providing them with a comfortable little home, I returned and reported for duty at Fort Larned.

CHAPTER XVI

A Courier

The scouts at Fort Larned, when I arrived there, were commanded by Dick Curtis—an old guide, frontiersman and Indian interpreter. There were some three hundred lodges of Kiowa and Comanche Indians camped near the fort. These Indians had not as yet gone upon the war-path, but were restless and discontented, and their leading chiefs, Satanta, Lone Wolf, Kicking Bird, Satank, Sittamore, and other noted warriors, were rather saucy.[1]

General Hazen,[2] who was at the post, was endeavoring to pacify the Indians and keep them from going on the war-path. I was appointed as his special scout, and one morning he notified me that he was going to Fort Harker, and wished me to accompany him as far as Fort Zarah, thirty miles distant. The General usually traveled in an ambulance,[3] but this trip he was to make in a six-mule wagon, under the escort of a squad of twenty infantrymen. So, early one morning in August, we started; arriving safely at Fort Zarah at twelve o'clock. General Hazen thought it unnecessary that we should go farther, and he proceeded on his way to Fort Harker without an escort, leaving instructions that we should return to Fort Larned the next day.

After the General had gone I went to the sergeant in command of the squad, and told him that I was going

45. A Big Joke

back that very afternoon, instead of waiting till the next morning; and I accordingly saddled up my mule and set out for Fort Larned. I proceeded uninterruptedly until I got about half-way between the two posts, when at Pawnee Rock I was suddenly "jumped" by about forty Indians, who came dashing up to me, extending their hands and saying, "How! How!"[4] They were some of the same Indians who had been hanging around Fort Larned in the morning. I saw that they had on their war-paint, and were evidently now out on the war-path.

My first impulse was to shake hands with them, as they seemed so desirous of it. I accordingly reached out my hand to one of them, who grasped it with a tight grip, and jerked me violently forward; another pulled my mule by the bridle, and in a moment I was completely surrounded. Before I could do anything at all, they had seized my revolvers from the holsters, and I received a blow on the head from a tomahawk which nearly rendered me senseless. My gun, which was lying across the saddle, was snatched from its place, and finally the Indian, who had hold of the bridle, started off towards the Arkansas River, leading the mule, which was being lashed by the other Indians who were following.

The savages were all singing, yelling and whooping, as only Indians can do, when they are having their little game all their own way. While looking towards the river I saw, on the opposite side, an immense village moving down along the bank, and then I became convinced that the Indians had left the post and were now starting out on the war-path. My captors crossed the stream with me, and as we waded through the shallow water they continued to lash the mule and myself. Finally they brought me before an important looking body of Indians, who proved to be the chiefs and principal warriors. I soon recognized old Satanta among them, as well as others whom I knew, and I supposed it was all over with me.

The Indians were jabbering away so rapidly among themselves that I could not understand what they were saying. Satanta at last asked me where I had been; and, as good luck would have it, a happy thought struck me. I told him I had been after a herd of cattle or "whoa-haws," as they called them. It so happened that the Indians had been out of meat for several weeks, as the large herd of cattle which had been promised them had not yet arrived, although expected by them.

The moment that I mentioned that I had been search-ing for the "whoa-haws," old Satanta began questioning me in a very eager manner. He asked me where the cattle were, and I replied that they were back only a few miles, and that I had been sent by General Hazen to inform him that the cattle were coming, and that they were intended for his people. This seemed to please the old rascal, who also wanted to know if there were any soldiers with the herd, and my reply was that there were. Thereupon the chiefs held a consultation, and presently Satanta asked me if General Hazen had really said that they should have the cattle. I replied in the affirmative, and added that I had been directed to bring the cattle to them. I followed this up with a very dignified inquiry, asking why his young men had treated me so. The old wretch intimated that it was only "a freak of the boys"; that the young men had wanted to see if I was brave; in fact, they had only meant to test my bravery, and that the whole thing was a joke.

The veteran liar was now beating me at my own game of lying; but I was very glad of it, as it was in my favor. I did not let him suspect that I doubted his veracity, but I remarked that it was a rough way to treat friends. He immediately ordered his young men to give me back my arms, and scolded them for what they had done. Of course, the sly old dog was now playing it very fine, as he was anxious to get possession of the cattle, with which he believed "there was a heap of soldiers coming." He had concluded it was not best to fight the soldiers if he could get the cattle peaceably.

Another council was held by the chiefs, and in a few minutes old Satanta came and asked me if I would go over and bring the cattle down to the opposite side of the river, so that they could get them. I replied, "Of course; that's my instruction from General Hazen."

Satanta said I must not feel angry at his young men, for they had only been acting in fun. He then inquired if I wished any of his men to accompany me to the cattle herd. I replied that it would be better for me to go alone, and then the soldiers could keep right on to Fort Larned, while I could drive the herd down on the bottom. So, wheeling my mule around, I was soon re-crossing the river, leaving old Satanta in the firm belief that I had told him a straight story, and was going for the cattle, which only existed in my imagination.

I hardly knew what to do, but thought that if I could get the river between the Indians and myself I would have a good three-quarters of a mile the start of them, and could then make a run for Fort Larned, as my mule was a good one.

Thus far my cattle story had panned out all right; but just as I reached the opposite bank of the river, I looked behind and saw that ten or fifteen Indians who had begun to suspect something crooked, were following me. The moment that my mule secured a good foothold on the bank, I urged him into a gentle lope towards the place where, according to my statement, the cattle were to be brought. Upon reaching a little ridge, and riding down the other side out of view, I turned my mule and headed him westward for Fort Larned. I let him out for all that he was worth, and when I came out on a little rise of ground, I looked back, and saw the Indian village in plain sight. My pursuers were now on the ridge which I had passed over, and were looking for me in every direction.

46. Ambushing the Indians

Presently they spied me, and seeing that I was running away, they struck out in swift pursuit, and in a few minutes it became painfully evident that they were gaining on me. They kept up the chase as far as Ash Creek, six miles from Fort Larned. I still led them half a mile, as their horses had not gained much during the last half of the race. My mule seemed to have gotten his second wind, and as I was on the old road I had played the whip and spurs on him without much cessation. The Indians likewise had urged their steeds to the utmost.

Finally, upon reaching the dividing ridge between Ash Greek and Pawnee Fork, I saw Fort Larned only four miles away. It was now sundown, and I heard the evening gun at the fort. The troops of the garrison little dreamed that there was a man flying for his life from the Indians and trying to reach the post. The Indians were once more gaining on me, and when I crossed the Pawnee Fork, two miles from the post, two or three of them were only a quarter of a mile behind me. Just as I had gained the opposite bank of the stream I was overjoyed to see some soldiers in a government wagon, only a short distance off. I yelled at the top of my voice, and riding up to them, told them that the Indians were after me.

Denver Jim, a well-known scout, asked how many there were, and upon my informing him that there were about a dozen, he said: "Let's drive the wagon into the trees, and we'll lay for 'em." The team was hurriedly driven in among the trees and low box-elder bushes, and there secreted.

We did not have to wait long for the Indians, who came dashing up, lashing their horses, which were panting and blowing. We let two of them pass by, but we opened a lively fire on the next three or four, killing two at the first crack. The others following, discovered that they had run into an ambush, and whirling off into the brush they turned and ran back in the direction whence they had come. The two who had passed heard the firing and made their escape. We scalped the two that we had killed, and appropriated their arms and equipments; and then catching their horses, we made our way into the post. The soldiers had heard us firing, and as we were approaching the fort the drums were being beaten, and the buglers were sounding the call to fall in. The officers had thought that Satanta and his Indians were coming in to capture the fort.

It seems that on the morning of that day, two hours after General Hazen had taken his departure, old Satanta drove into the post in an ambulance, which he had received some months before as a present from the government. He appeared to be angry and bent on mischief. In an interview with Captain Parker, the commanding officer, he asked why General Hazen had left the post without supplying the beef cattle which had been promised to him. The Captain told him that the cattle were surely on the road, but he could not explain why they were detained.

The interview proved to be a stormy one, and Satanta made numerous threats, saying that if he wished, he could capture the whole post with his warriors. Captain Parker, who was a brave man, gave Satanta to understand that he was reckoning beyond his powers, and would find it a more difficult undertaking than he had any idea of, as they were prepared for him at any moment. The interview finally terminated, and Satanta angrily left the officer's presence. Going over to the sutler's store he sold his ambulance to Mr. Tappan the post trader, and with a portion of the proceeds he secretly managed to secure some whisky from some bad men around the fort. There are always to be found around every frontier post some men who will sell whisky to the Indians at any time and under any circumstances, notwithstanding it is a flagrant violation of both civil and military regulations.

Satanta mounted his horse, and taking the whisky with him, he rode rapidly away and proceeded straight to his village. He had not been gone over an hour, when he returned to the vicinity of the post accompanied by his warriors who came in from every direction, to the number of seven or eight hundred. It was evident that the irate old rascal was "on his ear," so to speak, and it looked as if he intended to carry out his threat of capturing the fort. The garrison at once turned out and prepared to receive the red-skins, who, when within half a mile, circled around the fort and fired numerous shots into it, instead of trying to take it by assault.

While this circular movement was going on, it was observed that the Indian village in the distance was packing up, preparatory to leaving, and it was soon under way. The mounted warriors remained behind some little time, to give their families an opportunity to get away, as they feared that the troops might possibly in some manner intercept them. Finally, they encircled the post several times, fired some farewell rounds, and then galloped away over the prairie to overtake their fast departing village. On their way thither, they surprised and killed a party of wood-choppers down on the Pawnee Fork, as well as some herders who were guarding beef cattle; some seven or eight men in all, were killed, and it was evident that the Indians meant business.

The soldiers with the wagon—whom I had met at the crossing of the Pawnee Fork—had been out for the bodies of the men. Under the circumstances it was no wonder that the garrison, upon hearing the reports of our guns when we fired upon the party whom we ambushed, should have thought the Indians were coming back to give them another "turn."

We found that all was excitement at the post; double guards had been put on duty, and Captain Parker had all the scouts at his headquarters. He was endeavoring to get some one to take some important dispatches to General Sheridan at Fort Hays. I reported to him at once, and stated where I had met the Indians and how I had escaped from them.

"You was very fortunate, Cody, in thinking of that cattle story; but for that little game your hair would now be an ornament to a Kiowa's lodge," said he.

Just then Dick Curtis spoke up and said: "Cody, the Captain is anxious to send some dispatches to General Sheridan,[5] at Fort Hays, and none of the scouts here seem to be very willing to undertake the trip. They say they are not well enough acquainted with the country to find the way at night."

As a storm was coming up it was quite dark, and the scouts feared that they would lose the way; besides it was a dangerous ride, as a large party of Indians were known to be camped on Walnut Creek, on the direct road to Fort Hays. It was evident that Curtis was trying to induce me to volunteer. I made some evasive answer to Curtis, for

I did not care to volunteer after my long day's ride. But Curtis did not let the matter drop. Said he:

"I wish, Bill, that you were not so tired by your chase of to-day, for you know the country better than the rest of the boys, and I am certain that you could go through."

"As far as the ride to Fort Hays is concerned, that alone would matter but little to me," I said, "but it is a risky piece of work just now, as the country is full of hostile Indians; still if no other scout is willing to volunteer, I will chance it. I'll go, provided I am furnished with a good horse. I am tired of being chased on a government mule by Indians." At this Captain Nolan, who had been listening to our conversation, said:

"Bill, you may have the best horse in my company. You can take your choice if you will carry these dispatches. Although it is against regulations to dismount an enlisted man, I have no hesitancy in such a case of urgent necessity as this is, in telling you that you may have any horse you may wish."

"Captain, your first sergeant has a splendid horse, and that's the one I want. If he'll let me ride that horse, I'll be ready to start in one hour, storm or no storm," said I.

"Good enough, Bill; you shall have the horse; but are you sure you can find your way on such a dark night as this?"

"I have hunted on nearly every acre of ground between here and Fort Hays, and I can almost keep my route by the bones of the dead buffaloes," I confidently replied.

"Never fear, Captain, about Cody not finding the way; he is as good in the dark as he is in the daylight," said Curtis.

47. Whoa There!

An orderly was sent for the horse, and the animal was soon brought up, although the sergeant "kicked" a little against letting him go. After eating a lunch and filling a canteen with brandy, I went to headquarters and put my own saddle and bridle on the horse I was to ride. I then got the dispatches, and by ten o'clock was on the road to Fort Hays, which was sixty-five miles distant across the country. The scouts had all bidden me a hearty good-bye, and wished me success, not knowing when, if ever, they would again gaze upon "my warlike form," as the poet would say.

It was dark as pitch, but this I rather liked, as there was little probability of any of the red-skins seeing me unless I stumbled upon them accidentally. My greatest danger was that my horse might run into a hole and fall down, and in this way get away from me. To avoid any such accident, I tied one end of my rawhide lariat to the bridle and the other end to my belt. I didn't propose to be left on foot, alone out on the prairie.

It was, indeed, a wise precaution that I had taken, for within the next three miles the horse, sure enough, stepped into a prairie-dog's hole, and down he went, throwing me clear over his head. Springing to his feet, before I could catch hold of the bridle, he galloped away into the darkness; but when he reached the full length of the lariat, he found that he was picketed to Bison William. I brought him up standing, and after finding my gun, which had dropped to the ground, I went up to him and in a moment was in the saddle again, and went on my way rejoicing keeping straight on my course until I came to the ravines leading into Walnut Creek, twenty-five miles from Fort Larned, where the country became rougher, requiring me to travel slower and more carefully, as I feared the horse might fall over the bank, it being difficult to see anything five feet ahead. As a good horse is not very apt to jump over a bank, if left to guide himself, I let mine pick his own way. I was now proceeding as quietly as possible, for I was in the vicinity of a band of Indians who had recently camped in that locality. I thought that I had passed somewhat above the spot, having made a little circuit to the west with that intention; but as bad luck would have it this time, when I came up near the creek I suddenly rode in among a herd of horses. The animals became frightened and ran off in every direction.

I knew at once that I was among Indian horses, and had walked into the wrong pew; so without waiting to apologize, I backed out as quickly as possible. At this moment a dog, not fifty yards away, set up a howl, and then I heard some Indians engaged in conversation;—they were guarding the horses, and had been sleeping. Hearing my horse's retreating footsteps toward the hills, and thus becoming aware that there had been an enemy in their camp, they mounted their steeds and started for me.

I urged my horse to his full speed, taking the chances of his falling into holes, and guided him up the creek bottom. The Indians followed me as fast as they could by the noise I made, but I soon distanced them; and then crossed the creek.

When I had traveled several miles in a straight course, as I supposed, I took out my compass and by the light of a match saw that I was bearing two points to the east of north. At once changing my course to the direct route, I pushed rapidly on through the darkness towards Smoky

Hill River. At about three o'clock in the morning I began traveling more cautiously, as I was afraid of running into another band of Indians. Occasionally I scared up a herd of buffaloes or antelopes, or coyotes, or deer, which would frighten my horse for a moment, but with the exception of these slight alarms I got along all right.

After crossing Smoky Hill River, I felt comparatively safe as this was the last stream I had to cross. Riding on to the northward I struck the old Santa Fe trail,[6] ten miles from Fort Hays, just at break of day.

My horse did not seem much fatigued, and being anxious to make good time and get as near the post as possible before it was fairly daylight as there might be bands of Indians camped along Big Creek, I urged him forward as fast as he could go. As I had not "lost" any Indians, I was not now anxious to make their acquaintance, and shortly after *reveille* rode into the post. I proceeded directly to General Sheridan's headquarters, and was met at the door, by Colonel Moore, *aid-de-camp* on General Sheridan's staff who asked me on what business I had come.[7]

"I have dispatches for General Sheridan, and my instructions from Captain Parker, commanding Fort Larned, are that they shall be delivered to the General as soon as possible," said I.

Colonel Moore invited me into one of the offices, and said he would hand the dispatches to the General as soon as he got up.

"I prefer to give these dispatches to General Sheridan myself, and at once," was my reply.

The General, who was sleeping in the same building, hearing our voices, called out, "Send the man in with the

48. Delivering Dispatches to Sheridan

dispatches." I was ushered into the General's presence, and as we had met before he recognized me and said:

"Hello, Cody, is that you?"

"Yes, sir; I have some dispatches here for you, from Captain Parker," said I, as I handed the package over to him.

He hurriedly read them, and said they were important; and then he asked me all about General Hazen and where he had gone, and about the breaking out of the Kiowas and Comanches. I gave him all the information that I possessed, and related the events and adventures of the previous day and night.

"Bill," said he, "you must have had a pretty lively ride. You certainly had a close call when you ran into the Indians on Walnut Creek. That was a good joke that you played on old Satanta. I suppose you're pretty tired after your long journey?"

"I am rather weary, General, that's a fact, as I have been in the saddle since yesterday morning," was my reply, "but my horse is more tired than I am, and needs attention full as much if not more," I added. Thereupon the General called an orderly and gave instructions to have my animal well taken care of, and then he said, "Cody, come in and have some breakfast with me."

"No, thank you, General," said I, "Hays City is only a mile from here, and I prefer riding over there, as I know about every one in the town, and want to see some of my friends."

"Very well; do as you please, and come to the post afterwards as I want to see you," said he.

Bidding him good-morning, and telling him that I would return in a few hours, I rode over to Hays City, and at the

Perry House I met many of my old friends who were of course all glad to see me. I took some refreshments and a two hours nap, and afterward returned to Fort Hays, as I was requested.

As I rode up to the headquarters I noticed several scouts in a little group, evidently engaged in conversation on some important matter. Upon inquiry I learned that General Sheridan had informed them that he was desirous of sending a dispatch to Fort Dodge, a distance of ninety-five miles.

The Indians had recently killed two or three men while they were carrying dispatches between Fort Hays and Fort Dodge, and on this account none of the scouts seemed at all anxious to volunteer, although a reward of several hundred dollars was offered to any one who would carry the dispatches. They had learned of my experiences of the previous day, and asked me if I did not think it would be a dangerous trip. I gave it as my opinion that a man might possibly go through without seeing an Indian, but that the chances were ten to one that he would have an exceedingly lively run and a hard time before he reached his destination, if he ever got there at all.

Leaving the scouts to decide among themselves as to who was to go, I reported to General Sheridan, who also informed me that he wished some one to carry dispatches to Fort Dodge. While we were talking, his chief of scouts Dick Parr, entered and stated that none of the scouts had yet volunteered. Upon hearing this I got my "brave" up a little, and said:

"General, if there is no one ready to volunteer, I'll carry your dispatches myself."

"I had not thought of asking you to do this duty, Cody, as you are already pretty hard worked. But it is really important that these dispatches should go through," said the General.

"Well, if you don't get a courier by four o'clock this afternoon, I'll be ready for business at that time. All I want is a fresh horse," said I; "meantime I'll take a little more rest."

It was not much of a rest, however, that I got, for I went over to Hays City again and had "a time with the boys." I came back to the post at the appointed hour, and finding that no one had volunteered, I reported to General Sheridan. He had selected an excellent horse for me, and on handing me the dispatches he said:

"You can start as soon as you wish—the sooner the better; and good luck go with you, my boy."

In about an hour afterwards I was on the road, and just before dark I crossed Smoky Hill River. I had not yet urged my horse much, as I was saving his strength for the latter end of the route, and for any run that I might have to make in case the "wild-boys" should "jump" me. So far I had not seen a sign of Indians, and as evening came on I felt comparatively safe.

I had no adventures worth relating during the night, and just before daylight I found myself approaching Saw-log Crossing, on the Pawnee Fork, having then ridden about seventy miles.

A company of colored cavalry, commanded by Major Cox, was stationed at this point, and I approached their camp cautiously, for fear that the pickets might fire upon me—as the darkey soldiers were liable to shoot first and cry "halt" afterwards. When within hearing distance I yelled out at the top of my voice, and was answered by one of the pickets. I told him not to shoot, as I was a scout from Fort Hays; and then, calling the sergeant of the guard, I went up to the vidette[8] of the post, who readily recognized me. I entered the camp and proceeded to the tent of Major Cox, to whom I handed a letter from General Sheridan requesting him to give me a fresh horse. He at once complied with the request.

After I had slept an hour and had eaten a lunch, I again jumped into the saddle, and before sunrise I was once more on the road. It was twenty-five miles to Fort Dodge, and I arrived there between nine and ten o'clock, without having seen a single Indian.

After delivering the dispatches to the commanding officer, I met Johnny Austin, chief of scouts at this post, who was an old friend of mine. Upon his invitation I took a nap at his house, and when I awoke, fresh for business once more, he informed me that the Indians had been all around the post for the past two or three days, running off cattle and horses, and occasionally killing a stray man. It was a wonder to him that I had met with none of the red-skins on the way there. The Indians, he said, were also very thick on the Arkansas River, between Fort Dodge and Fort Larned, and making considerable trouble. Fort Dodge was located sixty-five miles west of Fort Larned, the latter post being on the Pawnee Fork, about five miles from its junction with the Arkansas River.

The commanding officer at Fort Dodge was anxious to send some dispatches to Fort Larned, but the scouts, like those at Fort Hays, were rather backward about

volunteering, as it was considered a very dangerous undertaking to make the trip. As Fort Larned was my post,
and as I wanted to go there anyhow, I said to Austin that I
would carry the dispatches, and if any of the boys wished
to go along, I would like to have them for company's sake.
Austin reported my offer to the commanding officer, who
sent for me and said he would be happy to have me take
his dispatches, if I could stand the trip on top of all that
I had already done.

"All I want is a good fresh horse, sir," said I.

"I am sorry to say that we haven't a decent horse here,
but we have a reliable and honest government mule, if that
will do you," said the officer.

"Trot out your mule," said I, "that's good enough for
me. I am ready at any time, sir."

The mule was forthcoming, and at dark I pulled out
for Fort Larned, and proceeded uninterruptedly to Coon
Creek, thirty miles out from Dodge. I had left the main
wagon road some distance to the south, and had traveled
parallel with it, thinking this to be a safer course, as the
Indians might be lying in wait on the main road for dispatch bearers and scouts.

At Coon Creek I dismounted and led the mule by the
bridle down to the water, where I took a drink, using my
hat for a dipper. While I was engaged in getting the water,
the mule jerked loose and struck out down the creek. I
followed him in hopes that he would catch his foot in the
bridle rein and stop, but this he seemed to have no idea
of doing. He was making straight for the wagon road,
and I did not know what minute he might run into a
band of Indians. He finally got on the road, but instead

of going back toward Fort Dodge, as I naturally expected he would do, he turned eastward toward Fort Larned, and kept up a little jog trot just ahead of me, but would not let me come up to him, although I tried it again and again. I had my gun in my hand, and several times I was strongly tempted to shoot him, and would probably have done so had it not been for fear of bringing Indians down upon me, and besides he was carrying the saddle for me. So I trudged on after the obstinate "critter," and if there ever was a government mule that deserved and received a good round cursing it was that one. I had neglected the precaution of tying one end of my lariat to his bit and the other to my belt, as I had done a few nights before, and I blamed myself for this gross piece of negligence.

Mile after mile I kept on after that mule, and every once in a while I indulged in strong language respecting the whole mule fraternity. From Coon Creek to Fort Larned it was thirty-five miles, and I finally concluded that my prospects were good for "hoofing" the whole distance. We—that is to say, the confounded mule and myself—were making pretty good time. There was nothing to hold the mule, and I was all the time trying to catch him—which urged him on. I made every step count, for I wanted to reach Fort Larned before daylight, in order to avoid if possible the Indians, to whom it would have been "pie" to have caught me there on foot.

The mule stuck to the road and kept on for Larned, and I did the same thing. Just as day was beginning to break, we—that is the mule and myself—found ourselves on a hill looking down into the valley of the Pawnee Fork, in which Fort Larned was located, only four miles away;

and when the morning gun belched forth we were within half a mile of the post.

"Now," said I, "Mr. Mule, it is my turn," and raising my gun to my shoulder, in "dead earnest" this time, I blazed away, hitting the animal in the hip. Throwing a second cartridge into the gun, I let him have another shot, and I continued to pour the lead into him until I had him completely laid out. Like the great majority of government mules, he was a tough one to kill, and he clung to life with all the tenaciousness of his obstinate nature. He was, without doubt, the toughest and meanest mule I ever saw, and he died hard.

The troops, hearing the reports of the gun, came rushing out to see what was the matter. They found that the mule had passed in his chips, and when they learned the cause they all agreed that I had served him just right. Taking the saddle and bridle from the dead body, I proceeded into the post and delivered the dispatches to Captain Parker. I then went over to Dick Curtis' house, which was headquarters for the scouts, and there put in several hours of solid sleep.

During the day General Hazen returned from Fort Harker, and he also had some important dispatches to send to General Sheridan. I was feeling quite elated over my big ride; and seeing that I was getting the best of the other scouts in regard to making a record, I volunteered to carry General Hazen's dispatches to Fort Hays. The General accepted my services, although he thought it was unnecessary for me to kill myself. I told him that I had business at Fort Hays, and wished to go there anyway, and it would make no difference to the other scouts, for none of them appeared willing to undertake the trip.

49. The Two Tramps

Accordingly, that night I left Fort Larned on an excellent horse, and next morning at daylight found myself once more in General Sheridan's headquarters at Fort Hays. The General was surprised to see me, and still more so when I told him of the time I had made in riding to Fort Dodge, and that I had taken dispatches from Fort Dodge to Fort Larned; and when, in addition to this, I mentioned my journey of the night previous, General Sheridan thought my ride from post to post, taken as a whole, was a remarkable one, and he said that he did not know of its equal. I can safely say that I have never heard of its being beaten in a country infested with hostile Indians.

To recapitulate: I had ridden from Fort Larned to Fort Zarah (a distance of sixty-five miles) and back in twelve hours, including the time when I was taken across the Arkansas by the Indians. In the succeeding twelve hours I had gone from Fort Larned to Fort Hays, a distance of sixty-five miles. In the next twenty-four hours I had gone from Fort Hays to Fort Dodge, a distance of ninety-five miles. The following night I had traveled from Fort Dodge thirty miles on muleback and thirty-five miles on foot to Fort Larned; and the next night sixty-five miles more to Fort Hays. Altogether I had ridden (and walked) 355 miles in fifty-eight riding hours, or an average of over six miles an hour. Of course, this may not be regarded as very fast riding, but taking into consideration the fact that it was mostly done in the night and over a wild country, with no roads to follow, and that I had to be continually on the look out for Indians, it was thought at the time to be a big ride, as well as a most dangerous one.

CHAPTER XVII

An Appointment

General Sheridan highly complimented me for what I had done, and informed me that I need not report back to General Hazen, as he had more important work for me to do. He told me that the Fifth Cavalry—one of the finest regiments in the army—was on its way to the Department of the Missouri, and that he was going to send it on an expedition against the Dog Soldier Indians, who were infesting the Republican River region.

"Cody," continued he, "I have decided to appoint you as guide and chief of scouts with the command. How does that suit you?"

"First-rate, General, and I thank you for the honor," I replied, as gracefully as I knew how.

The Dog Soldier Indians were a band of Cheyennes[1] and unruly, turbulent members of other tribes, who would not enter into any treaty, or keep a treaty if they made one, and who had always refused to go upon a reservation

After my conversation with the General, I went over to Hays City, where I met some of General Forsyth's[2] scouts, who had just returned from one of the severest battles ever fought with the Indians. As it will not be out of place in this connection, I will here give a brief history of that memorable event.

51. Gen'l Phil. Sheridan

The Indians had become quite troublesome, and General Sheridan had selected General George A. Forsyth to go out on an expedition, and punish them for their recent depredations. There was a scarcity of troops at Fort Hays at that time, so General Forsyth recruited a company of frontiersmen who could move rapidly, as they were to carry no luggage, and were to travel without the ordinary transportation. Thirty of these frontiersmen came from Fort Harker, and twenty from Fort Hays. It was certainly a small body of men, but nearly every one of them was an experienced hunter, guide, scout and Indian-fighter, and they could fight the red-skins in their own way.

In four days they were prepared to take the field, and on the morning of the 29th of August, 1868, they rode out of Fort Hays to meet the Indians. Lieutenant F. H. Beecher,[3] of the Third Infantry, nephew of Henry Ward Beecher,[4] was second in command; Brevet[5] Major-General W.H.H. McCall, who had been in the volunteer army,[6] acted as first sergeant; Dr. John Mowers, of Hays City, who had been a volunteer army surgeon, was the surgeon of the expedition; and Sharpe Grover was the chief guide.

Resting at Fort Wallace, they started September 10th, for the town of Sheridan, thirteen miles distant, where a band of Indians had attacked a train, killed two teamsters, and stolen some cattle. Arriving at Sheridan they easily found the Indian trail, and followed it for some distance. On the eighth day out from Fort Wallace, the command went into camp late in the afternoon, on the Arickaree,[7] which was then not more than eight or nine feet wide at that point, and only two or three inches deep. It was evident to the men that they were not far from the Indians, and it was decided that the next day they would find them and give them a fight.

Early next morning, September 19th, the cry of "Indians" startled the command. Every man jumped for his horse. A half-dozen red-skins, yelling and whooping and making a hideous racket, and firing their guns, rode up and attempted to stampede the horses, several of which, together with the four pack-mules, were so frightened that they broke loose and got away. The Indians then rode off, followed by a few shots. In a minute afterwards, hundreds of Indian warriors—it was estimated that there were nearly one thousand—came galloping down upon the command from every quarter, completely hemming them in.

Acting under the order of General Forsyth, the men retreated to a small island, tied their horses in a circle to the bushes, and then, throwing themselves upon the ground, they began the defense by firing at the approaching enemy, who came pretty close and gave them a raking fire. The besieged scouts at the first opportunity threw up a small breastwork with their knives. The firing, however, continued back and forth, and early in the fight Forsyth was twice seriously wounded—once in the right thigh, and once in the left leg. Dr. Mowers was also wounded in the head, and soon died. Two other men had been killed, and several wounded. All the horses of the command were killed by nine o'clock in the morning.

Shortly afterwards over three hundred Dog-Soldier Indians commanded by old "Roman Nose,"[8] charged down upon the little band of heroes, giving them volley after volley; but finally the scouts, at a favorable opportunity, returned their fire with telling effect. "Roman Nose" and "Medicine Man" were killed, and fell from their horses when within less than one rod of the scouts, who thereupon sent up a triumphant shout. The charging braves now weakened, and in a few moments they were driven back. It was a brilliant charge, and was most nobly and bravely repulsed. The scouts had again suffered severely, having several men wounded, among the number being Lieutenant Beecher who died that night. The Indians, too, had had quite a number killed, several of whom had fallen close to the earthworks. The dismounted Indian warriors still continued firing, but as the scouts had thrown up their intrenchments sufficiently to protect themselves by closely hugging the ground, little or no damage was done.

A second charge was made by the mounted Indians about two o'clock in the afternoon, and they were again repulsed with a severe loss. Darkness finally came on, and then ensued a cessation of hostilities. Two of the scouts had been killed, four fatally wounded, and fourteen others were wounded more or less severely. There were just twenty-eight able-bodied men left out of the fifty. The supplies had run out, and as Dr. Mowers had been mortally wounded and the medical stores captured, the wounded men could not be properly cared for.

Although they were entirely surrounded, and one hundred and ten miles from the nearest post, the men did not despair. They had an abundance of ammunition, plenty of water, underground only a short distance, and for food they had their horses and mules. At night two of the scouts, Tradeau and Stillwell, stole through the lines of the Indians, and started swiftly for Fort Wallace to obtain relief. It was a dangerous undertaking, but they were brave and experienced scouts. Stillwell was only nineteen or twenty years old, but he was, in every sense of the word, a thoroughbred frontiersman.

During the night the besieged scouts threw up their breastworks considerably higher and piled the dead animals on top. They dug down to water, and also stored away a lot of horse and mule meat in the sand to keep it fresh as long as possible. The Indians renewed their firing next morning, and kept it up all day, doing but little injury, however, as the scouts were now well entrenched; but many an Indian was sent to his happy hunting ground.

Night came again, and the prospects were indeed gloomy. An attempt was made by two more of the scouts

52. Battle on the Arickaree

to creep through the Indian lines, but they were detected
by the enemy and had to return to their comrades. The next
morning the Indians renewed hostilities as usual. Their
women and children began to disappear about noon, and
then the Indians tried to draw the scouts out by displaying
a white flag for a truce. They appeared to want to have a
talk with General Forsyth, but as their treachery was well-
known, the scouts did not fall into this trap. The Indians
had apparently become tired of fighting, especially as they
found that they had a most stubborn foe to deal with.

Night once more threw its mantle over the scene, and
under the cover of the darkness Donovan and Plyley, two

of the best scouts, stealthily made their way out of the camp, and started for Fort Wallace with a dispatch from General Forsyth, who gave a brief summary of the situation, and stated that if necessary he could hold out for six days longer.

When the day dawned again, only a small number of warriors could be seen, and they probably remained to watch the scouts and keep them corraled. The uninjured men attended to the wounded as well as they could under the adverse circumstances, but from want of proper treatment, evidences of gangrene appeared in some of the wounds on the sixth day. The mule and horse meat became totally unfit for use, but they had nothing else to eat, and had to eat it or starve. Under these trying circumstances the General told the men that any who wished to go might do so, and take their chances; but they all resolved to remain, and die together, if need be.

Relief came at last. Tradeau and Stillwell had safely reached Fort Wallace, and on the morning of the 25th of September, Colonel Carpenter and a detachment of cavalry arrived with supplies. This assistance to the besieged and starving scouts came like a vessel to ship-wrecked men drifting and starving on a raft in mid-ocean.

It was with the survivors of this terrible fight that I spent the few days at Hays City, prior to the arrival of the Fifth Cavalry.

CHAPTER XVIII

Scouting

On the third day of October the Fifth Cavalry arrived at Fort Hays, and I at once began making the acquaintance of the different officers of the regiment. I was introduced by General Sheridan to Colonel William Royall, who was in command of the regiment. He was a gallant officer, and an agreeable and pleasant gentleman. He is now stationed at Omaha as Inspector General in the Department of the Platte.[1] I also became acquainted with Major W. H. Brown, Major Walker, Captain Sweetman, Quartermaster E. M. Hayes, and in fact all the officers of the regiment.

General Sheridan, being anxious to punish the Indians who had lately fought General Forsyth, did not give the regiment much of a rest, and accordingly on the 5th of October it began its march for the Beaver Creek country. The first night we camped on the South fork of Big Creek, four miles west of Hays City. By this time I had become pretty well acquainted with Major Brown and Captain Sweetman, who invited me to mess with them on this expedition; and a jolly mess we had. There were other scouts in the command besides myself, and I particularly remember Tom Renahan, Hank Fields and a character called "Nosey" on account of his long nose.

On the morning of the 6th we pulled out to the north,

53. Bringing Meat into Camp

and during the day I was very favorably struck with the appearance of the regiment. It was a beautiful command, and when strung out on the prairie with a train of seventy-five six-mule wagons, ambulances and pack mules, I felt very proud of my position as guide and chief of scouts of such a warlike expedition.

Just as we were about to go into camp on the Saline river that night, we ran on to a band of about fifteen Indians, who, seeing us, dashed across the creek, followed by some bullets which we sent after them; but as the small band proved to be a scouting party, we pursued them only a mile or two, when our attention was directed to a herd of buffaloes—they being very plenty—and we succeeded in killing ten or fifteen for the command.

The next day we marched thirty miles, and late in the afternoon we went into camp on the South fork of the Solomon. At this encampment Colonel Royall asked me to go out and kill some buffaloes for the boys.

"All right, Colonel, send along a wagon or two to bring in the meat," I said.

"I am not in the habit of sending out my wagons until I know that there is something to be hauled in; kill your buffalo first and then I'll send out the wagons," was the Colonel's reply. I said no more, but went out on a hunt, and after a short absence returned and asked the Colonel to send his wagons over the hill for the half dozen buffaloes I had killed.

The following afternoon he again requested me to go out and get some fresh buffalo meat. I didn't ask him for any wagons this time, but rode out some distance, and coming up with a small herd, I managed to get seven of them headed straight for the encampment, and instead of shooting them just then, I ran them at full speed right into the camp, and then killed them all, one after the other in rapid succession. Colonel Royall witnessed the whole proceeding, which puzzled him somewhat, as he could see no reason why I had not killed them on the prairie. He came up, rather angrily, and demanded an explanation. "I can't allow any such business as this, Cody," said he, "what do you mean by it?"

"I didn't care about asking for any wagons this time, Colonel; so I thought I would make the buffaloes furnish their own transportation," was my reply. The Colonel saw the point in a moment, and had no more to say on the subject.

54. "Indians!"

No Indians had been seen in the vicinity during the day, and Colonel Royall having carefully posted his pickets, supposed everything was serene for the night. But before morning we were roused from our slumbers by hearing shots fired, and immediately afterwards one of the mounted pickets came galloping into camp, saying that there were Indians close at hand. The companies all fell into line, and were soon prepared and anxious to give the red-skins battle; but as the men were yet new in the Indian country a great many of them were considerably excited. No Indians, however, made their appearance, and upon going to the picket-post where the picket said he had seen them, none could be found, nor could any traces of them be discovered. The sentinel—who was an Irishman—insisted that there certainly had been red-skins there.

"But you must be mistaken," said Colonel Royall.

"Upon me sowl, Colonel, I'm not; as shure ez me name's Pat Maloney, one of thim rid divils hit me on the head wid a club, so he did," said Pat; and so, when morning came, the mystery was further investigated and was easily solved. Elk tracks were found in the vicinity and it was undoubtedly a herd of elks that had frightened Pat; as he had turned to run, he had gone under a limb of a tree, against which he hit his head, and supposed he had been struck by a club in the hands of an Indian. It was hard to convince Pat however, of the truth.

A three days uninteresting march brought us to Beaver Creek where we camped and from which point scouting parties were sent out in different directions. Neither of these parties discovering Indians they all returned to camp about the same time, finding it in a state of great

55. Gen'l E. A. Carr

excitement, it having been attacked a few hours previous by a party of Indians, who had succeeded in killing two men and in making off with sixty horses belonging to Co. H.

That evening the command started on the trail of these Indian horse-thieves; Major Brown with two companies and three days rations pushing ahead in advance of the main command. Being unsuccessful, however, in overtaking the Indians, and getting nearly out of provisions—it being our eighteenth day out, the entire command marched towards the nearest railroad point, and camped on the Saline River; distant three miles from Buffalo Tank.

While waiting for supplies we received a new

commanding officer, Brevet Major-General E. A. Carr, who was the senior major of the regiment, and who ranked Colonel Royall. He brought with him the now celebrated Forsyth scouts, who were commanded by Lieutenant Pepoon, a regular army officer.

It was also while waiting in this camp that Major Brown received a new lieutenant to fill a vacancy in his company. On the day that this officer was to arrive, Major Brown had his private ambulance brought out, and invited me to accompany him to the railroad station to meet his lieutenant, whose name was A. B. Bache. He proved to be a fine gentleman, and a brave, dashing officer. On the way to the dépôt Major Brown had said, "Now, Cody, when we come back we'll give Bache a lively ride and shake him up a little."

Major Brown was a jolly good fellow, but sometimes he would get "a little off," and as this was one of his "off days" he was bound to amuse himself in some original and mischievous way. Reaching the dépôt just as the train came in, we easily found the Lieutenant, and giving him the back seat in the ambulance we were soon headed for camp.

Pretty soon Major Brown took the reins from his driver, and at once began whipping the mules. After getting them into a lively gallop he pulled out his revolver and fired several shots. The road was terribly rough and the night was so dark that we could hardly see where we were going. It was a wonderful piece of luck that we were not tipped over and our necks broken. Finally Bache said, good-humoredly:

"Is this the way you break in all your Lieutenants, Major?"

"Oh, no; I don't do this as a regular thing, but it's the way we frequently ride in this country," said the Major; "just keep your seat, Mr. Bache, and we'll take you through on time." The Major appropriated the reply of the old California stage driver, Hank Monk, to Horace Greeley.[2]

We were now rattling down a steep hill at full speed, and just as we reached the bottom, the front wheels struck a deep ditch over which the mules had jumped. We were all brought up standing by the sudden stoppage of the ambulance. Major Brown and myself were nearly pitched out on the wheels, while the Lieutenant came flying headlong from the back seat to the front of the vehicle.

"Take a back seat, Lieutenant," coolly said Major Brown.

"Major, I have just left that seat," said Bache.

We soon lifted the wagon out of the ditch, and then resumed our drive, running into camp under full headway, and creating considerable amusement. Every one recognized the ambulance and knew at once that Major Brown and I were out on a "lark," and therefore there was not much said about our exploit. Halting with a grand flourish in front of his tent, Major Brown jumped out in his most gallant style and politely asked his lieutenant in. A very pleasant evening was spent there, quite a number of the officers calling to make the acquaintance of the new officer, who entertained the visitors with an amusing account of the ride from the dépôt.

Next morning at an early hour, the command started out on a hunt for Indians. General Carr having a pretty good idea where he would be most likely to find them, directed me to guide him by the nearest route to Elephant Rock on Beaver Creek.

Upon arriving at the south fork of the Beaver on the second day's march, we discovered a large, fresh Indian trail which we hurriedly followed for a distance of eight miles, when suddenly we saw on the bluffs ahead of us, quite a large number of Indians.

General Carr ordered Lieutenant Pepoon's scouts and Company M to the front. This company was commanded by Lieutenant Schinosky, a Frenchman by birth and a reckless dare-devil by nature, who was anxious to have a hair-lifting match. Having advanced his company nearly a mile ahead of the main command, about four hundred Indians suddenly charged down upon him and gave him a lively little fight, until he was supported by our full force.

The Indians kept increasing in numbers all the while until it was estimated that we were fighting from eight hundred to one thousand of them. The engagement became quite general, and several were killed and wounded on each side. The Indians were evidently fighting to give their families and village, a chance to get away. We had undoubtedly surprised them with a larger force than they had expected to see in that part of the country. We fought them until dark, all the time driving them before us. At night they annoyed us considerably by firing down into our camp from the higher hills, and several times the command was ordered out to dislodge them from their position and drive them back.

After having returned from one of these little sallies, Major Brown, Captain Sweetman, Lieutenant Bache and myself were taking supper together, when "whang!" came a bullet into Lieutenant Bache's plate, breaking a hole through it. The bullet came from the gun of one of the

56. A Crack Shot

Indians, who had returned to the high bluff over-looking our camp. Major Brown declared it was a crack shot, because it broke the plate. We finished our supper without having any more such close calls.

At daylight next morning we struck out on the trail, and soon came to the spot where the Indians had camped the day before. We could see that their village was a very large one, consisting of about five hundred lodges; and we pushed forward rapidly from this point on the trail which ran back toward Prairie Dog Creek.

About two o'clock we came in sight of the retreating village, and soon the warriors turned back to give us battle. They set fire to the prairie grass in front of us, and on all sides, in order to delay us as much as possible. We kept up a running fight for the remainder of the afternoon, and the Indians repeatedly attempted to lead us off the track of their flying village, but their trail was easily followed, as they were continually dropping tepee poles, camp kettles, robes, furs and all heavy articles belonging to them. They were evidently scattering, and it finally became difficult for us to keep on the main trail. When darkness set in, we went into camp, it being useless to try to follow the Indians after nightfall.

Next morning we were again on the trail, which led north, and back towards the Beaver Creek, which stream it crossed within a few miles of the spot where we had first discovered the Indians, they having made nearly a complete circle, in hopes of misleading us. Late in the afternoon, we again saw them going over a hill far ahead of us, and towards evening the main body of warriors came back and fought us once more; but we continued to drive them until darkness set in, when we camped for the night.

The Indians soon scattered in every direction, but we followed the main trail to the Republican river, where we made a cut-off, and then went north towards the Platte river. We found, however, that the Indians by traveling night and day had got a long start, and the General concluded that it was useless to follow them any further, as we had pushed them so hard, and given them such a scare that they would leave the Republican country and go north across the Union Pacific railroad. Most of the Indians, as he had predicted, did cross the Platte river, near Ogallala, on the Union Pacific, and thence continued northward.

That night we returned to the Republican river and camped in a grove of cottonwoods, which I named Carr's Grove, in honor of the commanding officer.

The General told me that the next day's march would be towards the head-waters of the Beaver, and he asked me the distance. I replied that it was about twenty-five miles, and he said we would make it the next day. Getting an early start in the morning, we struck out across the prairie, my position as guide being ahead of the advance guard. About two o'clock General Carr overtook me, and asked how far I supposed it was to water. I thought it was about eight miles, although we could see no sign or indication of any stream in our front.

"Pepoon's scouts say that you are going in the wrong direction," said the General, "and in the way you are bearing it will be fifteen miles before you can strike any of the branches of the Beaver; and that when you do, you will find no water, for the Beavers are dry at this time of the year at that point."

"General, I think the scouts are mistaken," said I, "for the Beaver has more water near its head than it has below; and at the place where we will strike the stream we will find immense beaver dams, large enough and strong enough to cross the whole command, if you wish."

"Well, Cody, go ahead," said he, "I'll leave it to you, but remember that I don't want a dry camp."

"No danger of that," said I, and then I rode on, leaving him to return to the command. As I had predicted, we found water seven or eight miles further on, where we came upon a beautiful little stream—a tributary of the Beaver—hidden in the hills. We had no difficulty in selecting a good halting place, and obtaining fresh spring water and excellent grass. The General, upon learning from me that the stream—which was only eight or nine miles long—had no name, took out his map and located it, and named it Cody's Creek, which name it still bears.

We pulled out early next morning for the Beaver, and when we were approaching the stream I rode on ahead of the advance guard, in order to find a crossing. Just as I turned a bend of the creek, "bang!" went a shot, and down went my horse—myself with him. I disentangled myself, and jumped behind the dead body. Looking in the direction whence the shot had come, I saw two Indians, and at once turned my gun loose on them, but in the excitement of the moment I missed my aim. They fired two or three more shots, and I returned the compliment, wounding one of their horses.

On the opposite side of the creek, going over the hill, I observed a few lodges moving rapidly away, and also some mounted warriors, who could see me, and who kept blazing away with their guns. The two Indians who had fired at me and had killed my horse were retreating across the creek on a beaver dam. I sent a few shots after them to accelerate their speed, and also fired at the ones on the other side of the stream. I was undecided as to whether it was best to run back to the command on foot or hold my position. I knew that within a few minutes the troops would come up, and if they heard the firing they would come rapidly.

The Indians, seeing that I was alone, turned and charged down the hill, and were about to re-cross the creek to corral me, when the advance guard of the command put in an appearance on the ridge, and dashed forward to my rescue. The red-skins whirled and made off.

When General Carr came up, he ordered Company I to go in pursuit of the band. I accompanied Lieutenant Brady, who commanded, and we had a running fight with the Indians, lasting several hours. We captured several head of their horses and most of their lodges. At night we returned to the command, which by this time had crossed the creek on the beaver dam.

We scouted for several days along the river, and had two or three lively skirmishes. Finally our supplies began to run low, and General Carr gave orders to return to Fort Wallace, which we reached three days afterwards, and where we remained several days.

While the regiment was waiting here for orders, I spent most of the time in hunting buffaloes, and one day while I was out with a small party, we were "jumped" by about fifty Indians. We had a severe fight of at least an hour, when we succeeded in driving the enemy. They lost four

57. A Hard Crowd

of their warriors, and probably concluded that we were a hard crowd. I had some excellent marksmen with me, and they did some fine work, sending the bullets thick and fast where they would do the most good. Two or three of our horses had been hit, and one man had been wounded; we were ready and willing to stay with the red-skins as long as they wished—but they finally gave it up however, as a bad job, and rode off. We finished our hunt, and went back to the post loaded down with plenty of buffalo meat, and received the compliments of the General for our little fight.

CHAPTER XIX

A Tough Time

General Carr soon received orders from General Sheridan that he was to make a winter's campaign in the Canadian river country, and that we were to proceed to Fort Lyon, on the Arkansas river, in Colorado, and there fit out for the expedition. Leaving Fort Wallace in November, 1868, we arrived at Fort Lyon in the latter part of the month, and outfitted for the coming expedition.

General Penrose had left this post three weeks previously with a command of some three hundred men. He had taken no wagons with him and his supply train was composed only of pack mules. General Carr was ordered to follow with supplies on his trail and overtake him as soon as possible. I was particularly anxious to catch up with Penrose's command, as my old friend Wild Bill was among his scouts. We followed the trail very easily for the first three days, and then we were caught in Freeze-Out canyon by a fearful snow storm, which compelled us to go into camp for a day. The ground now being covered with snow, we found that it would be almost impossible to follow Penrose's trail any further, especially as he had left no sign to indicate the direction he was going. General Carr sent for me and said that as it was very important that we should not lose the trail, he wished that I would take

58. Camping in the Snow

some scouts with me, and while the command remained in camp, push on as far as possible and see if I could not discover some traces of Penrose or where he had camped at any time.

Accompanied by four men I started out in the blinding snow storm, taking a southerly direction. We rode twenty-four miles, and upon reaching a tributary of the Cimarron, we scouted up and down the stream for a few miles and finally found one of Penrose's old camps. It was now late in the afternoon, and as the command would come up the next day, it was not necessary for all of us to return with the information to General Carr. So riding down into a sheltered place in a bend of the creek, we built a fire and broiled some venison from a deer which we had shot during the day, and after eating a substantial meal, I left the four men there, while I returned to bring up the troops.

It was eleven o'clock at night when I got back to the camp. A light was still burning in the General's tent, he having remained awake, anxiously awaiting my return. He was glad to see me, and was overjoyed at the information I brought, for he had great fears concerning the safety of General Penrose. He roused up his cook and ordered him to get me a good hot supper, all of which I greatly appreciated. I passed the night in the General's tent, and next morning rose refreshed and prepared for a big day's work.

The command took up its march next day for the Cimarron, and had a hard tramp of it on account of the snow having drifted to a great depth in many of the ravines, and in some places the teamsters had to shovel their way through. We arrived at the Cimarron at sundown, and went into a nice warm camp. Upon looking around next morning, we found that Penrose, having been unencumbered by wagons, had kept on the west side of the Cimarron, and the country was so rough that it was impossible for us to stay on his trail with our wagons; but knowing that he would certainly follow down the river, General Carr concluded to take the best wagon route along the stream, which I discovered to be on the east side. Before we could make any headway with our wagon train we had to leave the river and get out on the divide. We were very fortunate that day in finding a splendid road for some distance, until we were all at once brought up standing on a high table-land, overlooking a beautiful winding creek that lay far below us in the valley. The question that troubled us, was, how we were to get the wagons down. We were now in the foot-hills of the Rattoon Mountains, and the bluff we were on was very steep.

"Cody, we're in a nice fix now," said General Carr.

"Oh, that's nothing," was my reply.

"But you can never take the train down," said he.

"Never you mind the train, General. You say you are looking for a good camp. How does that beautiful spot down in the valley suit you?" I asked him.

"That will do. I can easily descend with the cavalry, but how to get the wagons down there is a puzzler to me," said he.

"By the time you've located your camp, your wagons shall be there," said I.

"All right, Cody, I'll leave it to you, as you seem to want to be boss," replied he pleasantly. He at once ordered the command to dismount and lead the horses down the mountain-side. The wagon train was a mile in the rear, and when it came up, one of the drivers asked: "How are we going down there?"

"Run down, slide down or fall down—any way to get down," said I.

"We never can do it; it's too steep; the wagons will run over the mules," said another wagon-master.

"I guess not; the mules have got to keep out of the way," was my reply.

Telling Wilson, the chief wagon-master, to bring on his mess-wagon,[1] which was at the head of the train, I said I would try the experiment at least. Wilson drove the team and wagon to the brink of the hill, and following my directions he brought out some extra chains with which we locked both wheels on each side, and then rough-locked[2] them. We then started the wagon down the hill. The wheel-horses—or rather the wheel-mules—were good on the hold-back, and we got along finely until we nearly reached the bottom, when the wagon crowded the mules so hard that they started on a run and galloped down into the valley and to the place where General Carr had located his camp. Three other wagons immediately followed in the same way, and in half an hour every wagon was in camp, without the least accident having occurred. It was indeed an exciting sight to see the six-mule teams come straight down the mountain and finally break into a full run. At times it looked as if the wagons would turn a somersault and land on the mules.

This proved to be a lucky march for us as far as gaining on Penrose was concerned, for the route he had taken on the west side of the stream turned out to be a bad one, and we went with our immense wagon train as far in one day as Penrose had in seven. His command had marched on to a plateau or high table-land so steep, that not even a pack mule could descend it, and he was obliged to retrace his steps a long ways, thus losing three days time as we afterwards learned.

While in this camp we had a lively turkey hunt. The trees along the banks of the stream were literally alive with wild turkeys, and after unsaddling the horses between two and three hundred soldiers surrounded a grove of timber and had a grand turkey round-up, killing four or five hundred of the birds, with guns, clubs and stones. Of course, we had turkey in every style after this hunt—roast turkey, boiled turkey, fried turkey, "turkey on toast," and so on; and we appropriately called this place Camp Turkey.

From this point on, for several days, we had no trouble in following Penrose's trail, which led us in a southeasterly direction towards the Canadian River. No Indians were seen, nor any signs of them found. One day, while riding in advance of the command, down San Francisco Creek, I heard some one calling my name from a little bunch of willow brush on the opposite bank, and, upon looking closely at the spot, I saw a negro.

"Sakes alive! Massa Bill, am dat you?" asked the man, whom I recognized as one of the colored soldiers of the Tenth Cavalry. I next heard him say to some one in the brush: "Come out o' heah. Dar's Massa Buffalo Bill." Then he sang out, "Massa Bill, is you got any hawd tack?"[3]

"Nary a hard tack; but the wagons will be along presently, and then you can get all you want," said I.

"Dat's de best news I'se heerd foah sixteen long days, Massa Bill," said he.

"Where's your command? Where's General Penrose?" I asked.

"I dunno," said the darkey; "we got lost, and we's been a starvin' eber since."

By this time two other negroes had emerged from their place of concealment. They had deserted Penrose's command—which was out of rations and nearly in a starving condition—and were trying to make their way back to Fort Lyon. General Carr concluded, from what they could tell him, that General Penrose was somewhere on Polladora Creek; but we could not learn anything definite from the starved "mokes,"[4] for they knew not where they were themselves.

Having learned that General Penrose's troops were in such bad shape, General Carr ordered Major Brown to start out the next morning with two companies of cavalry and fifty pack-mules loaded with provisions, and to make all possible speed to reach and relieve the suffering soldiers. I accompanied this detachment, and on the third day out we found the half-famished soldiers camped on the Polladora. The camp presented a pitiful sight, indeed. For over two weeks the men had had only quarter rations, and were now nearly starved to death. Over two hundred horses and mules were lying dead, having died from fatigue and starvation. General Penrose, having feared that General Carr would not find him, had sent back a company of the Seventh Cavalry to Fort Lyon for supplies; but no word as yet had been heard from them. The rations which Major Brown brought to the command came none too soon, and were the means of saving many a life.

About the first man I saw after reaching the camp was

59. A Welcome Visitor

my old, true and tried friend, Wild Bill. That night we had a jolly reunion around the camp-fires.

General Carr, upon arriving with his force, took command of all the troops, he being the senior officer and ranking General Penrose. After selecting a good camp, he unloaded the wagons and sent them back to Fort Lyon for fresh supplies. He then picked out five hundred of the best men and horses, and, taking his pack-train with him, he started south for the Canadian River, distant about forty miles, leaving the rest of the troops at the supply camp.

I was ordered to accompany this expedition. We struck

the south fork of the Canadian River, or Rio Colorado, at a point a few miles above the old *adobe* walls,[5] which at one time had composed a fort, and was the place where Kit Carson once had a big Indian fight. We were now within twelve miles of a new supply dépôt, called Camp Evans, which had been established for the Third Cavalry and Evans's Expedition from New Mexico.[6] The scouts who had brought in this information also reported that they expected the arrival at Camp Evans of a bull-train from New Mexico with a large quantity of beer for the soldiers. This news was "pie"[7] for Wild Bill and myself, and we determined to lie low for that beer outfit. That very evening it came along, and the beer that was destined for the soldiers at Camp Evans never reached its destination. It went straight down the thirsty throats of General Carr's command. It appears that the Mexicans living near Fort Union had manufactured the beer, and were taking it through to Camp Evans to sell to the troops, but it struck a lively market without going so far. It was sold to our boys in pint cups, and as the weather was very cold we warmed the beer by putting the ends of our picket-pins[8] heated red-hot into the cups. The result was one of the biggest beer jollifications I ever had the misfortune to attend.

One evening General Carr summoned me to his tent, and said he wished to send some scouts with dispatches to Camp Supply, which were to be forwarded from there to Sheridan. He ordered me to call the scouts together at once at his headquarters, and select the men who were to go. I asked him if I should not go myself, but he replied that he wished me to remain with the command, as he could not spare me. The distance to Camp Supply was about two hundred miles, and owing to the very cold weather it was anything but a pleasant trip. Consequently none of the scouts were anxious to undertake it. It was finally settled, however, that Wild Bill, a half-breed called Little Geary, and three other scouts should carry the dispatches, and they accordingly took their departure next day, with instructions to return to the command as soon as possible.

For several days we scouted along the Canadian River, but found no signs of Indians. General Carr then went back to his camp, and soon afterwards our wagon train came in from Fort Lyon with a fresh load of provisions. Our animals being in poor condition, we remained in different camps along San Francisco Creek and the north fork of the Canadian, until Wild Bill and his scouts returned from Camp Supply.

Among the scouts of Penrose's command were fifteen Mexicans, and between them and the American scouts there had existed a feud; when General Carr took command of the expedition—uniting it with his own—and I was made chief of all the scouts, this feud grew more intense, and the Mexicans often threatened to clean us out; but they postponed the undertaking from time to time, until one day, while we were all at the sutler's[9] store, the long-expected fight took place, and resulted in the Mexicans getting severely beaten.

General Carr, upon hearing of the row, sent for Wild Bill and myself, he having concluded, from the various statements which had been made to him, that we were the instigators of the affair. But after listening to what we had to say, he thought that the Mexicans were as much to blame as we were.

It is not to be denied that Wild Bill and myself had been partaking too freely of "tanglefoot" that evening; and General Carr said to me: "Cody, there are plenty of antelopes in the country, and you can do some hunting for the camp while we stay here."

"All right, General, I'll do it."

After that I put in my time hunting, and with splendid success, killing from fifteen to twenty antelopes a day, which kept the men well supplied with fresh meat.

At length, our horses and mules having become sufficiently recruited to travel, we returned to Fort Lyon, arriving there in March, 1869, where the command was to rest and recruit for thirty days, before proceeding to the Department of the Platte, whither it had been ordered.

CHAPTER XX

An Exciting Chase

General Carr, at my request, kindly granted me one month's leave of absence to visit my family in St. Louis, and ordered Captain Hayes, our quartermaster, to let me ride my mule and horse to Sheridan, distant 140 miles, where I was to take the cars.[1] I was instructed to leave the animals in the quartermaster's corral at Fort Wallace until I should come back, but instead of doing this I put them both in the care of my old friend Perry, the hotel-keeper at Sheridan. After a twenty days absence in St. Louis, pleasantly spent with my family, I returned to Sheridan, and there learned that my mule and horse had been seized by the government.

It seems that the quartermaster's agent at Sheridan had reported to General Bankhead, commanding Fort Wallace, and to Captain Laufer, the quartermaster, that I had left the country and had sold a government horse and mule to Mr. Perry, and of course Captain Laufer took possession of the animals and threatened to have Perry arrested for buying government property. Perry explained to him the facts in the case and said that I would return in a few days; but the captain would pay no attention to his statements.

I immediately went over to the office of the quartermaster's agent, and had Perry point him out to me. I at once laid hold of him, and in a short time had treated him to just such a thrashing as his contemptible lie deserved.

He then mounted a horse, rode to Fort Wallace, and reported me to General Bankhead and Captain Laufer, and obtained a guard to return with and protect him.

The next morning I secured a horse from Perry, and proceeding to Fort Wallace demanded my horse and mule from General Bankhead, on the ground that they were quartermaster Hayes' property and belonged to General Carr's command, and that I had obtained permission to ride them to Sheridan and back. General Bankhead, in a gruff manner ordered me out of his office and off the reservation, saying that if I didn't take a hurried departure he would have me forcibly put out. I told him to do it and be hanged; I might have used a stronger expression, and upon second thought, I believe I did. I next interviewed Captain Laufer and demanded of him also the horse and mule, as I was responsible for them to Quartermaster Hayes. Captain Laufer intimated that I was a liar and that I had disposed of the animals. Hot words ensued between us, and he too ordered me to leave the post. I replied that General Bankhead had commanded me to do the same thing, but that I had not yet gone; and that I did not propose to obey any orders of an inferior officer.

Seeing that it was of no use to make any further effort to get possession of the animals I rode back to Sheridan, and just as I reached there I met the quartermaster's agent coming out from supper, with his head tied up. It occurred to me that he had not received more than one half the punishment justly due him, and that now would be a good time to give him the balance—so I carried the idea into immediate execution. After finishing the job in good style, I informed him that he could not stay in that town while I remained there, and convinced him that Sheridan was not large enough to hold us both at the same time; he accordingly left the place and again went to Fort Wallace, this time reporting to General Bankhead that I had driven him away, and had threatened to kill him.

That night while sleeping at the Perry House, I was awakened by a tap on the shoulder and upon looking up I was considerably surprised to see the room filled with armed negroes who had their guns all pointed at me. The first words I heard came from the sergeant, who said:

"Now look a-heah, Massa Bill, ef you makes a move we'll blow you off de farm, shuah!" Just then Captain Ezekiel entered and ordered the soldiers to stand back.

"Captain, what does this mean?" I asked.

"I am sorry, Bill, but I have been ordered by General Bankhead to arrest you and bring you to Fort Wallace," said he.

"That's all right," said I, "but you could have made the arrest alone, without having brought the whole Thirty-eighth Infantry with you."

"I know that, Bill," replied the Captain, "but as you've not been in very good humor for the last day or two, I didn't know how you would act."

I hastily dressed, and accompanied Captain Ezekiel to Fort Wallace, arriving there at two o'clock in the morning.

"Bill, I am really sorry," said Captain Ezekiel, as we alighted, "but I have orders to place you in the guard-house, and I must perform my duty."

"Very well, Captain; I don't blame you a bit," said I; and into the guard-house I went as a prisoner for the first and only time in my life. The sergeant of the—guard who was an old friend of mine, belonging to Captain Graham's company, which was stationed there at the time—did not put me into a cell, but kindly allowed me to stay in his room and occupy his bed, and in a few minutes I was snoring away as if nothing unusual had occurred.

Shortly after *reveille* Captain Graham called to see me. He thought it was a shame for me to be in the guard-house, and said that he would interview General Bankhead in my behalf as soon as he got up. The Captain had a nice breakfast prepared for me, and then departed. At guard-mount[2] I was not sent for, contrary to my expectations, and thereupon I had word conveyed to Captain Graham, who was officer of the day, that I wanted to see General Bankhead. The Captain informed me that the General absolutely refused to hold any conversation whatever with me.

At this time there was no telegraph line between Fort Wallace and Fort Lyon, and therefore it was impossible for me to telegraph to General Carr, and I determined to send a dispatch direct to General Sheridan. I accordingly wrote out a long telegram informing him of my difficulty, and had it taken to the telegraph office for transmission; but the operator, instead of sending it at once as he should have done, showed it to General Bankhead, who tore it up, and instructed the operator not to pay any attention to what I might say, as he was running that post. Thinking it very strange that I received no answer during the day I went to the telegraph office, accompanied by a guard, and learned from the operator what he had done. "See here, my young friend," said I, "this is a public telegraph line, and I want my telegram sent, or there'll be trouble."

I re-wrote my dispatch and handed it to him, accompanied with the money to pay for the transmission, saying, as I did so: "Young man, I wish that telegram sent direct to Chicago. You know it is your duty to send it, and it must go."

He knew very well that he was compelled to transmit the message, but before doing so he called on General Bankhead and informed him of what I had said, and told him that he would certainly have to send it, for if he didn't he might lose his position. The General, seeing that the telegram would have to go, summoned me to his headquarters, and the first thing he said, after I got into his presence was:

"If I let you go, sir, will you leave the post at once and not bother my agent at Sheridan again?"

"No, sir;" I replied, "I'll do nothing of the kind. I'll remain in the guard-house until I receive an answer from General Sheridan."

"If I give you the horse and mule will you proceed at once to Fort Lyon?"

"No, sir; I have some bills to settle at Sheridan and some other business to transact," replied I.

"Well, sir; will you at least agree not to interfere any further with the quartermaster's agent at Sheridan?"

"I shall not bother him any more, sir, as I have had all I want from him," was my answer.

General Bankhead thereupon sent for Captain Laufer and ordered him to turn the horse and mule over to me. In a few minutes more I was on my way to Sheridan, and after settling my business there, I proceeded to Fort Lyon, arriving two days afterwards. I related my adventures to

General Carr, Major Brown, and other officers, who were greatly amused thereby.

"I'm glad you've come, Bill," said General Carr, "as I have been wanting you for the last two weeks. While we have been at this post several valuable animals, as well as a large number of government horses and mules have been stolen, and we think that the thieves are still in the vicinity of the fort, but as yet we have been unable to discover their rendezvous. I have had a party out for the last few days in the neighborhood of old Fort Lyon, and they have found fresh tracks down there and seem to think that the stock is concealed somewhere in the timber, along the Arkansas river. Bill Green, one of the scouts who has just come up from there, can perhaps tell you something more about the matter."

Green, who had been summoned, said that he had discovered fresh trails before striking the heavy timber opposite old Fort Lyon, but that in the tall grass he could not follow them. He had marked the place where he had last seen fresh mule tracks, so that he could find it again.

"Now, Cody, you're just the person we want," said the General.

"Very well, I'll get a fresh mount, and to-morrow I'll go down and see what I can discover," said I.

"You had better take two men besides Green, and a pack mule with eight or ten days' rations," suggested the General, "so that if you find the trail you can follow it up, as I am very anxious to get back this stolen property. The scoundrels have taken one of my private horses and also Lieutenant Forbush's favorite little black race mule."

Next morning I started out after the horse-thieves,

being accompanied by Green, Jack Farley, and another scout. The mule track, marked by Green, was easily found, and with very little difficulty I followed it for about two miles into the timber and came upon a place where, as I could plainly see from numerous signs, quite a number of head of stock had been tied among the trees and kept for several days. This was evidently the spot where the thieves had been hiding their stolen stock until they had accumulated quite a herd. From this point it was difficult to trail them, as they had taken the stolen animals out of the timber one by one and in different directions, thus showing that they were experts at the business and experienced frontiersmen, for no Indian could have exhibited more cunning in covering up a trail than did they.

I abandoned the idea of following their trail in this immediate locality, so calling my men together, I told them that we would ride out for about five miles and make a complete circuit about the place, and in this way we would certainly find the trail on which they had moved out. While making the circuit we discovered the tracks of twelve animals—four mules and eight horses—in the edge of some sand-hills, and from this point we had no trouble in trailing them down the Arkansas river, which they had crossed at Sand Creek,[3] and then had gone up the latter stream, in the direction of Denver, to which place they were undoubtedly bound. When nearing Denver their trail became so obscure that we at last lost it; but by inquiring of the settlers along the road which they had taken, we occasionally heard of them.

When within four miles of Denver—this was on a Thursday—we learned that the horse-thieves had passed there two days before. I came to the conclusion they would attempt to dispose of the animals in Denver, and being aware that Saturday was the great auction day there, I thought it best to remain where we were at a hotel, and not go into the city until that day. It certainly would not have been advisable for me to have gone into Denver mean-time—because I was well-known there, and if the thieves had learned of my presence in the city they would at once have suspected my business.

Early Saturday morning, we rode into town and stabled our horses at the Elephant Corral. I secured a room from Ed. Chase, overlooking the corral, and then took up my post of observation. I did not have long to wait, for a man, whom I readily recognized as one of our old packers, rode into the corral mounted upon Lieutenant Forbush's rac-ing mule, and leading another government mule, which I also identified. It had been recently branded, and over the "U.S." was a plain "D.B." I waited for the man's com-panion to put in an appearance, but he did not come, and my conclusion was that he was secreted outside of the city with the rest of the animals.

Presently the black mule belonging to Forbush was put up at auction. Now, thought I, is the time to do my work. So, walking through the crowd, who were bidding for the mule, I approached the man who had offered him for sale. He recognized me and endeavored to escape, but I seized him by the shoulder, saying: "I guess, my friend, that you'll have to go with me. If you make any resistance, I'll shoot you on the spot." He was armed with a pair of pistols, which I took away from him. Then informing the auctioneer that I was a United States detective, and showing him—as well as an inquisitive officer—my commission as such, I told him to stop the sale, as the mule was stolen property, and that I had arrested the thief, whose name was Williams.

Farley and Green, who were near at hand, now came forward, and together we took the prisoner and the mules three miles down the Platte River; there, in a thick bunch of timber, we all dismounted and made preparations to hang Williams from a limb, if he did not tell us where his partner was. At first he denied knowing anything about any partner, or any other stock; but when he saw that we were in earnest, and would hang him at the end of the given time—five minutes—unless he "squealed," he told us that his "pal" was at an unoccupied house three miles further down the river.

We immediately proceeded to the spot indicated, and as we came within sight of the house we saw our stock grazing near by. Just as we rode up to the door, another one of our old packers, whom I recognized as Bill Bevins,[4] stepped to the front, and I covered him instantly with my rifle before he could draw his revolver. I ordered him to throw up his hands, and he obeyed the command. Green then disarmed him and brought him out. We looked through the house and found their saddles, pack-saddles, blankets, overcoats, lariats and two Henry rifles, which we took possession of. The horses and mules we tied in a bunch, and with the whole outfit we returned to Denver, where we lodged Williams and Bevins in jail, in charge of my friend, Sheriff Edward Cook. The next day we took them out, and, tying each one on a mule, we struck out on our return trip to Fort Lyon.

At the hotel outside the city, where we had stopped on Thursday and Friday, we were joined by our man with the pack-mule. That night we camped on Cherry Creek, seventeen miles from Denver. The weather—it being in April—was cold and stormy, but we found a warm and cosy camping place in a bend of the creek. We made our beds in a row, with our feet towards the fire. The prisoners so far had appeared very docile, and had made no attempt to escape, and therefore I did not think it necessary to hobble them. We made them sleep on the inside, and it was so arranged that some one of us should be on guard all the time.

At about one o'clock in the night it began snowing, while I was watching. Shortly before three o'clock, Jack Farley, who was then on guard, and sitting on the foot of the bed, with his back to the prisoners, was kicked clear into the fire by Williams, and the next moment Bevins, who had got hold of his shoes—which I had thought were out of his reach—sprang up and jumped over the fire, and started on a run. I sent a shot after him as soon as I awoke sufficiently to comprehend what was taking place. Williams attempted to follow him, and as he did so, I whirled around and knocked him down with my revolver. Farley by this time had gathered himself out of the fire, and Green had started after Bevins, firing at him on the run; but the prisoner made his escape into the brush. In his flight, unfortunately for him, and luckily for us, he dropped one of his shoes.

Leaving Williams in the charge of Farley and "Long Doc," as we called the man with the pack-mule, Green and myself struck out after Bevins as fast as possible. We heard him breaking through the brush, but knowing that it would be useless to follow him on foot, we went back to the camp and saddled up two of the fastest horses, and at daylight we struck out on his trail, which was plainly visible in the snow. He had got an hour and a half the start of us. His tracks led us in the direction of the mountains and the South Platte River, and as the country through which he was passing was covered with prickly pears, we knew that he could not escape stepping on them with his one bare foot, and hence we were likely to overtake him in a short time. We could see, however, from the long jumps that he was taking, that he was making excellent time, but we frequently noticed, after we had gone some distance, that the prickly pears and stones along his route were cutting his bare foot, as nearly every track of it was spotted with blood.

We had run our horses some twelve miles when we saw Bevins crossing a ridge about two miles ahead. Urging our horses up to their utmost speed, we reached the ridge just as he was descending the divide towards the South Platte, which stream was very deep and swift at this point. It became evident that if he should cross it ahead of us, he would have a good chance of making his escape. So pushing our steeds as fast as possible, we rapidly gained on him, and when within a hundred yards of him I cried to him to halt or I would shoot. Knowing I was a good shot, he stopped, and, coolly sitting down, waited till we came up.

"Bevins, you've given us a good run," said I.

"Yes," said he, "and if I had had fifteen minutes more of a start and got across the Platte, I would have laughed at the idea of your ever catching me."

Bevins's run was the most remarkable feat of the kind

61. The Recapture of Bevins

ever known, either of a white man, or an Indian. A man who could run bare-footed in the snow eighteen miles through a prickly pear patch, was certainly a "tough one," and that's the kind of a person Bill Bevins was. Upon looking at his bleeding foot I really felt sorry for him. He asked me for my knife, and I gave him my sharp-pointed bowie, with which he dug the prickly pear briars out of his foot. I considered him as "game" a man as I had ever met.

"Bevins, I have got to take you back," said I, "but as you can't walk with that foot, you can ride my horse and I'll foot it."

We accordingly started back for our camp, with Bevins on my horse, which was led either by Green or myself, as we alternately rode the other horse. We kept a close watch on Bevins, for we had ample proof that he needed watching. His wounded foot must have pained him terribly but not a word of complaint escaped him. On arriving at the camp we found Williams bound as we had left him and he seemed sorry that we had captured Bevins.

After breakfasting we resumed our journey, and nothing worth of note again occurred until we reached the Arkansas river, where we found a vacant cabin and at once took possession of it for the night. There was no likelihood of Bevins again trying to escape, for his foot had swollen to an enormous size, and was useless. Believing that Williams could not escape from the cabin, we unbound him. We then went to sleep, leaving Long Doc on guard, the cabin being comfortably warmed and well lighted by the fire. It was a dark, stormy night—so dark that you could hardly see your hand before you. At about ten o'clock, Williams asked Long Doc to allow him to step to the door for a moment.

Long Doc, who had his revolver in his hand, did not think it necessary to wake us up, and believing that he could take care of the prisoner, he granted his request. Williams thereupon walked to the outer edge of the door, while Long Doc, revolver in hand, was watching him from the inside. Suddenly Williams made a spring to the right, and before Doc could even raise his revolver, he had dodged around the house. Doc jumped after him, and fired just as he turned a corner, the report bringing us all to our feet, and in an instant we knew what had happened. I at once covered Bevins with my revolver, but as I saw that he could hardly stir, and was making no demonstration, I lowered the weapon. Just then Doc came in swearing "a blue streak," and announced that Williams had escaped. There was nothing for us to do except to gather our horses close to the cabin and stand guard over them for the rest of the night, to prevent the possibility of Williams sneaking up and stealing one of them. That was the last I ever saw or heard of Williams.

We finally got back to Fort Lyon with Bevins, and General Carr, to whom I immediately reported, complimented us highly on the success of our trip, notwithstanding we had lost one prisoner. The next day we took Bevins to Boggs' ranch on Picket Wire Creek, and there turned him over to the civil authorities, who put him in a log jail to await his trial. He never was tried, however, for he soon made his escape, as I expected he would do. I heard no more of him until 1872, when I learned that he was skirmishing around on Laramie Plains at his old tricks. He sent word by the gentleman from whom I gained this information, that if he ever met me again he would kill me on sight. He

62. Robbing a Stage Coach

finally was arrested and convicted for robbery, and was confined in the prison at Laramie City. Again he made his escape, and soon afterwards he organized a desperate gang of outlaws who infested the country north of the Union Pacific railroad, and when the stages began to run between Cheyenne and Deadwood, in the Black Hills, they robbed the coaches and passengers, frequently making large hauls of plunder. They kept this up for some time, till finally most of the gang were caught, tried, convicted, and sent to the penitentiary for a number of years. Bill Bevins and nearly all of his gang are now confined in the Nebraska state prison, to which they were transferred, from Wyoming.

CHAPTER XXI

A Military Expedition

A day or two after my return to Fort Lyon, the Fifth Cavalry were ordered to the Department of the Platte, and took up their line of march for Fort McPherson, Nebraska. We laid over one day at Fort Wallace, to get supplies, and while there I had occasion to pass General Bankhead's headquarters. His orderly called to me, and said the General wished to see me. As I entered the General's office he extended his hand and said: "I hope you have no hard feelings toward me, Cody, for having you arrested when you were here. I have just had a talk with General Carr and Quartermaster Hayes, and they informed me that you had their permission to ride the horse and mule, and if you had stated this fact to me there would have been no trouble about the matter whatever."

"That is all right, General," said I; "I will think no more of it. But I don't believe that your quartermaster's agent will ever again circulate false stories about me."

"No," said the General; "he has not yet recovered from the beating that you gave him."

From Fort Wallace we moved down to Sheridan, where the command halted for us to lay in a supply of forage which was stored there. I was still messing[1] with Major Brown, with whom I went into the village to purchase a supply of provisions for our mess; but unfortunately we were in too jolly a mood to fool away money on "grub." We bought several articles, however, and put them into the ambulance and sent them back to the camp with our cook. The Major and myself did not return until *reveille* next morning. Soon afterwards the General sounded "boots and saddles,"[2] and presently the regiment was on its way to McPherson.

It was very late before we went into camp that night, and we were tired and hungry. Just as Major Brown was having his tent put up, his cook came to us and asked where the provisions were that we had bought the day before.

"Why, did we not give them to you—did you not bring them to camp in the ambulance?" asked Major Brown.

"No, sir; it was only a five-gallon demijohn[3] of whiskey, a five-gallon demijohn of brandy, and two cases of Old Tom-Cat gin," said the cook.

"The mischief!" I exclaimed; "didn't we spend any money on grub at all?"

"No, sir," replied the cook.

"Well, that will do for the present," said Major Brown.

It seems that our minds had evidently been running on a different subject than provisions while we were loitering in Sheridan, and we found ourselves, with a two hundred and fifty mile march ahead of us, without anything more inviting than ordinary army rations.

At this juncture Captain Denny came up, and the Major apologized for not being able to invite him to take supper with us; but we did the next best thing, and asked him to take a drink. He remarked that that was what he was looking for, and when he learned of our being out of commissary supplies, and that we had bought nothing except whiskey, brandy and gin, he said, joyously:

"Boys, as we have an abundance, you can eat with us, and we will drink with you."

It was a satisfactory arrangement, and from that time forward we traded our liquids for their solids. When the rest of the officers heard of what Brown and I had done, they all sent us invitations to dine with them at any time. We returned the compliment by inviting them to drink with us whenever they were dry. Although I would not advise anybody to follow our example, yet it is a fact that we got more provisions for our whiskey than the same money, which we paid for the liquor, would have bought; so after all it proved a very profitable investment.

On reaching the north fork of the Beaver and riding down the valley towards the stream, I suddenly discovered a large fresh Indian trail. On examination I found it to be scattered all over the valley on both sides of the creek, as if a very large village had recently passed down that way. Judging from the size of the trail, I thought there could not be less than four hundred lodges, or between twenty-five hundred and three thousand warriors, women and children in the band. I galloped hack to the command, distant about three miles, and reported the news to General Carr, who halted the regiment, and, after consulting a few minutes, ordered me to select a ravine, or as low ground as possible, so that he could keep the troops out of sight until we could strike the creek.

We went into camp on the Beaver, and the General ordered Lieutenant Ward to take twelve men and myself and follow up the trail for several miles, and find out how fast the Indians were traveling. I was soon convinced, by the many camps they had made, that they were traveling slowly, and hunting as they journeyed. We went down the Beaver on this scout about twelve miles, keeping our horses well concealed under the banks of the creek, so as not to be discovered.

At this point, Lieutenant Ward and myself, leaving our horses behind us, crawled to the top of a high knoll, where we could have a good view for some miles distant down the stream. We peeped over the summit of the hill, and not over three miles away we could see a whole Indian village in plain sight, and thousands of ponies grazing around on the prairie. Looking over to our left on the opposite side of the creek, we observed two or three parties of Indians coming in, loaded down with buffalo meat.

"This is no place for us, Lieutenant," said I; "I think we have important business at the camp to attend to as soon as possible."

"I agree with you," said he, "and the quicker we get there the better it will be for us."

We quickly descended the hill and joined the men below. Lieutenant Ward hurriedly wrote a note to General Carr, and handing it to a corporal, ordered him to make all possible haste back to the command and deliver the message. The man started off on a gallop, and Lieutenant Ward said: "We will march slowly back until we meet the troops, as I think the General will soon be here, for he will start immediately upon receiving my note."

In a few minutes we heard two or three shots in the direction in which our dispatch courier had gone, and soon after we saw him come flying around the bend of the creek, pursued by four or five Indians. The Lieutenant, with his squad of soldiers and myself, at once charged upon them, when they turned and ran across the stream.

"This will not do," said Lieutenant Ward, "the whole Indian village will now know that soldiers are near by.

"Lieutenant, give me that note, and I will take it to the General," said I.

He gladly handed me the dispatch, and spurring my horse I dashed up the creek. After having ridden a short distance, I observed another party of Indians also going to the village with meat; but instead of waiting for them to fire upon me, I gave them a shot at long range. Seeing one man firing at them so boldly, it surprised them, and they did not know what to make of it. While they were thus considering, I got between them and our camp. By this time they had recovered from their surprise, and, cutting their buffalo meat loose from their horses, they came after me at the top of their speed; but as their steeds were tired out, it did not take me long to leave them far in the rear.

I reached the command in less than an hour, delivered the dispatch to General Carr, and informed him of what I had seen. He instantly had the bugler sound "boots and saddles," and all the troops—with the exception of two companies, which we left to guard the train—were soon galloping in the direction of the Indian camp.

We had ridden about three miles when we met Lieutenant Ward, who was coming slowly towards us. He reported that he had run into a party of Indian buffalo-hunters, and had killed one of the number, and had had one of his horses wounded. We immediately pushed forward and after marching about five miles came within sight of hundreds of mounted Indians advancing up the creek to meet us. They formed a complete line in front of us. General Carr, being desirous of striking their village, ordered the troops to charge, break through their line, and keep straight on. This movement would, no doubt, have been successfully accomplished had it not been for the rattle-brained and dare-devil French Lieutenant Schinosky, commanding Company B, who, misunderstanding General Carr's orders, charged upon some Indians at the left, while the rest of the command dashed through the enemy's line, and was keeping straight on, when it was observed that Schinosky and his company were surrounded by four or five hundred red-skins. The General, to save the company, was obliged to sound a halt and charge back to the rescue. The company, during this short fight, had several men and quite a number of horses killed.

All this took up valuable time, and night was coming on. The Indians were fighting desperately to keep us from reaching their village, which being informed by couriers of what was taking place, was packing up and getting away. During that afternoon it was all we could do to hold our own in fighting the mounted warriors, who were in our front and contesting every inch of the ground. The General had left word for our wagon train to follow up with its escort of two companies, but as it had not made its appearance he entertained some fears that it had been surrounded, and to prevent the possible loss of the supply train we had to go back and look for it. About 9 o'clock that evening we found it, and went into camp for the night.

Next morning we passed down the creek and there was not an Indian to be seen. They had all disappeared and gone on with their village. Two miles further on we came to where a village had been located, and here we found nearly everything belonging or pertaining to an Indian camp, which had been left in the great hurry to get away. These articles were all gathered up and burned. We then pushed out on the trail as fast as possible. It led us to the northeast towards the Republican; but as the Indians had a night the start of us we entertained but little hope of overtaking them that day. Upon reaching the Republican in the afternoon the General called a halt, and as the trail was running more to the east, he concluded to send his wagon train on to Fort McPherson by the most direct route, while he would follow on the trail of the red-skins.

Next morning at daylight we again pulled out and were evidently gaining rapidly on the Indians for we could occasionally see them in the distance. About 11 o'clock that day while Major Babcock was ahead of the main command with his company, and while we were crossing a deep ravine, we were surprised by about three hundred warriors who commenced a lively fire upon us. Galloping out of the ravine on to the rough prairie the men dismounted and returned the fire. We soon succeeded in driving the enemy before us, and were so close upon them at one time, that they abandoned and threw away nearly all their lodges and camp equipages, and everything that had any considerable weight. They left behind them their played-out horses, and for miles we could see Indian furniture strewn along in every direction. The trail became divided, and the Indians scattered in small bodies, all over the prairie. As night was approaching and our horses were about giving out, a halt was called. A company was detailed to collect all the Indian horses running loose over the country, and to burn the other Indian property.

The command being nearly out of rations I was sent to the nearest point, Old Fort Kearney, about sixty miles distant for supplies.

Shortly after we reached Fort McPherson, which continued to be the headquarters of the Fifth Cavalry for some time. We remained there for ten days, fitting out for a new expedition to the Republican river country, and were reinforced by three companies of the celebrated Pawnee Indian scouts, commanded by Major Frank North; his officers being Captain Lute North, brother of the Major, Captain Cushing, his brother-in-law, Captain Morse, and Lieutenants Beecher, Matthews and Kislandberry. General Carr recommended at this time to General Augur, who was in command of the Department, that I be made chief of scouts in the Department of the Platte, and informed me that in this position I would receive higher wages than I had been getting in the Department of the Missouri. This appointment I had not asked for.

I made the acquaintance of Major Frank North,[4] and I found him, and his officers, perfect gentlemen, and we were all good friends from the very start. The Pawnee scouts had made quite a reputation for themselves as they had performed brave and valuable services, in fighting against the Sioux, whose bitter enemies they were; being thoroughly acquainted with the Republican and Beaver country, I was glad that they were to be with the expedition, and they did good service.[5]

During our stay at Fort McPherson I made the acquaintance of Lieutenant George P. Belden, known as the

"White Chief," whose life was written by Colonel Brisbin, U.S. army.[6] I found him to be an intelligent, dashing fellow, a splendid rider and an excellent shot. An hour after our introduction he challenged me for a rifle match, the preliminaries of which were soon arranged. We were to shoot ten shots each for fifty dollars, at two hundred yards, off hand. Belden was to use a Henry rifle, while I was to shoot my old "Lucretia." This match I won and then Belden proposed to shoot a one hundred yard match, as I was shooting over his distance. In this match Belden was victorious. We were now even, and we stopped right there.

While we were at this post General Augur and several of his officers, and also Thomas Duncan, Brevet Brigadier and Lieutenant Colonel of the Fifth Cavalry, paid us a visit for the purpose of reviewing the command. The regiment turned out in fine style and showed themselves to be well drilled soldiers, thoroughly understanding military tactics. The Pawnee scouts were also reviewed and it was very amusing to see them in their full regulation uniform. They had been furnished a regular cavalry uniform and on this parade some of them had their heavy overcoats on, others their large black hats, with all the brass accoutrements attached; some of them were minus pantaloons and only wore a breech clout.[7] Others wore regulation pantaloons but no shirts on and were bareheaded; others again had the seat of the pantaloons cut out, leaving only leggins; some of them wore brass spurs, but had no boots or moccasins on. They seemed to understand the drill remarkably well for Indians. The commands, of course, were given to them in their own language by Major North, who could talk it as well as any full-blooded Pawnee. The Indians were well mounted and felt proud and elated because they had been made United States soldiers. Major North, has had for years complete power over these Indians and can do more with them than any man living. That evening after the parade was over the officers and quite a number of ladies visited a grand Indian dance given by the Pawnees, and of all the Indians I have seen, their dances excel those of any other tribe.[8]

Next day the command started; when encamped, several days after, on the Republican river near the mouth of the Beaver, we heard the whoops of Indians, followed by shots in the vicinity of the mule herd, which had been taken down to water. One of the herders came dashing into camp with an arrow sticking into him. My horse was close at hand, and, mounting him bare-back, I at once dashed off after the mule herd, which had been stampeded. I supposed certainly that I would be the first man on the ground. I was mistaken, however, for the Pawnee Indians, unlike regular soldiers, had not waited to receive orders from their officers, but had jumped on their ponies without bridles or saddles, and placing ropes in their mouths, had dashed off in the direction whence the shots had come, and had got there ahead of me. It proved to be a party of about fifty Sioux, who had endeavored to stampede our mules, and it took them by surprise to see their inveterate enemies—the Pawnees—coming at full gallop towards them. They were not aware that the Pawnees were with the command, and as they knew that it would take regular soldiers sometime to turn out, they thought they would have ample opportunity to secure the herd before the troops could give chase.

We had a running fight of fifteen miles, and several of the enemy were killed. During this chase I was mounted on an excellent horse, which Colonel Royall had picked out for me, and for the first mile or two I was in advance of the Pawnees. Presently a Pawnee shot by me like an arrow and I could not help admiring the horse that he was riding. Seeing that he possessed rare running qualities, I determined if possible to get possession of the animal in some way. It was a large buckskin or yellow horse, and I took a careful view of him so that I would know him when I returned to camp.

After the chase was over I rode up to Major North and inquired about the buckskin horse.

"Oh yes," said the Major, "that is one of our favorite steeds."

"What chance is there to trade for him?" I asked.

"It is a government horse," said he, "and the Indian who is riding him is very much attached to the animal."

"I have fallen in love with the horse myself," said I, "and I would like to know if you have any objections to my trading for him if I can arrange it satisfactorily with the Indian?"

He said: "None whatever, and I will help you to do it; you can give the Indian another horse in his place."

A few days after this, I persuaded the Indian, by making him several presents, to trade horses with me, and in this way I became the owner of the buckskin steed, not as my own property, however, but as a government horse that I could ride. I gave him the name of "Buckskin Joe" and he proved to be a second Brigham. That horse I rode on and off during the summers of 1869, 1870, 1871 and 1872, and he was the horse that the Grand Duke Alexis rode on his buffalo hunt. In the winter of 1872, after I had left Fort McPherson, Buckskin Joe was condemned and sold at public sale, and was bought by Dave Perry, at North Platte, who in 1877 presented him to me, and I still own him. He is now at my ranch on the Dismal river, stone blind, but I shall keep him until he dies.

The command scouted several days up the Beaver and Prairie Dog rivers, occasionally having running fights with war parties of Indians, but did not succeed in getting them into a general battle. At the end of twenty days we found ourselves back on the Republican.

Hitherto the Pawnees had not taken much interest in me, but while at this camp I gained their respect and admiration by showing them how I killed buffaloes. Although the Pawnees were excellent buffalo killers, for Indians, I have never seen one of them who could kill more than four or five in one run. A number of them generally surround the herd and then dash in upon them, and in this way each one kills from one to four buffaloes. I had gone out in company with Major North and some of the officers, and saw them make a "surround." Twenty of the Pawnees circled a herd and succeeded in killing only thirty-two.

While they were cutting up the animals another herd appeared in sight. The Indians were preparing to surround it, when I asked Major North to keep them back and let me show them what I could do. He accordingly informed the Indians of my wish and they readily consented to let me have the opportunity. I had learned that Buckskin Joe was an excellent buffalo horse, and felt confident that I would astonish the natives; galloping in among the buffaloes, I certainly did so by killing thirty-six in less than a half-mile run. At nearly every shot I killed a buffalo, stringing the dead animals out on the prairie, not over fifty feet apart. This manner of killing was greatly admired by the Indians who called me a big chief, and from that time on, I stood high in their estimation.

CHAPTER XXII

A Desperate Fight

On leaving camp, the command took a westward course up the Republican, and Major North with two companies of his Pawnees and two or three companies of cavalry, under the command of Colonel Royall, made a scout to the north of the river. Shortly after we had gone into camp, on the Black Tail Deer Fork, we observed a band of Indians coming over the prairie at full gallop, singing and yelling and waving their lances and long poles. At first we supposed them to be Sioux, and all was excitement for a few moments. We noticed, however, that our Pawnee Indians made no hostile demonstrations or preparations towards going out to fight them, but began singing and yelling themselves. Captain Lute North stepped up to General Carr and said:

"General, those are our men who are coming, and they have had a fight. That is the way they act when they come back from a battle and have taken any scalps."

The Pawnees came into camp on the run. Captain North calling to one of them—a sergeant—soon found out that they had run across a party of Sioux who were following a large Indian trail. These Indians had evidently been in a fight, for two or three of them had been wounded and they were conveying the injured persons on *travois*.[1]

The Pawnees had "jumped" them and had killed three or four more of them.

Next morning the command, at an early hour, started out to take up this Indian trail which they followed for two days as rapidly as possible; it becoming evident from the many camp fires which we passed, that we were gaining on the Indians. Wherever they had encamped we found the print of a woman's shoe, and we concluded that they had with them some white captive. This made us all the more anxious to overtake them, and General Carr accordingly selected all his best horses, which could stand a hard run, and gave orders for the wagon train to follow as fast as possible, while he pushed ahead on a forced march. At the same time I was ordered to pick out five or six of the best Pawnees, and go on in advance of the command, keeping ten or twelve miles ahead on the trail, so that when we overtook the Indians we could find out the location of their camp, and send word to the troops before they came in sight, thus affording ample time to arrange a plan for the capture of the village.

After having gone about ten miles in advance of the regiment, we began to move very cautiously, as we were now evidently nearing the Indians. We looked carefully over the summits of the hills before exposing ourselves to plain view, and at last we discovered the village, encamped in the sand-hills south of the South Platte river at Summit Springs. Here I left the Pawnee scouts to keep watch, while I went back and informed General Carr that the Indians were in sight.

The General at once ordered his men to tighten their saddles and otherwise prepare for action. Soon all was excitement among the officers and soldiers, every one being anxious to charge the village. I now changed my horse for old Buckskin Joe, who had been led for me thus far, and was comparatively fresh. Acting on my suggestion, the General made a circuit to the north, believing that if the Indians had their scouts out, they would naturally be watching in the direction whence they had come. When we had passed the Indians and were between them and the Platte river, we turned to the left and started toward the village.

By this manoeuver we had avoided discovery by the Sioux scouts, and we were confident of giving them a complete surprise. Keeping the command wholly out of sight, until we were within a mile of the Indians, the General halted the advance guard until all closed up, and then issued an order, that, when he sounded the charge, the whole command was to rush into the village.

As we halted on the top of the hill overlooking the camp of the unsuspecting Indians, General Carr called out to his bugler: "Sound the charge!" The bugler for a moment became intensely excited, and actually forgot the notes. The General again sang out: "Sound the charge!" and yet the bugler was unable to obey the command. Quartermaster Hayes—who had obtained permission to accompany the expedition—was riding near the General, and comprehending the dilemma of the man, rushed up to him, jerked the bugle from his hands and sounded the charge himself in clear and distinct notes. As the troops rushed forward, he threw the bugle away, then drawing his pistols, was among the first men that entered the village.

The Indians had just driven up their horses and were

63. Indian Village

preparing to make a move of the camp, when they saw
the soldiers coming down upon them. A great many of
them succeeded in jumping upon their ponies, and, leaving
every thing behind them, advanced out of the village and
prepared to meet the charge; but upon second thought
they quickly concluded that it was useless to try to check
us, and, those who were mounted rapidly rode away, while
the others on foot fled for safety to the neighboring hills.
We went through their village shooting right and left at
everything we saw. The Pawnees, the regular soldiers and
the officers were all mixed up together, and the Sioux were
flying in every direction.

General Carr had instructed the command that when
they entered the village, they must keep a sharp look out
for white women, as he was confident the Indians had some
captives. The company which had been ordered to take
possession of the village after its capture, soon found two

white women, one of whom had just been killed and the other wounded. They were both Swedes, and the survivor could not talk English. A Swedish soldier, however, was soon found who could talk with her. The name of this woman was Mrs. Weichel, and her story as told to the soldier was, that as soon as the Indians saw the troops coming down upon them, a squaw—Tall Bull's wife—had killed Mrs. Alderdice, the other captive, with a hatchet, and then wounded her. This squaw had evidently intended to kill both women to prevent them from telling how cruelly they had been treated.

The attack lasted but a short time, and the Indians were driven several miles away.[2] The soldiers then gathered in the herd of Indian horses, which were running at large over the country and drove them back to the camp. After taking a survey of what we had accomplished, it was found that we had killed about one hundred and forty Indians, and captured one hundred and twenty squaws and papooses, two hundred lodges, and eight hundred horses and mules. The village proved to be one of the richest I had ever seen. The red-skins had everything pertaining to an Indian camp, besides numerous articles belonging to the white settlers whom they had killed on the Saline. The Pawnees, as well as the soldiers, ransacked the camp for curiosities, and found enough to start twenty museums, besides a large amount of gold and silver. This money had been stolen from the Swedish settlers whom they had murdered on the Saline. General Carr ordered that all the tepees, the Indian lodges, buffalo robes, all camp equipage and provisions, including dried buffalo meat, amounting to several tons, should be gathered in piles and burned.

A grave was dug in which the dead Swedish woman, Mrs. Alderdice, was buried. Captain Kane, a religious officer, read the burial service, as we had no chaplain with us.

While this was going on, the Sioux warriors having recovered from their surprise, had come back and a battle took place all around the camp. I was on the skirmish line, and I noticed an Indian, who was riding a large bay horse, and giving orders to his men in his own language—which I could occasionally understand—telling them that they had lost everything, that they were ruined, and he entreated them to follow him, and fight until they died. His horse was an extraordinary one, fleet as the wind, dashing here and there, and I determined to capture him if possible, but I was afraid to fire at the Indian for fear of killing the horse.

I noticed that the Indian, as he rode around the skirmish line, passed the head of a ravine not far distant, and it occurred to me that if I could dismount and creep to the ravine I could, as he passed there, easily drop him from his saddle without danger of hitting the horse. Accordingly I crept into and secreted myself in the ravine, reaching the place unseen by the Indians, and I waited there until Mr. Chief came riding by.

When he was not more than thirty yards distant I fired, and the next moment he tumbled from his saddle, and the horse kept on without his rider. Instead of running toward the Indians, however, he galloped toward our men, by one of whom he was caught. Lieutenant Mason, who had been very conspicuous in the fight and who had killed two or three Indians himself, single-handed, came galloping up to the ravine and jumping from his horse, secured the fancy war bonnet from the head of the dead

64. The Killing of Tall Bull

chief, together with all his other accoutrements. We both then rejoined the soldiers, and I at once went in search of the horse; I found him in the possession of Sergeant McGrath, who had caught him. The Sergeant knew that I had been trying to get the animal and having seen me kill his rider, he handed him over to me at once.

Little did I think at that time that I had captured a horse

which, for four years afterwards was the fastest runner in the state of Nebraska, but such proved to be the fact.

I jumped on his back and rode him down to the spot where the prisoners were corraled. One of the squaws among the prisoners suddenly began crying in a pitiful and hysterical manner at the sight of this horse, and upon inquiry I found that she was Tall Bull's wife, the same squaw that had killed one of the white women and wounded the other. She stated that this was her husband's favorite war-horse, and that only a short time ago she had seen Tall Bull[3] riding him. I gave her to understand that her liege lord had passed in his mortal chips and that it would be sometime before he would ride his favorite horse again, and I informed her that henceforth I should call the gallant steed "Tall Bull," in honor of her husband.

Late in the evening our wagon train arrived, and placing the wounded woman, Mrs. Weichel, in the ambulance—she having been kindly attended to by the surgeons,—and gathering up the prisoners—the squaws and papooses—and captured stock, we started at once for the South Platte River, eight miles distant, and there went into camp.

Next morning General Carr issued an order that all the money found in the village should be turned over to the adjutant. About one thousand dollars was thus collected, and the entire amount was given to Mrs. Weichel. The command then proceeded to Fort Sedgwick, from which point the particulars of our fight, which took place on Sunday, July 11th, 1869, were telegraphed to all parts of the country.

We remained at this post for two weeks, during which General Augur, of the Department of the Platte, paid us a visit, and highly complimented the command for the gallant service it had performed. For this fight at Summit Springs General Carr and his command were complimented not only in General Orders, but received a vote of thanks from the Legislatures of Nebraska and Colorado—as Tall Bull and his Indians had long been a terror to the border settlements—and the resolutions of thanks were elegantly engrossed and sent to General Carr.

The wounded white woman was cared for in the hospital at this post, and after her recovery she soon married the hospital steward, her former husband having been killed by the Indians.

Our prisoners were sent to the Whetstone Agency,[4] on the Missouri River, where Spotted Tail and the friendly Sioux were then living. The captured horses and mules were distributed among the officers, scouts and soldiers. Among the animals that I thus obtained were my Tall Bull horse, and a pony which I called "Powder Face," and which afterwards became quite celebrated, as he figured prominently in the stories of Ned Buntline.

One day, while we were lying at Fort Sedgwick, General Carr received a telegram from Fort McPherson stating that the Indians had made a dash on the Union Pacific Railroad, and had killed several section-men and run off some stock near O'Fallon's Station; also that an expedition was going out from Fort McPherson to catch and punish the redskins if possible. The General ordered me to accompany the expedition, and accordingly that night I proceeded by rail to McPherson Station, and from thence rode on horseback to the fort. Two companies, under command of Major Brown, had been ordered out, and next morning, just as we were about to start, Major Brown said to me:

"By the way, Cody, we are going to have quite an important character with us as a guest on this scout. It's old Ned Buntline, the novelist."

Just then I noticed a gentleman, who was rather stoutly built, and who wore a blue military coat, on the left breast of which were pinned about twenty gold medals and badges of secret societies. He walked a little lame as he approached us, and I at once concluded that he was Ned Buntline.

"He has a good mark to shoot at on the left breast," said I to Major Brown, "but he looks like a soldier." As he came up, Major Brown said:

"Cody, allow me to introduce you to Colonel E.Z.C. Judson, otherwise known as Ned Buntline."[5]

"Colonel Judson, I am glad to meet you," said I; "the Major tells me that you are to accompany us on the scout."

"Yes, my boy, so I am," said he; "I was to deliver a temperance lecture to-night, but no lectures for me when there is a prospect for a fight. The Major has kindly offered me a horse, but I don't know how I'll stand the ride, for I haven't done any riding lately; but when I was a young man I spent several years among the fur companies of the Northwest, and was a good rider and an excellent shot."

"The Major has given you a fine horse, and you'll soon find yourself at home in the saddle," said I.

The command soon pulled out for the South Platte River, which was very wide and high, owing to recent mountain rains, and in crossing it we had to swim our horses in some places. Buntline was the first man across. We reached O'Fallon's at eleven o'clock, and in a short time I succeeded in finding the Indian trail; the party seemed to be a small one, which had come up from the south. We followed their track to the North Platte, but as they had a start of two days, Major Brown abandoned the pursuit, and returned to Fort McPherson, while I went back to Fort Sedgwick, accompanied by Buntline.

During this short scout, Buntline had asked me a great many questions, and he was determined to go out on the next expedition with me, providing he could obtain permission from the commanding officer. I introduced him to the officers—excepting those he already knew—and invited him to become my guest while he remained at the post, and gave him my pony Powder Face to ride.

By this time I had learned that my horse Tall Bull was a remarkably fast runner, and therefore when Lieutenant Mason, who was quite a sport and owned a racer, challenged me to a race, I immediately accepted it. We were to run our horses a single dash of half a mile for one hundred dollars a side. Several of the officers, and also Reub. Wood, the post-trader, bantered me for side bets, and I took them all until I had put up my last cent on Tall Bull.

The ground was measured off, the judges were selected, and all other preliminaries were arranged. We rode our horses ourselves, and coming up to the score nicely we let them go. I saw from the start that it would be mere play to beat the Lieutenant's horse, and therefore I held Tall Bull in check, so that none could see how fast he really could run. I easily won the race, and pocketed a snug little sum of money. Of course everybody was now talking horse. Major North remarked that if Tall Bull could beat the Pawnees' fast horse, I could break his whole command.

The next day the troops were paid off, the Pawnees with the rest, and for two or three days they did nothing but run horse-races, as all the recently captured horses had to be tested to find out the swiftest among them. Finally the Pawnees wanted to run their favorite horse against Tall Bull, and I accordingly arranged a race with them. They raised three hundred dollars and bet it on their horse, while of course, I backed Tall Bull with an equal amount, and in addition took numerous side bets. The race was a single dash of a mile, and Tall Bull won it without any difficulty. I was ahead on this race about seven hundred dollars, and the horse was fast getting a reputation. Heretofore nobody would bet on him, but now he had plenty of backers.

I also made a race for my pony Powder Face, against a fast pony belonging to Captain Lute North. I selected a small boy, living at the post to ride Powder Face, while an Indian boy was to ride the other pony. The Pawnees as usual wanted to bet on their pony, but as I had not yet fully ascertained the running qualities of Powder Face, I did not care about risking very much money on him. Had I known him as well then as I did afterwards I would have backed him for every dollar I had, for he proved to be one of the swiftest ponies I ever saw, and had evidently been kept as a racer.

The race was to be four hundred yards, and when I led the pony over the track he seemed to understand what he was there for. North and I finally put the riders on, and it was all I could do to hold the fiery little animal after the boy became seated on his back. He jumped around and made such quick movements, that the boy was not at all confident of being able to stay on him. The order to start was at last given by the judges, and as I brought Powder Face up to the score and the word "go" was given, he jumped away so quickly that he left his rider sitting on the ground; notwithstanding he ran through and won the race without him. It was an easy victory, and after that I could get up no more races. Thus passed the time while we were at Fort Sedgwick.

General Carr having obtained a leave of absence, Colonel Royall was given the command of an expedition that was ordered to go out after the Indians, and in a few days—after having rested a couple of weeks—we set out for the Republican; having learned that there were plenty of Indians in that section of the country. At Frenchman's Fork we discovered an Indian village, but did not surprise it, for its people had noticed us approaching, and were retreating when we reached their camping-place. We chased them down the stream, and they finally turned to the left, went north, and crossed the South Platte river five miles above Ogallala. We pushed rapidly after them, following them across the North Platte and on through the sand-hills towards the Niobrara; but as they were making much better time than we, the pursuit was abandoned.

While we were in the sand-hills, scouting the Niobrara country, the Pawnee Indians brought into camp, one night, some very large bones, one of which a surgeon of the expedition pronounced to be the thigh-bone of a human being. The Indians claimed that the bones they had found were those of a person belonging to a race of people who a long time ago lived in this country. That there was once a race of men on the earth whose size was about three times that of an ordinary man, and they were so swift and powerful that they could run along-side of a buffalo, and taking the animal in one arm could tear

off a leg and eat the meat as they walked. These giants denied the existence of a Great Spirit, and when they heard the thunder or saw the lightning they laughed at it and said that they were greater than either. This so displeased the Great Spirit that he caused a great rain-storm to come, and the water kept rising higher and higher so that it drove those proud and conceited giants from the low grounds to the hills, and thence to the mountains, but at last even the mountain tops were submerged, and then those mammoth men were all drowned. After the flood had subsided, the Great Spirit came to the conclusion that he had made man too large and powerful, and that he would therefore correct the mistake by creating a race of men of smaller size and less strength. This is the reason, say the Indians, that modern men are small and not like the giants of old, and they claim that this story is a matter of Indian history, which has been handed down among them from time immemorial.

As we had no wagons with us at the time this large and heavy bone was found, we were obliged to leave it.

CHAPTER XXIII

Administering Justice

On returning to Fort McPherson we found that Brevet
Major General W. H. Emory, Colonel of the Fifth Cavalry,
and Brevet Brigadier General Thomas Duncan, Lieutenant Colonel of the regiment, had arrived there during
our absence. General Emory had been appointed to the
command of the District of the Republican, with headquarters at Fort McPherson. As the command had been
continually in the field, it was generally thought that we
were to have a long rest; and it looked as if this post was
to be my home and headquarters for some time to come.
I accordingly sent to St. Louis for my wife and daughter to
join me there. General Emory promised to build a house
for me, but before the building was completed my family
arrived.

During the fall of 1869 there were two or three scouting
expeditions sent out; but nothing of very great importance
was accomplished by them. I found Fort McPherson to
be a lively and pleasant post to be stationed at, especially
as there was plenty of game in the vicinity, and within a
day's ride there were large herds of deer, antelope and elk.

During the winter of 1869–70 I spent a great deal of
time in pursuit of game, and during the season we had two
hunting parties of Englishmen there; one party being that

of Mr. Flynn, and the other that of George Boyd Houghton, of London—the well known caricaturist.[1] Among their amusements were several horse races, which I arranged, and in which Tall Bull and Powder Face were invariably the winners. Tall Bull by this time had such a reputation as a running horse, that it was difficult to make a race for him. I remember one however, in which he ran against a horse in Captain Spaulding's Company of the Second Cavalry.

This race was rather a novel affair. I had made a bet that Tall Bull would beat the Second Cavalry horse around a one mile track, and, during the time that he was running, I would jump off and on the horse eight times. I rode the horse bareback; seized his mane with my left hand, rested my right on his withers, and while he was going at full speed, I jumped to the ground, and sprang again upon his back, eight times in succession. Such feats I had seen performed in the circus and I had practiced considerably at it with Tall Bull, so that I was certain of winning the race in the manner agreed upon.

Early one morning, in the spring of 1870, the Indians, who had approached during the night, stole some twenty-one head of horses from Mr. John Burke—a Government contractor—Ben. Gallagher and Jack Waite. They also ran off some horses from the post; among the number being my pony Powder Face. The commandant at once ordered out Lieutenant Thomas with Company I of the Fifth Cavalry, and directed me to accompany them as trailer. We discovered the trail after some little difficulty, as the Indians were continually trying to hide it, and followed it sixty miles, when darkness set in.

We were now within about four miles of Red Willow

Creek and I felt confident the Indians would camp that night in that vicinity. Advising Lieutenant Thomas to halt his company and "lay low" I proceeded on to the creek, where, moving around cautiously, I suddenly discovered horses feeding in a bend of the stream on the opposite side. I hurried back to the troops with the information, and Lieutenant Thomas moved his company to the bank of the creek, with the intention of remaining there until daylight, and then, if possible, surprise the Indians.

Just at break of day we mounted our horses, and after riding a short distance we ascended a slight elevation, when, not over one hundred yards distant, we looked down into the Indian camp. The Indians, preparing to make an early start, had driven up their horses and were in the act of mounting, when they saw us charging down upon them. In a moment they sprang upon their ponies and dashed away. Had it not been for the creek, which lay between us and them, we would have got them before they could have mounted their horses; but as it was rather miry, we were unexpectedly delayed. The Indians fired some shots at us while we were crossing, but as soon as we got across we went for them in hot pursuit. A few of the red-skins had not had time to mount and had started on foot down the creek toward the brush. One of these was killed.

A number of our soldiers, who had been detailed before the charge to gather up any of the Indian horses that would be stampeded, succeeded in capturing thirty-two. I hurriedly looked over them to see if Powder Face was among them; but he was not there. Starting in pursuit of the fugitives I finally espied an Indian mounted on my favorite, dashing away and leading all the others. We continued the chase for two or three miles, overtaking a couple who were mounted upon one horse. Coming up behind them I fired my rifle, when about thirty feet distant; the ball passed through the backs of both, and they fell headlong to the ground; but I made no stop however just then, for I had my eye on the gentleman who was riding Powder Face. It seemed to be fun for him to run away from us, and run away he did, for the last I saw of him was when he went over a divide, about three miles away. I bade him adieu. On my way back to the Indian camp I stopped and secured the war bonnets and accoutrements of the pair I had killed, and at the same time gently "raised their hair."[2]

We were feeling rather tired and hungry, as we had started out on the trail thirty-six hours before without a breakfast or taking any food with us; but not a murmur or complaint was heard among the men. In the abandoned Indian camp, however, we found enough dried buffalo meat to give us all a meal, and after remaining there for two hours, to rest our animals, we started on our return to Fort McPherson, where we arrived at night, having traveled 130 miles in two days.

This being the first fight Lieutenant Thomas had ever commanded in, he felt highly elated over his success, and hoped that his name would be mentioned in the special orders for gallantry; sure enough when we returned both he, myself and the whole command received a complimentary mention in a special order. This he certainly deserved for he was a brave, energetic, dashing little officer. The war bonnets which I had captured I turned over to General Carr, with the request that he present them to General Augur, whose daughters were visiting at the post at the time.

Shortly after this, another expedition was organized at Fort McPherson for the Republican river country. It was commanded by General Duncan, who was a jolly, blustering old fellow, and the officers who knew him well, said that we would have a good time, as he was very fond of hunting. He was a good fighter, and one of the officers said that an Indian bullet never could hurt him, as he had been shot in the head with a cannon ball which had not injured him in the least; another said the ball glanced off and killed one of the toughest mules in the army.

The Pawnee scouts who had been mustered out of service, during the winter of 1869 and '70, were reorganized to accompany this expedition. I was glad of this, as I had become quite attached to one of the officers, Major North, and to many of the Indians. The only white scout we had at the post, besides myself at that time, was John Y. Nelson, whose Indian name was Cha-Sha-Cha-Opoyeo,[3] which interpreted means Red-Willow-Fill-the-Pipe. This man is a character in his way; he has a Sioux squaw for a wife, and consequently a half-breed family. John is a good fellow, though as a liar he has but few equals and no superior.

We started out from the post with the regimental band playing the lively air of "The Girl I Left Behind Me." We made but a short march that day, and camped at night at the head of Fox Creek. Next morning General Duncan sent me word by his orderly that I was to bring up my gun and shoot at a mark with him; but I can assure the reader that I did not feel much like shooting anything except myself, for on the night before, I had returned to Fort McPherson and spent several hours in interviewing the sutler's store, in company with Major Brown. I looked around for my gun, and found that I had left it behind. The last I could remember about it was that I had it at the sutler's store. I informed Major Brown of my loss, who said that I was a nice scout to start out without a gun. I replied that that was not the worst of it, as General Duncan had sent for me to shoot a match with him, and I did not know what to do; for if the old gentleman discovered my predicament, he would very likely severely reprimand me.

"Well, Cody," said he, "the best you can do is to make some excuse, and then go and borrow a gun from some of the men, and tell the General that you lent yours to some man to go hunting with to-day. While we are waiting here, I will send back to the post and get your rifle for you."

I succeeded in obtaining a gun from John Nelson, and then marching up to the General's headquarters I shot the desired match with him, which resulted in his favor.

This was the first scout the Pawnees had been out on under command of General Duncan, and in stationing his guards around the camp he posted them in a manner entirely different from that of General Carr and Colonel Royall, and he insisted that the different posts should call out the hour of the night thus:

"Post No. 1, nine o'clock, all is well! Post No. 2, nine o'clock, all is well!" etc.

The Pawnees, who had their regular turns at standing upon guard, were ordered to call the hour the same as the white soldiers. This was very difficult for them to do, as there were but few of them who could express themselves in English. Major North explained to them that when the man on post next to them should call out the hour, they must call it also as near like him as possible. It was very amusing to hear them do this. They would try to remember what the other man had said on the post next to them. For instance, a white soldier would call out: "Post No. 1, half-past nine o'clock, all is well!" The Indian standing next to him knew that he was bound to say something in English, and he would sing out something like the following:

"Poss number half pass five cents—go to——! I don't care!"

This system was really so ridiculous and amusing that the General had to give it up, and the order was accordingly countermanded.

Nothing of any great interest occurred on this march, until one day, while proceeding up Prairie Dog Creek,[4] Major North and myself went out in advance of the command several miles and killed a number of buffaloes. Night was approaching, and I began to look around for a suitable camping ground for the command. Major North dismounted from his horse and was resting, while I rode down to the stream to see if there was plenty of grass in the vicinity. I found an excellent camping spot, and returning to Major North told him that I would ride over the hill a little way, so that the advance guard could see me. This I did, and when the advance came in sight I dismounted and laid down upon the grass to rest.

Suddenly I heard three or four shots, and in a few moments Major North came dashing up towards me, pursued by eight or ten Indians. I instantly sprang into my saddle, and fired a few shots at the Indians, who by this time had all come in sight, to the number of fifty. We turned our horses and ran, the bullets flying after us thick and fast— my whip being shot from my hand and daylight being put through the crown of my hat. We were in close quarters, when suddenly Lieutenant Valkmar came galloping up to our relief with several soldiers, and the Indians seeing them whirled and retreated. As soon as Major North got in sight of his Pawnees, he began riding in a circle. This was a sign to them that there were hostile Indians in front, and in a moment the Pawnees broke ranks pell-mell and, with Major North at their head, started for the flying warriors. The rest of the command pushed rapidly forward also, and chased the enemy for three or four miles, killing three of them.

But this was a wrong move on our part, as their village was on Prairie Dog Creek, while they led us in a different direction; one Indian only kept straight on up the creek— a messenger to the village. Some of the command, who had followed him, stirred up the village and accelerated its departure. We finally got back to the main force, and then learned that we had made a great mistake. Now commenced another stern chase.

The second day that we had been following these Indians we came upon an old squaw, whom they had left on the prairie to die. Her people had built for her a little shade or lodge, and had given her some provisions, sufficient to last her on her trip to the Happy Hunting grounds. This the Indians often do when pursued by an enemy, and one of their number becomes too old and feeble to travel any longer. This squaw was recognized by John Nelson who said that she was a relative of his wife. From her we learned that the flying Indians were known as Pawnee Killer's band, and that they had lately killed Buck's surveying party, consisting of eight or nine men; the massacre having occurred a few days before on Beaver Creek. We knew that they had had a fight with surveyors, as we found quite a number of surveying instruments, which had been left in the abandoned camp. We drove these Indians across the Platte river and then returned to Fort McPherson, bringing the old squaw with us, from there she was sent to the Spotted Tail Agency.

During my absence, my wife had given birth to a son, and he was several weeks old when I returned. No name had yet been given him and I selected that of Elmo Judson, in honor of Ned Buntline; but this the officers and scouts objected to. Major Brown proposed that we should call him Kit Carson, and it was finally settled that that should be his name.

During the summer we made one or two more scouts and had a few skirmishes with the Indians: but nothing of any great importance transpired. In the fall of 1870, while I was a witness in a court martial at Fort D. A. Russell I woke up one morning and found that I was dead broke;— this is not an unusual occurrence to a frontiersman, or an author I may add, especially when he is endeavoring to kill time—to raise necessary funds I sold my race horse Tall Bull to Lieutenant Mason, who had long wanted him.

In the winter of 1870 and 1871 I first met George Watts Garland, an English gentleman, and a great hunter, whom I had the pleasure of guiding on several hunts and with whom I spent some weeks. During the winter I also took several parties out on the Loupe River country, hunting and trapping. Although I was still chief of scouts I did not have much to do, as the Indians were comparatively quiet, thus giving me plenty of time for sporting.

In the spring of 1871 several short scouting expeditions were sent out from Fort McPherson, but all with minor results.

About this time General Emory was considerably annoyed by petty offenses committed in the vicinity of the post, and as there was no justice of the peace in the neighborhood, he was anxious to have such an officer there to attend to the civilians; one day he remarked to me that I would make an excellent justice.

"General, you compliment me rather too highly, for I don't know any more about law than a government mule does about book-keeping," said I.

"That doesn't make any difference," said he, "for I know that you will make a good 'Squire."[5] He accordingly had the county commissioners appoint me to the office of justice of the peace, and I soon received my commission.

One morning a man came rushing up to my house and stated that he wanted to get out a writ of replevin,[6] to recover possession of a horse which a stranger was taking out of the country. I had no blank forms, and had not yet received the statutes of Nebraska to copy from, so I asked the man:

"Where is the fellow who has got your horse?"

"He is going up the road, and is about two miles away," replied he.

"Very well," said I, "I will get the writ ready in a minute or two."

I saddled up my horse, and then taking my old reliable gun, "Lucretia," I said to the man: "That's the best writ of replevin that I can think of; come along, and we'll get that horse, or know the reason why."

We soon overtook the stranger who was driving a herd of horses, and as we came up to him, I said:

"Hello, sir; I am an officer, and have an attachment for that horse," and at the same time I pointed out the animal.

"Well, sir, what are you going to do about it?" he inquired.

"I propose to take you and the horse back to the post," said I.

"You can take the horse," said he, "but I haven't the time to return with you."

"You'll have to take the time, or pay the costs here and now," said I.

"How much are the costs?"

"Twenty dollars."

"Here's your money," said he, as he handed me the greenbacks.

I then gave him a little friendly advice, and told him that he was released from custody. He went on his way a wiser and a poorer man, while the owner of the horse and myself returned to the fort. I pocketed the twenty dollars, of course. Some people might think it was not a square way of doing business, but I didn't know any better just then. I had several little cases of this kind, and I became better posted on law in the course of time, being assisted by Lieutenant Burr Reilly, of the Fifth Cavalry, who had been educated for a lawyer.

One evening I was called upon to perform a marriage ceremony. The bridegroom was one of the sergeants of the post. I had "braced up" for the occasion by imbibing rather freely of stimulants, and when I arrived at the house, with a copy of the Statutes of Nebraska, which I had recently

66. A Wedding Ceremony

received, I felt somewhat confused. Whether my bewilderment was owing to the importance of the occasion and the large assembly, or to the effect of Louis Woodin's "tanglefoot," I cannot now distinctly remember—but my suspicions have always been that it was due to the latter cause. I looked carefully through the statutes to find the marriage ceremony, but my efforts were unsuccessful. Finally the time came for the knot to be tied. I told the couple to stand up, and then I said to the bridegroom:

"Do you take this woman to be your lawful wedded wife, to support and love her through life?"

"I do," was the reply.

Then addressing myself to the bride, I said, "Do you take this man to be your lawful wedded husband through life, to love, honor and obey him?"

"I do," was her response.

"Then join hands," said I to both of them; "I now pronounce you to be man and wife, and whomsoever God and Buffalo Bill have joined together let no man put asunder. May you live long and prosper. Amen."

This concluded the interesting ceremony, which was followed by the usual festivities on such occasions. I was highly complimented for the elegant and eloquent manner in which I had tied the matrimonial knot.

During the summer of 1871, Professor Marsh,[7] of Yale College, came out to McPherson, with a large party of students to have a hunt and to look for fossils. Professor Marsh had heard of the big bone which had been found by the Pawnees in the Niobrara country, and he intended to look for that as well as other bones. He accordingly secured the services of Major Frank North and the Pawnees as an escort. I was also to accompany the bone-hunters, and would have done so had it not been for the fact that just at that time I was ordered out with a small scouting party to go after some Indians.

The day before the Professor arrived at the fort, I had been out hunting on the north side of the North Platte River, near Pawnee Springs, with several companions, when we were suddenly attacked by Indians, who wounded one of our number, John Weister. We stood the Indians off for a little while, and Weister got even with them by killing one of their party. The Indians, however, outnumbered us, and at last we were forced to make a run for our lives. In this we succeeded, and reached the fort in safety. The General wanted to have the Indians pursued, and said he could not spare me to accompany Professor Marsh.

67. A Ride For Life

However, I had the opportunity to make the acquaintance of the eminent Professor, whom I found to be not only a well-posted person but a very entertaining gentleman. He gave me a geological history of the country; told me in what section fossils were to be found; and otherwise entertained me with several scientific yarns, some of which seemed too complicated and too mysterious to be believed by an ordinary man like myself; but it was all clear to him. I rode out with him several miles, as he was starting on his bone-hunting expedition, and I greatly enjoyed the ride. His party had been provided with Government transportation and his students were all mounted on Government horses.

As we rode along he delivered a scientific lecture, and

he convinced me that he knew what he was talking about. I finally bade him good-bye, and returned to the post. While the fossil-hunters were out on their expedition, we had several lively little skirmishes with the Indians. After having been absent some little time Professor Marsh and his party came back with their wagons loaded down with all kinds of bones, and the Professor was in his glory. He had evidently struck a bone-yard, and "gad!"[8] wasn't he happy! But they had failed to find the big bone which the Pawnees had unearthed the year before.

CHAPTER XXIV

Hunting Expeditions

Early in the month of September, 1871, information was received at Fort McPherson that General Sheridan and a party of invited friends were coming out to the post to have a grand hunt in the vicinity, and to explore the country from McPherson to Fort Hays, in Kansas. On the morning of September 22d they arrived in a special car at North Platte, a station on the Union Pacific, distant eighteen miles from Fort McPherson.

The party consisted of General Sheridan, Lawrence R. Jerome, James Gordon Bennett, of the *New York Herald*; Leonard W. Jerome, Carroll Livingston, Major J. G. Hecksher, General Fitzhugh, General H. E. Davies, Captain M. Edward Rogers, Colonel J. Schuyler Crosby, Samuel Johnson, General Anson Stager, of the Western Union Telegraph Company; Charles Wilson, editor of the *Chicago Evening Journal*; General Rucker, Quartermaster-General, and Dr. Asch—the two last-named being of General Sheridan's staff.[1] They were met at the station by General Emory and Major Brown, with a cavalry company as escort and a sufficient number of vehicles to carry the distinguished visitors and their baggage.

A brisk drive of less than two hours over a hard and smooth road brought them to the fort, where they found the garrison, consisting of five companies of the Fifth Cavalry, under the command of General Carr, out on parade awaiting their arrival. The band played some martial music, and the cavalry passed very handsomely in review before General Sheridan. The guests were then most hospitably received, and assigned to comfortable quarters.

Lieutenant Hayes, the quartermaster of the expedition, arranged everything for the comfort of the party. One hundred cavalry under command of Major Brown were detailed as an escort. A train of sixteen wagons was provided to carry the baggage, supplies, and forage for the trip; and, besides these, there were three four-horse ambulances in which the guns were carried, and in which members of the party who became weary of the saddle might ride and rest. At General Sheridan's request I was to accompany the expedition; he introduced me to all his friends, and gave me a good send-off.

During the afternoon and evening the gentlemen were all entertained at the post in a variety of ways, including dinner and supper parties, and music and dancing; at a late hour they retired to rest in their tents at the camp which they occupied outside the post—named Camp Rucker in honor of General Rucker.

At five o'clock next morning a cavalry bugle sounded the *reveille*, and soon all were astir in the camp, preparatory to pulling out for the first day's march. I rose fresh and eager for the trip, and as it was a nobby[2] and high-toned outfit which I was to accompany, I determined to put on a little style myself. So I dressed in a new suit of light buckskin, trimmed along the seams with fringes of the same material; and I put on a crimson shirt handsomely ornamented on the bosom, while on my head I wore a broad *sombrero*. Then mounting a snowy white horse—a gallant stepper—I rode down from the fort to the camp, rifle in hand. I felt first-rate that morning, and looked well.

The expedition was soon under way. Our road for ten miles wound through a wooded ravine called Cottonwood Cañon, intersecting the high ground, or divide, as it is called, between the Platte and Republican Rivers. Upon emerging from the cañon we found ourselves upon the plains. First in the line rode General Sheridan, followed by his guests, and then the orderlies. Then came the ambulances, in one of which were carried five greyhounds, brought along to course the antelope and rabbit. With the ambulances marched a pair of Indian ponies belonging to Lieutenant Hayes—captured during some Indian fight—and harnessed to a light wagon, which General Sheridan occasionally used. These little horses, but thirteen hands high, showed more vigor and endurance than any other of the animals we had with us. Following the ambulances came the main body of the escort and the supply wagons.

We marched seventeen miles the first day, and went into camp on Fox Creek, a tributary of the Republican. No hunting had as yet been done; but I informed the gentlemen of the party that we would strike the buffalo country the next day. A hundred or more questions were then asked me by this one and that one, and the whole evening was spent principally in buffalo talk, sandwiched with stories of the plains—both of war and of the chase. Several of the party, who were good vocalists, gave us some excellent music. We closed the evening by christening the camp, naming it Camp Brown, in honor of the gallant officer in command of the escort.

At three o'clock next morning the bugle called us to an early start. We had breakfast at half-past four, and at six were in the saddle. All were eager to see and shoot the buffaloes which I assured them we would certainly meet during the day. After marching five miles, the advance guard, of which I had the command, discovered six buffaloes grazing at a distance of about two miles from us. We returned to the hunters with this information, and they at once consulted with me as to the best way to attack the "enemy."

Acting upon my suggestions, Fitzhugh, Crosby, Lawrence Jerome, Livingston, Hecksher and Rogers, accompanied by myself as guide, rode through a convenient cañon to a point beyond the buffaloes, so that we were to the windward of the animals. The rest of the party made a detour of nearly five miles, keeping behind the crest of a hill. We charged down upon the buffaloes, at full gallop, and just then the other party emerged from their concealment and witnessed the exciting chase. The buffaloes started off in a line, single file. Fitzhugh, after a lively gallop, led us all and soon came alongside the rear buffalo, at which he fired. The animal faltered, and then with another shot Fitzhugh brought him to the ground. Crosby dashed by him and leveled another of the herd, while Livingston dropped a third. Those who were not directly engaged in the hunt now came up and congratulated the men upon their success, and Fitzhugh was at once hailed as the winner of the buffalo cup; while all sympathized with Hecksher, whose chance had been the best at the start, but who lost by reason of his horse falling and rolling over him.

The hunt being over, the column moved forward on its march passing through a prairie-dog town, several miles in extent. These animals are found throughout the plains, living together in a sort of society; their numberless burrows in their "towns" adjoin each other, so that great care is necessary in riding through these places, as the ground is so undermined as often to fall in under the weight of a horse. Around the entrance to their holes the ground is piled up almost a foot high; on these little elevations the prairie-dogs sit upon their hind legs, chattering to each other and observing whatever passes on the plains. They will permit a person to approach quite near, but when they have viewed him closely, they dive into their dens with wonderful quickness. They are difficult to kill, and if hit, generally succeed in crawling underground before they can be captured. Rattlesnakes and small owls are generally found in great numbers in the prairie-dog towns, and live in the same holes with the dogs on friendly terms. A few of the prairie-dogs were killed, and were found to be very palatable eating.

A short distance beyond the dog town we discovered a settlement of five white men, who proved to be the two Clifford brothers, Arthur Ruff, Dick Seymour and John Nelson—the latter already referred to in these pages. Each of them had a squaw wife and numerous half-breed children, living in tents of buffalo skins. They owned a herd of horses and mules and a few cattle, and had cultivated a small piece of land. Their principal occupation was hunting, and they had a large number of buffalo hides, which, they had tanned in the Indian manner.

Upon reaching Pleasant Valley, on Medicine Creek, our

68. Prairie-Dog Village

party divided into two detachments—one hunting along the bank of the stream for elk or deer, and the other remaining with the main body of the escort. The elk hunters met with no success whatever, but the others ran across plenty of buffaloes, and nearly everybody killed one or more before the day was over. Lawrence Jerome made an excellent shot; while riding in an ambulance he killed a buffalo which attempted to cross the line of march.

At about four o'clock P.M., we arrived at Mitchell's Fork of the Medicine, having traveled thirty-five miles during that day, and there we went into camp—calling it Camp Jack Hayes, in honor of Lieutenant Hayes.

On the next morning, the 25th, we moved out of camp at eight o'clock. The party was very successful through the day in securing game, Hecksher, Fitzhugh, Livingston and Lieutenant Hayes; and in fact all did good shooting.

Lawrence Jerome persuaded me to let him ride Buckskin Joe, the best buffalo horse in the whole outfit, and on his back he did wonders among the buffaloes. Leonard Jerome, Bennett and Rogers also were very successful in buffalo hunting.

Our camp of this night was named Camp Asch to commemorate our surgeon, Dr. Asch. The evening was pleasantly spent around the camp fires in relating the adventures of the day.

Upon crossing the Republican river on the morning of the 26th, we came upon an immense number of buffaloes scattered over the country in every direction, as far as the eye could reach and all had an opportunity to do as much hunting as they wished. The wagons and troops moved slowly along in the direction of the next camp, while the hunters went off separately, or by twos and threes, in different directions, and all were rewarded with abundant success. Lawrence Jerome, however, had his career suddenly checked. He had dismounted to make a steady and careful shot, and thoughtlessly let go of the bridle. The buffalo failing to take a tumble, as he ought to have done, started off at a lively gait, followed by Buckskin Joe—the horse being determined to do some hunting on his own account—the last seen of him, he was a little ahead of the buffalo, and gaining slightly, leaving his late rider to his own reflections and the prospect of a tramp; his desolate condition was soon discovered and another horse warranted not to run under any provocation, was sent to him. It maybe stated here that three days afterwards, as I subsequently learned, Buckskin Joe, all saddled and bridled, turned up at Fort McPherson.

We pitched our tents for the night in a charming spot on the bank of Beaver Creek. The game was so abundant that we remained there one day. This stopping place was called Camp Cody, in honor of the reader's humble servant.

The next day was spent in hunting jack-rabbits, coyotes, elks, antelopes and wild turkeys. We had a splendid dinner as will be seen from the following:

BILL OF FARE.

SOUP.

Buffalo Tail.

FISH.

Cisco broiled, fried Dace.

ENTREES.

Salmi of Prairie Dog, Stewed Rabbit, Fillet of Buffalo, Aux Champignons.

ROAST.

Elk, Antelope, Black-tailed Deer, Wild Turkey.

BROILED.

Teal, Mallard, Antelope Chops, Buffalo-Calf Steaks, Young Wild Turkey.

VEGETABLES.

Sweet Potatoes, Mashed Potatoes, Green Peas.

DESSERT.

Tapioca Pudding.

WINES.

Champagne Frappe, Champagne au Naturel, Claret, Whiskey, Brandy, Bass' Ale.

COFFEE.

This I considered a pretty square meal for a party of hunters, and everybody did ample justice to it.

In the evening a court-martial was held, at which I presided as chief justice. We tried one of the gentlemen for aiding and abetting in the loss of a government horse, and for having something to do with the mysterious disappearance of a Colt's pistol. He was charged also with snoring in a manner that was regarded as fiendish, and with committing a variety of other less offenses too numerous to mention.

The accused made a feeble defense as to the pistol, and claimed that instead of losing a government horse, the fact was that the horse had lost him. His statements were all regarded as "too thin," and finally failing to prove good character, he confessed all, and threw himself upon the mercy of the court. The culprit was Lawrence Jerome.

As chief justice I delivered the opinion of the court, which my modesty does not prevent me from saying, was done in an able and dignified manner; as an act of clemency I suspended judgment for the time being, remarking that while the camp fire held out to burn, the vilest sinner might return; and in hope of the accused's amendment, I would defer pronouncing sentence. The trial afforded its considerable amusement, and gave me a splendid opportunity to display the legal knowledge which I had acquired while acting as justice of the peace at Fort McPherson.

On the morning of the 28th the command crossed the South Beaver, distant nine miles from Camp Cody, and then striking a fair road we made a rapid march until we reached our camp on Short Nose or Prairie Dog Creek, about 2 P.M., after having made twenty-four miles. The remainder of the afternoon was spent in hunting buffaloes and turkeys. Camp Stager was the name given to this place, in honor of General Stager, of the Western Union Telegraph Company.

The next day we made a march of twenty-four miles, and then halted at about 1 P.M. on the North Solomon River. This day we killed three buffaloes, two antelopes, two raccoons, and three teal ducks. Near our camp, which we named Camp Leonard Jerome, was a beaver dam some six feet high and twenty yards wide; it was near the junction of two streams, and formed a pond of at least four acres.

On the 30th we traveled twenty-five miles, and during the march nine turkeys, two rabbits, and three or four buffaloes were killed. We went into camp on the bank of the South Fork of the Solomon River and called the place Camp Sam Johnson. We were now but forty-five miles from Fort Hays, the point at which General Sheridan and his guests expected to strike the Kansas Pacific Railway, and thence return home. That evening I volunteered to ride to Fort Hays and meet the party next day, bringing with me all the letters that might be at the post. Taking the best horse in the command I started out, expecting to make the trip in about four hours.

The next morning the command got an early start and traveled thirty miles to Saline River, where they made their last camp on the plains. As some of the party were attacking a herd of buffaloes, I rode in from Fort Hays and got into the middle of the herd, and killed a buffalo or two before the hunters observed me. I brought a large number of letters, which proved welcome reading matter.

In the evening we gathered around the camp-fire for the last time. The duty of naming the camp, which was called Camp Davies, having been duly performed, we all united in making that night the pleasantest of all that we had spent together. We had eloquent speeches, songs, and interesting anecdotes. I was called upon, and entertained the gentlemen with some lively Indian stories.

The excursionists reached Fort Hays, distant fifteen miles, on the morning of October 2d, where we pitched our tents for the last time, and named the camp in honor of Mr. Hecksher. That same afternoon General Sheridan and his guests took the train for the East, after bidding Major Brown, Lieutenant Hayes and myself a hearty good-bye, and expressing themselves as greatly pleased with their hunt, and the manner in which they had been escorted and guided.

It will be proper and fair to state here that General Davies afterwards wrote an interesting account of this hunt and published it in a neat volume of sixty-eight pages, under the title of "Ten Days on the Plains." I would have inserted the volume bodily in this book, were it not for the fact that the General has spoken in a rather too complimentary manner of me. However, I have taken the liberty in this chapter to condense from the little volume, and in some places I have used the identical language of General Davies without quoting the same; in fact, to do the General justice, I ought to close this chapter with several lines of quotation marks to be pretty generally distributed by the reader throughout my account of our ten days' hunt.

Soon after the departure of General Sheridan's party, we returned to Fort McPherson and found General Carr about to start out on a twenty days' scout, not so much for the purpose of finding Indians, but more for the object of taking some friends on a hunt. His guests were a couple of Englishmen,—whose names I cannot now remember—and Mr. McCarthy, of Syracuse, New York, who was a relative of General Emory. The command consisted of three companies of the Fifth Cavalry, one company of Pawnee Indians, and twenty-five wagons. Of course I was called on to accompany the expedition.

One day, after we had been out from the post for some little time, I was hunting on Deer Creek, in company with Mr. McCarthy, about eight miles from the command. I had been wishing for several days to play a joke on him, and had arranged a plan with Captain Lute North to carry it into execution. I had informed North at about what time we would be on Deer Creek, and it was agreed that he should appear in the vicinity with some of his Pawnees, who were to throw their blankets around them, and come dashing down upon us, firing and whooping in true Indian style; while he was to either conceal or disguise himself.

This programme was faithfully and completely carried out. I had been talking about Indians to McCarthy, and he had become considerably excited, when just as we turned a bend of the creek, we saw not half a mile from us about twenty Indians, who instantly started for us on a gallop, firing their guns and yelling at the top of their voices.

"McCarthy, shall we dismount and fight, or run?" said I.

He didn't wait to reply, but wheeling his horse, started at full speed down the creek, losing his hat and dropping his gun; away he went, never once looking back to see if he was being pursued. I tried to stop him by yelling at him and saying that it was all right, as the Indians were Pawnees. Unfortunately he did not hear me, but kept straight on, not stopping his horse until he reached the camp.

I knew that he would tell General Carr that the Indians had jumped him, and that the General would soon start out with the troops. So as soon as the Pawnees rode up to me I told them to remain there while I went after my friend. I rode after him as fast as possible, but he had arrived at the command some time before me and when I got there the General had, as I had suspected he would do, ordered out two companies of cavalry to go in pursuit of the Indians. I told the General that the Indians were only some Pawnees, who had been out hunting and that they had merely played a joke upon us. I forgot to inform him that I had put up the trick, but as he was always fond of a good joke himself, he did not get very angry. I had picked up McCarthy's hat and gun which I returned to him, and it was some time afterwards before he discovered who was at the bottom of the affair.

When we returned to Fort McPherson we found there

69. McCarthy's Fright

Mr. Royal Buck, whose father had been killed with his entire party by Pawnee Killer's band of Indians on the Beaver Creek. He had a letter from the commanding officer of the Department requesting that he be furnished with an escort to go in search of the remains of his father and the party. Two companies of cavalry were sent with him and I accompanied them as guide. As the old squaw, which we had captured, and of which mention is made in a previous chapter, could not exactly tell us the place on Beaver Creek where the party had been killed, we searched the country over for two days and discovered no signs of the murdered men. At last, however, our efforts were rewarded with success. We found pieces of their wagons and among other things an old letter or two which Mr. Buck recognized

70. Finding the Remains of the Buck Party

as his father's handwriting. We then discovered some of the remains, which we buried; but nothing further. It was now getting late in the fall and we accordingly returned to Fort McPherson.[3]

A short time after this the Fifth Cavalry was ordered to Arizona, a not very desirable country to soldier in. I had become greatly attached to the officers of the regiment, having been continually with them for over three years, and had about made up my mind to accompany them, when a letter was received from General Sheridan instructing the commanding officer "not to take Cody" with him, and saying that I was to remain in my old position. In a few days the command left for its destination, taking the cars at McPherson Station, where I bade my old friends adieu. During the next few weeks I had but little to do, as the post was garrisoned by infantry, awaiting the arrival of the Third Cavalry.

CHAPTER XXV

Hunting with a Grand Duke

About the first of January, 1872, General Forsyth and Dr. Asch, of Sheridan's staff came out to Fort McPherson to make preparations for a big buffalo hunt for the Grand Duke Alexis, of Russia;[1] and as this was to be no ordinary affair, these officers had been sent by General Sheridan to have all the necessary arrangements perfected by the time the Grand Duke should arrive. They learned from me that there were plenty of buffaloes in the vicinity and especially on the Red Willow, sixty miles distant. They said they would like to go over on the Red Willow and pick out a suitable place for the camp; they also inquired the location of the Spotted Tail, Sioux Indians. Spotted Tail had permission from the Government to hunt the buffalo, with his people during the winter, in the Republican river country. It was my opinion that they were located somewhere on the Frenchman's Fork about one hundred and fifty miles from Fort McPherson.

General Sheridan's commissioners informed me, that he wished me to visit Spotted Tail's camp, and induce about one hundred of the leading warriors and chiefs, to come to the point where it should be decided to locate the Alexis hunting camp, and to be there by the time the Grand Duke should arrive, so that he could see a body of

71. Spotted Tail

American Indians and observe the manner in which they killed buffaloes. The Indians would also be called upon to give a grand war dance in honor of the distinguished visitor.

Next morning General Forsyth and Dr. Asch, accompanied by Captain Hayes, who had been left at Fort McPherson in charge of the Fifth Cavalry horses, taking an ambulance and a light wagon, to carry their tents, and provisions sufficient to last them two or three days; started, under my guidance, with a small escort, for Red Willow Creek, arriving there at night. The next day we selected a pleasant camping place on a little knoll in the valley of the Red Willow. General Forsyth and his party returned to the post the next day while I left for Spotted Tail's camp.

The weather was very cold and I found my journey by no means a pleasant one as I was obliged to camp out with only my saddle blankets; and besides, there was more or less danger from the Indians themselves; for, although Spotted Tail himself was friendly, I was afraid I might have difficulty in getting into his camp. I was liable at any moment to run into a party of his young men who might be out hunting, and as I had many enemies among the Sioux, I would be running considerable risk in meeting them.

At the end of the first day I camped on Stinking Water, a tributary of the Frenchman's Fork, where I built a little fire in the timber; but it was so very cold I was not able to sleep much. Getting an early start in the morning I followed up the Frenchman's Fork and late in the afternoon I could see, from the fresh horse tracks and from the dead buffaloes lying here and there, recently killed, that I was nearing Spotted Tail's camp. I rode on for a few miles further, and then hiding my horse in a low ravine, I crawled up a high hill, where I obtained a good view of the country. I could see for four or five miles up the creek, and got sight of a village and of two or three hundred ponies in its vicinity. I waited until night came and then I succeeded in riding into the Indian camp unobserved.

I had seen Spotted Tail's camp when he came from the north and I knew the kind of lodge he was living in. As I entered the village I wrapped a blanket around my head so that the Indians could not tell whether I was a white or a red man. In this way I rode around until I found Spotted Tail's lodge. Dismounting from my horse I opened his tent door and looked in and saw the old chief lying on some robes. I spoke to him and he recognized me at once and invited me to enter. Inside the lodge I found a white man, an old frontiersman, Todd Randall, who was Spotted

Tail's agent and who had lived a great many years with the Indians. He understood their language perfectly and did all the interpreting for Spotted Tail. Through him I readily communicated with the chief and informed him of my errand. I told him that the warriors and chiefs would greatly please General Sheridan if they would meet him in about ten sleeps at the old Government crossing of the Red Willow. I further informed him that there was a great chief from across the water who was coming there to visit him. Spotted Tail replied that he would be very glad to go; that the next morning he would call his people together and select those who would accompany him. I told Spotted Tail how I had entered his camp. He replied that I had acted wisely; that although his people were friendly, yet some of his young men had a grudge against me, and I might have had difficulty with them had I met them away from the village. He directed his squaw to get me something to eat, and ordered that my horse be taken care of, and upon his invitation I spent the remainder of the night in his lodge.

Next morning the chiefs and warriors assembled according to orders, and to them was stated the object of my visit. They were asked:

"Do you know who this man is?"

"Yes, we know him well," replied one, "that is Pa-he-haska," (that being my name among the Sioux, which translated means "Long Hair") "that is our old enemy," a great many of the Indians, who were with Spotted Tail at this time, had been driven out of the Republican country.

"That is he," said Spotted Tail. "I want all my people to be kind to him and treat him as my friend."

72. Grand Duke Alexis

I noticed that several of them were looking daggers at me. They appeared as if they wished to raise my hair then and there. Spotted Tail motioned and I followed him into his lodge, and thereupon the Indians dispersed. Having the assurance of Spotted Tail that none of the young men would follow me I started back for the Red Willow, arriving the second night.

There I found Captain Egan with a company of the Second Cavalry and a wagon train loaded with tents, grain,

73. Indian Exercises

provisions, etc. The men were leveling off the ground and were making preparations to put up large wall tents for the Grand Duke Alexis and his *suite,*[2] and for General Sheridan, his staff and other officers, and invited guests of the party. Proceeding to Fort McPherson I reported what had been done. Thereupon Quartermaster Hayes selected from the five or six hundred horses in his charge, seventy-five of the very best, which were sent to the Red Willow, to be used by Alexis and his party at the coming hunt. In a day or two a large supply of provisions, liquors, etc., arrived from Chicago, together with bedding and furniture for the tents; all of which were sent over to Camp Alexis.

At last, on the morning of the 12th of January, 1872, the Grand Duke and party arrived at North Platte by special train; in charge of a Mr. Francis Thompson. Captain Hayes and myself, with five or six ambulances, fifteen or twenty extra saddle-horses and a company of cavalry under Captain Egan, were at the dépôt in time to receive them. Presently General Sheridan and a large, fine-looking young man, whom we at once concluded to be the Grand Duke came out of the cars and approached us. General Sheridan at once introduced me to the Grand Duke as Buffalo Bill, for he it was, and said that I was to take charge of him and show him how to kill buffalo.

In less than half an hour the whole party were dashing away towards the south, across the South Platte and towards the Medicine; upon reaching which point we halted for a change of horses and a lunch. Resuming our ride we reached Camp Alexis in the afternoon. General Sheridan was well pleased with the arrangements that had been made and was delighted to find that Spotted Tail and his Indians had arrived on time. They were objects of great curiosity to the Grand Duke, who spent considerable time in looking at them, and watching their exhibitions of horsemanship, sham fights, etc. That evening the Indians gave the grand war dance, which I had arranged for.

General Custer, who was one of the hunting party, carried on a mild flirtation with one of Spotted Tail's daughters, who had accompanied her father thither, and it was noticed also that the Duke Alexis paid considerable attention to another handsome red-skin maiden. The night passed pleasantly, and all retired with great expectations of having a most enjoyable and successful buffalo hunt. The Duke Alexis asked me a great many questions as to how we shot buffaloes, and what kind of a gun or pistol we used, and if he was going to have a good horse. I told him that he was to have my celebrated buffalo horse Buckskin Joe, and when we went into a buffalo herd all he would have to do was to sit on the horse's back and fire away.

At nine o'clock next morning we were all in our saddles, and in a few minutes were galloping over the prairies in search of a buffalo herd. We had not gone far before we observed a herd some distance ahead of us crossing our way; after that we proceeded cautiously, so as to keep out of sight until we were ready to make a charge.

Of course the main thing was to give Alexis the first chance and the best shot at the buffaloes, and when all was in readiness we dashed over a little knoll that had hidden us from view, and in a few minutes we were among them. Alexis at first preferred to use his pistol instead of a gun. He fired six shots from this weapon at buffaloes only twenty feet away from him, but as he shot wildly, not one of his bullets took effect. Riding up to his side and seeing that his weapon was empty, I exchanged pistols with him. He again fired six shots, without dropping a buffalo.

Seeing that the animals were bound to make their escape without his killing one of them, unless he had a better weapon, I rode up to him, gave him my old reliable "Lucretia," and told him to urge his horse close to the buffaloes, and I would then give him the word when to shoot. At the same time I gave old Buckskin Joe a blow with my whip, and with a few jumps the horse carried the Grand Duke to within about ten feet of a big buffalo bull.

"Now is your time," said I. He fired, and down went the buffalo. The Grand Duke stopped his horse, dropped his gun on the ground, and commenced waving his hat.

When his *suite* came galloping up, he began talking to them in a tongue which I could not understand. Presently General Sheridan joined the group, and the ambulances were brought up. Very soon the corks began to fly from the champagne bottles, in honor of the Grand Duke Alexis, who had killed the first buffalo.

It was reported in a great many of the newspapers that I shot the first buffalo for Alexis, while in some it was stated that I held the buffalo while His Royal Highness killed it. But the way I have related the affair is the correct version.

It was thought that we had had about sport enough for one day, and accordingly I was directed by General Sheridan to guide the party back to camp, and we were soon on our way thither. Several of the party, however, concluded to have a little hunt on their own account, and presently we saw them galloping over the prairie in different directions in pursuit of buffaloes.

While we were crossing a deep ravine, on our way to camp, we ran into a small band of buffaloes that had been frightened by some of the hunters. As they rushed past us, not more than thirty yards distant, Alexis raised his pistol, fired and killed a buffalo cow. It was either an extraordinary good shot or a "scratch"[3]—probably the latter, for it surprised the Grand Duke as well as everybody else. We gave him three cheers, and when the ambulance came up we took a pull at the champagne in honor of the Grand Duke's success. I was in hopes that he would kill five or six more buffaloes before we reached camp, especially if a basket of champagne was to be opened every time he dropped one.

General Sheridan directed me to take care of the hides

74. Two Lance Killing a Buffalo

and heads of the buffaloes which Alexis had killed, as the Duke wished to keep them as souvenirs of the hunt. I also cut out the choice meat from the cow and brought it into camp, and that night at supper Alexis had the pleasure of dining on broiled buffalo steak obtained from the animal which he had shot himself.

We remained at this camp two or three days, during which we hunted most of the time, the Grand Duke himself killing eight buffaloes.

One day Alexis desired to see how the Indians hunted buffaloes and killed them with bow and arrow; so Spotted Tail, selecting some of his best hunters, had them surround a herd, and bring the animals down, not only with arrows, but with lances. The Grand Duke was told to follow upon the heels of one celebrated Indian hunter, whose name was "Two Lance," and watch him bring down the game; for this chief had the reputation of being able to send an arrow through and through the body of a buffalo. Upon this occasion he did not belie his reputation, for he sent an arrow *through* a buffalo, which fell dead at the shot, and the arrow was given to Alexis as a souvenir of his hunt on the American Plains.

When the Grand Duke was satisfied with the sport, orders were given for the return to the railroad. The conveyance provided for the Grand Duke and General Sheridan was a heavy double-seated open carriage, or rather an Irish dog-cart, and it was drawn by four spirited cavalry horses which were not much used to the harness. The driver was Bill Reed, an old overland stage driver and wagon master; on our way in, the Grand Duke frequently expressed his admiration of the skillful manner in which Reed handled the reins.

General Sheridan informed the Duke that I also had been a stage-driver in the Rocky Mountains, and thereupon His Royal Highness expressed a desire to see me drive. I was in advance at the time, and General Sheridan sang out to me:

"Cody, get in here and show the Duke how you can drive. Mr. Reed will exchange places with you and ride your horse."

"All right, General," said I, and in a few moments I had the reins and we were rattling away over the prairie. When we were approaching Medicine Creek, General Sheridan said: "Shake 'em up a little, Bill, and give us some old-time stage-driving." I gave the horses a crack or two of the whip, and they started off at a very rapid gait. They had a light load to pull, and kept increasing their speed at every jump, and I found it difficult to hold them. They fairly flew over the ground, and at last we reached a steep hill, or divide, which, led down into the valley of the Medicine. There was no brake on the wagon, and the horses were not much on the hold-back. I saw that it would be impossible to stop them. All I could do was to keep them straight in the track and let them go it down the hill, for three miles; which distance, I believe, was made in about six minutes. Every once in a while the hind wheels would strike a rut and take a bound, and not touch the ground again for fifteen or twenty feet. The Duke and the General were kept rather busy in holding their positions on the seats, and when they saw that I was keeping the horses straight in the road, they seemed to enjoy the dash which we were making. I was unable to stop the team until they ran into the camp where we were to obtain a fresh relay, and there I succeeded in checking them. The Grand Duke said he didn't want any more of that kind of driving, as he preferred to go a little slower.

On arriving at the railroad, the Duke invited me into his car, and made me some valuable presents, at the same time giving me a cordial invitation to visit him, if ever I should come to his country.

General Sheridan took occasion to remind me of an invitation to visit New York which I had received from some of the gentlemen who accompanied the General on the hunt from Fort McPherson to Hays City, in September of the previous year. Said he:

"You will never have a better opportunity to accept that

invitation than now. I have had a talk with General Ord[4] concerning you, and he will give you a leave of absence whenever you are ready to start. Write a letter to General Stager, of Chicago, that you are now prepared to accept the invitation, and he will send you a pass."

Thanking the General for his kindness, I then bade him and the Grand Duke good-bye, and soon their train was out of sight.

CHAPTER XXVI

Sight-Seeing

General Ord, commanding the Department of the Platte at the time, and who had been out on the Alexis hunt, had some business to attend to at Fort McPherson, and I accepted his invitation to ride over to the post with him in an ambulance. On the way thither he asked me how I would like to have an officer's commission in the regular army. He said that General Sheridan and himself had had some conversation about the matter, and if I wanted a commission, one could easily be procured for me. I thanked General Ord for his kindness, and said that although an officer's commission in the regular army was a tempting prize, yet I preferred to remain in the position I was then holding. He concluded by stating that if at any time I should wish a commission, all that I would have to do to secure it would be to inform him of my desire.

Having determined to visit New York, I acted upon General Sheridan's suggestion and wrote to General Stager, from whom in a few days I received my railroad passes. Obtaining thirty days' leave of absence from the department, I struck out for the East. On arriving in Chicago, in February, 1872, I was met at the dépôt by Colonel M. V. Sheridan, who said that his brother, the General, had not yet returned, but had sent word that I was to be his

75. An Embarrassing Situation

and the Colonel's guest, at their house, while I remained in Chicago.

I spent two or three days very pleasantly in the great city of the West, meeting several of the gentlemen who had been out on the Sheridan hunt in September—General Stager, Colonel Wilson, editor of the *Journal*; Mr. Sam Johnson, General Rucker and others—by all of whom I was most cordially received and well entertained. I was introduced to quite a number of the best people of the city, and was invited to several "swell" dinners. I also accompanied General Sheridan—who meantime had returned to the city—to a ball at Riverside—an aristocratic suburb.

On this occasion I became so embarrassed that it was more difficult for me to face the throng of beautiful ladies, than it would have been to confront a hundred hostile Indians. This was my first trip to the East, and I had not yet become accustomed to being stared at. And besides this, the hundreds of questions which I was called upon to answer further embarrassed and perplexed me.

According to the route laid out for me by General Stager, I was to stop at Niagara Falls, Buffalo and Rochester on my way to New York, and he provided me with all the necessary railroad passes. Just as I was about to leave Chicago I met Professor Henry A. Ward, of Rochester, for whom during the previous year or two I had collected a large number of specimens of wild animals. He was on his way to Rochester, and kindly volunteered to act as my guide until we reached that point. We spent one day in viewing the wonders of Niagara, and I stopped one day at Rochester and was shown the beauties of that handsome city by Professor Ward, and I had the honor of receiving an invitation to dine with the Mayor.

On arriving at New York I was met at the dépôt by Mr. J. G. Hecksher, who had been appointed as "a committee of one" to escort me to the Union Club, where James Gordon Bennett, Leonard W. Jerome and others were to give me an informal reception, and where I was to make my headquarters during my visit in the great metropolis. I had an elegant dinner at the club rooms, with the gentlemen who had been out on the September hunt, and other members of the club.

After dinner, in company with Mr. Hecksher—who acted as my guide—I started out on the trail of my friend, Ned Buntline, whom we found at the Brevoort Place Hotel. He was delighted to see me, and insisted on my becoming his guest. He would listen to no excuses, and on introducing me to Messrs. Overton & Blair, proprietors of the Brevoort, they also gave me a pressing invitation to make my home at their house. I finally compromised the matter by agreeing to divide my time between the Union Club, the Brevoort House, and Ned Buntline's quarters.

The next few days I spent in viewing the sights of New York, everything being new and startling, convincing me that as yet I had seen but a small portion of the world. I received numerous dinner invitations, as well as invitations to visit different places of amusement and interest; but as they came in so thick and fast, I soon became badly demoralized and confused. I found I had accepted invitations to dine at half a dozen or more houses on the same day and at the same hour. James Gordon Bennett had prepared a dinner for me, at which quite a large number of his friends were to be present, but owing to my confusion, arising from the many other invitations I had received, I forgot all about it, and dined elsewhere. This was "a bad break," but I did not learn of my mistake until next day, when at the Union Club House several gentlemen, among them Lawrence Jerome, inquired "where in the world I had been," and why I had not put in an appearance at Bennett's dinner. They said that Bennett had taken great pains to give me a splendid reception, that the party had waited till nine o'clock for me, and that my non-arrival caused considerable disappointment. I apologized as well as I could, by saying that I had been out on a scout and had got lost, and had forgotten all about the dinner; and expressed my regret for the disappointment I had created by my forgetfulness. August Belmont, the banker, being near said:

"Never mind, gentlemen, I'll give Cody a dinner at my house."

"Thank you, sir," said I; "I see you are determined that I shall not run short of rations while I am in the city. I'll be there, sure."

Both Mr. Jerome and Mr. Hecksher told me that I must not disappoint Mr. Belmont, for his dinners were splendid affairs. I made a note of the date, and at the appointed time I was promptly at Mr. Belmont's mansion, where I spent a very enjoyable evening.

Mr. Bennett, who was among the guests, having forgiven my carelessness, invited me to accompany him to the Liederkranz[1] masked ball, which was to take place in a few evenings, and would be a grand spectacle. Together we attended the ball, and during the evening I was well entertained. The dancers kept on their masks until midnight, and the merry and motley throng presented a brilliant scene, moving gracefully beneath the bright gas-light to the inspiriting music. To me it was a novel and entertaining sight, and in many respects reminded me greatly of an Indian war-dance.

Acting upon the suggestion of Mr. Bennett, I had dressed myself in my buckskin suit, and I naturally attracted considerable attention; especially when I took part in the dancing and exhibited some of my backwoods steps, which, although not as graceful as some, were a great deal more emphatic. But when I undertook to do artistic danc-ing, I found I was decidedly out of place in that crowd, and I accordingly withdrew from the floor.

I occasionally passed an evening at Niblo's Garden, viewing the many beauties of "The Black Crook," which was then having its long run, under the management of Jarrett & Palmer,[2] whose acquaintance I had made, and who extended to me the freedom of the theater.

Ned Buntline and Fred Maeder had dramatized one of the stories which the former had written about me for the *New York Weekly*. The drama was called "Buffalo Bill, the King of Border Men." While I was in New York it was produced at the Bowery Theater; J. B. Studley, an excel-lent actor, appearing in the character of "Buffalo Bill," and Mrs. W. G. Jones, a fine actress, taking the part of my sister, a leading *rôle*. I was curious to see how I would look when represented by some one else, and of course I was present on the opening night, a private box having been reserved for me. The theater was packed, every seat being occupied as well as the standing-room. The drama was played smoothly, and created a great deal of enthusiasm.

The audience, upon learning that the real "Buffalo Bill" was present, gave several cheers between the acts, and I was called on to come out on the stage and make a speech. Mr. Freleigh, the manager, insisted that I should comply with the request, and that I should be introduced to Mr. Studley. I finally consented, and the next moment I found myself standing behind the footlights and in front of an audience for the first time in my life. I looked up, then down, then on each side, and everywhere I saw a sea of human faces, and thousands of eyes all staring at me. I confess that I felt very much embarrassed—never more so in my life—and I knew not what to say. I made a desperate effort, and a few words escaped me, but what they were I could not for the life of me tell, nor could any one else in the house. My utterances were inaudible even to the leader of the orchestra, Mr. Dean, who was sitting only a few feet in front of me. Bowing to the audience, I beat a hasty retreat into one of the cañons of the stage. I never felt more relieved in my life than when I got out of the view of that immense crowd. That evening Mr. Freleigh offered to give me five hundred dollars a week to play the part of "Buffalo Bill" myself. I thought that he was certainly joking, especially as he had witnessed my awkward performance; but when he assured me that he was in earnest, I told him that it would be useless for me to attempt anything of the kind, for I never could talk to a crowd of people like that, even if it was to save my neck, and that he might as well try to make an actor out of a government mule. I thanked him for the generous offer, which I had to decline owing to a lack of confidence in myself; or as some people might express it, I didn't have the requisite cheek to undertake a thing of that sort. The play of "Buffalo Bill" had a very successful run of six or eight weeks, and was afterwards produced in all the principal cities of the country, everywhere being received with genuine enthusiasm.

I had been in New York about twenty days when General Sheridan arrived in the city. I met him soon after he got into town. In answer to a question how I was enjoying myself, I replied that I had struck the best camp I had ever seen, and if he didn't have any objections I would like to have my leave of absence extended about ten days. This he willingly did, and then informed me that my services would soon be required at Fort McPherson, as there was to be an expedition sent out from that point.

At Westchester, Pennsylvania, I had some relatives living whom I had never seen, and now being so near, I determined to make them a visit. Upon mentioning the matter to Buntline, he suggested that we should together take a trip to Philadelphia, and thence run out to Westchester. Accordingly the next day found us in the "City of Brotherly Love," and in a few hours we arrived at the home of my uncle, General Henry R. Guss, the proprietor of the Green Tree Hotel, who gave us a cordial reception.

Inviting us into the parlor, my uncle brought in the members of his family, among them an elderly lady, who was my grandmother, as he informed me. He told me that my Aunt Eliza, his first wife, was dead, and that he had married a second time; Lizzie Guss, my cousin, I thought was the most beautiful girl I had ever seen. They were all very anxious to have us remain several days, but as I had some business to attend to in New York, I was obliged to return that day. Assuring them, however, that I would visit them again soon, I bade them adieu, and with Buntline took the train for New York.

The time soon arrived for my departure for the West; so packing up my traps I started for home, and on the way thither I spent a day with my Westchester relatives, who did everything in their power to entertain me during my brief stay with them.

CHAPTER XXVII

Honors

Upon reaching Fort McPherson, I found that the Third Cavalry, commanded by General Reynolds, had arrived from Arizona, in which Territory they had been on duty for some time, and where they had acquired quite a reputation on account of their Indian fighting qualities.

Shortly after my return, a small party of Indians made a dash on McPherson Station, about five miles from the fort, killing two or three men and running off quite a large number of horses. Captain Meinhold and Lieutenant Lawson with their company were ordered out to pursue and punish the Indians if possible. I was the guide of the expedition and had as an assistant J. B. Omohundro,[1] better known as "Texas Jack" and who was a scout at the post.

Finding the trail, I followed it for two days, although it was difficult trailing because the red-skins had taken every possible precaution to conceal their tracks. On the second day Captain Meinhold went into camp on the South Fork of the Loupe, at a point where the trail was badly scattered. Six men were detailed to accompany me on a scout in search of the camp of the fugitives. We had gone but a short distance when we discovered Indians camped, not more than a mile away, with horses grazing near by. They were only a small party, and I determined to charge upon them with my six men, rather than return to the command, because I feared they would see us as we went back and then they would get away from us entirely. I asked the men if they were willing to attempt it, and they replied that they would follow me wherever I would lead them. That was the kind of spirit that pleased me, and we immediately moved forward on the enemy, getting as close to them as possible without being seen.

I finally gave the signal to charge, and we dashed into the little camp with a yell. Five Indians sprang out of a willow tepee, and greeted us with a volley, and we returned the fire. I was riding Buckskin Joe, who with a few jumps brought me up to the tepee, followed by my men. We nearly ran over the Indians who were endeavoring to reach their horses on the opposite side of the creek. Just as one was jumping the narrow stream a bullet from my old "Lucretia" overtook him. He never reached the other bank, but dropped dead in the water. Those of the Indians who were guarding the horses, seeing what was going on at the camp, came rushing to the rescue of their friends. I now counted thirteen braves, but as we had already disposed of two, we had only eleven to take care of. The odds were nearly two to one against us.

While the Indian reinforcements were approaching the camp I jumped the creek with Buckskin Joe to meet them, expecting our party would follow me; but as they could not induce their horses to make the leap, I was the only one who got over. I ordered the sergeant to dismount his men, and leaving one to hold the horses, to come over with the rest and help me drive the Indians off. Before they could do this, two mounted warriors closed in on me and were shooting at short range. I returned their fire and had the satisfaction of seeing one of them fall from his horse. At this moment I felt blood trickling down my forehead, and hastily running my hand through my hair I discovered that I had received a scalp wound. The Indian, who had shot me, was not more than ten yards away, and when he saw his partner tumble from his saddle, he turned to run.

By this time the soldiers had crossed the creek to assist me, and were blazing away at the other Indians. Urging Buckskin Joe forward, I was soon alongside of the chap who had wounded me, when raising myself in the stirrups I shot him through the head.

The reports of our guns had been heard by Captain Meinhold, who at once started with his company up the creek to our aid, and when the remaining Indians, whom we were still fighting, saw these reinforcements coming they whirled their horses and fled; as their steeds were quite fresh they made their escape. However, we killed six out of the thirteen Indians, and captured most of their stolen stock. Our loss was one man killed, and one man—myself—slightly wounded. One of our horses was killed, and Buckskin Joe was wounded, but I didn't discover the fact until some time afterwards as he had been shot in the breast and showed no signs of having received a scratch of any kind. Securing the scalps of the dead Indians and other trophies we returned to the fort.

I made several other scouts during the summer with different officers of the Third Cavalry, one being with Major Alick Moore, a good officer, with whom I was out for thirty days. Another long one was with Major Curtis, with whom I followed some Indians from the South Platte

76. Texas Jack

river to Fort Randall on the Missouri river in Dakota, on which trip the command ran out of rations and for fifteen days subsisted entirely upon the game we killed.

In the fall of 1872 the Earl of Dunraven[2] and Dr. Kingsley with several friends came to Fort McPherson with a letter from General Sheridan, asking me to accompany them on an elk hunt. I did so, and I afterwards spent several weeks in hunting with the Earl of Dunraven, who was a thorough sportsman and an excellent hunter. It was while I was out with the Earl, that a Chicago party—friends of General Sheridan—arrived at Fort McPherson for the purpose of going out on a hunt. They, too, had a letter from the General requesting me to go with them. The Earl had not yet finished his hunt, but as I had been out with him for several weeks, and he had by this time learned where to find plenty of elks and other game, I concluded to leave him and accompany the Chicago party. I informed him of my intention and gave him my reasons for going, at the same time telling him that I would send him one of my scouts, Texas Jack, who was a good hunter, and would be glad to accompany him. The Earl seemed to be somewhat offended at this, and I don't think he has ever forgiven me for "going back on him." Let that be as it may, he found Texas Jack a splendid hunter and guide, and Jack has been his guide on several hunts since.

Among the gentlemen who composed the Chicago party were E. P. Green,—son-in-law of Remington, the rifle manufacturer,—Alexander Sample, Mr. Milligan, of the firm of Heath & Milligan, of Chicago, and several others, whose names I do not now remember. Mr. Milligan was a man full of life, and was continually "boiling over with fun." He was a regular velocipede,[3] so to speak, and was here, there, and everywhere. He was exceedingly desirous of having an Indian fight on the trip, not that he was naturally a blood-thirsty man but just for variety he wanted a little "Indian pie." He was in every respect the life of the party, during the entire time that we were out.

One day while he was hunting with Sample and myself we came in sight of a band of thirty mounted Indians.

"Milligan, here's what you've been wanting for some time," said I, "for yonder is a war party of Indians and no mistake; and they'll come for us, you bet."

"I don't believe this is one of my fighting days," replied Milligan, "and it occurs to me that I have urgent business at the camp."

Our camp was five or six miles distant on the Dismal river, and our escort consisted of a company of cavalry commanded by Captain Russell. The soldiers were in camp, and Milligan thought that Captain Russell ought to be at once notified of the appearance of these Indians. Knowing that we could reach the camp in safety, for we were well mounted, I continued to have considerable amusement at Milligan's expense, who finally said:

"Cody, what's making my hat raise up so. I can hardly keep it on my head."

Sample, who was as cool as a cucumber, said to Milligan: "There must be something wrong with your hair. It must be trying to get on end."

"It's all very fine for you fellows to stand here and talk," replied Milligan, "but I am not doing justice to my family by remaining. Sample, I think we are a couple of old fools to have come out here, and I never would have done so if it had not been for you."

By this time the Indians had discovered us and were holding a consultation, and Milligan turned his horse in the direction of the camp. I never believed that he was half as scared as he seemed to be, but that he was merely pretending so that we could enjoy our joke. However, we did not wait any longer but rode into camp and notified Captain Russell, who immediately started with his company to pursue the band.

While we were riding along with the company Milligan said to Sample: "Now, Alick, let them come on. We may yet go back to Chicago covered with glory."

We struck the trail going north, but as we had not come out on a scout for Indians, we concluded not to follow them; although Milligan was now very anxious to proceed and clean them out.

The hunt came to an end in a day or two, and we escorted the visiting hunters to North Platte, where they took the train for Chicago. Before their departure they extended to me a very cordial invitation to come to their city on a visit, promising that I should be well taken care of.

Soon after this I had the pleasure of guiding a party of gentlemen from Omaha on a buffalo hunt. Among the number were Judge Dundy,[4] Colonel Watson B. Smith, and U.S. District Attorney Neville. We left Fort McPherson in good trim. I was greatly amused at the "style" of Mr. Neville, who wore a stove-pipe hat and a swallow-tail coat, which made up a very comical rig for a buffalo hunter. As we galloped over the prairie, he jammed his hat down over his ears to keep it from being shaken off his head, and in order to stick to his horse, he clung to the pommel of his saddle. He was not much of a rider, and he went bouncing up and down, with his swallow-tails flopping in the air. The sight I shall never forget, for it was enough to make a "horse laugh," and I actually believe old Buckskin Joe did laugh.

However, we had a splendid hunt, and on the second

day I lariated, or roped, a big buffalo bull and tied him to a tree,—a feat which I had often performed, and which the gentlemen requested me to do on this occasion for their benefit, as they had heard of my skill with the lariat. I captured several other buffaloes in the same way. The gentlemen returned to Omaha well pleased with their hunt.

In the fall of the year, 1872, a convention was held at Grand Island, when some of my friends made me their candidate to represent the Twenty-sixth District in the legislature of Nebraska; but as I had always been a Democrat and the State was largely Republican, I had no idea of being elected. In fact I cared very little about it, and therefore made no effort whatever to secure an election. However, I was elected and that is the way in which I acquired my title of Honorable.[5]

CHAPTER XXVIII

An Actor

During the summer and fall of 1872, I received numerous letters from Ned Buntline, urging me to come East and go upon the stage to represent my own character. "There's money in it," he wrote, "and you will prove a big card, as your character is a novelty on the stage."

At times I almost determined to make the venture; but the recollection of that night when I stood on the stage of the Bowery Theatre and was unable to utter a word above a whisper, would cause me to stop and think and become irresolute. I feared that I would be a total failure, and wrote Buntline to that effect. But he insisted that I would soon get over all that embarrassment, and become accustomed to the stage, so that I would think no more of appearing before five thousand people than I would before half a dozen. He proposed to organize a good company, and wished me to meet him in Chicago, where the opening performance would be given.

I remained undecided as to what I ought to do. The officers at the fort as well as my family and friends to whom I had mentioned the matter, laughed at the idea of my ever becoming an actor. That I, an old scout who had never seen more than twenty or thirty theatrical performances in my life, should think of going upon the stage, was ridiculous in the extreme—so they all said.

A few days after my election to the legislature a happy event occurred in my family circle, in the birth of a daughter whom we named Orra;[1] about the same time I received another letter from Buntline, in which he requested me to appear on the stage for a few months as an experiment; and he said that if I made a failure or did not like the business, I could easily return to my old life.

My two sisters who had been living with us had married,—Nellie, to A. C. Jester, a cattle man, and May, to Ed. Bradford, a railroad engineer—and consequently left us; and my wife had been wishing for a long time to visit her parents in St. Louis. Taking these and other things into consideration I finally resolved to resign my seat in the legislature and try my luck behind the footlights. I informed General Reynolds of my determination, telling him at the same time that at the end of the month, November, I would resign my position under him. The General regretted to hear this, and advised me not to take the step, for I was leaving a comfortable little home, where I was sure of making a good living for my family; while, on the other hand, I was embarking upon a sea of uncertainty. Having once made up my mind, however, nothing could change it.

While I was selling my horses and other effects, preparatory to leaving the fort, one of my brother scouts, Texas Jack, said that he would like to accompany me. Now as Jack had also appeared as the hero in one of Ned Buntline's stories, I thought that he would make as good a "star" as myself, and it was accordingly arranged that Jack should go with me. On our way East we stopped in Omaha a day or two to visit General Augur and other officers, and also the gentlemen who were out on the Judge Dundy hunt. Judge Dundy and his friends gave a dinner party in my honor at the leading restaurant and entertained me very handsomely during my stay in the city.

At Omaha I parted with my family, who went to St. Louis, while Jack and myself proceeded to Chicago. Ned Buntline and Mr. Milligan, having been apprised of our coming by a telegram, met us at the dépôt. Mr. Milligan accompanied us to the Sherman House, where he had made arrangements for us to be his guests while we remained in the city. I didn't see much of Buntline that evening, as he hurried off to deliver a temperance lecture in one of the public halls. The next day we met him by appointment, and the first thing he said, was:

"Boys, are you ready for business?"

"I can't answer that," replied I, "for we don't know what we are going to do."

"It's all arranged," said he, "and you'll have no trouble whatever. Come with me. We'll go and see Nixon, manager of the Amphitheatre. That's the place where we are to play. We'll open there next Monday night." Jack and myself accordingly accompanied him to manager Nixon's office without saying a word, as we didn't know what to say.

"Here we are, Mr. Nixon," said Buntline; "here are the stars for you. Here are the boys; and they are a fine pair to draw too. Now, Nixon, I am prepared for business."

Nixon and Buntline had evidently had a talk about the terms of our engagement. Buntline, it seems, was to furnish the company, the drama, and the pictorial printing, and was to receive sixty per cent. of the gross receipts for his share; while Nixon was to furnish the theater, the *attachés*, the orchestra, and the local printing; and receive forty per cent. of the gross receipts.

"I am ready for you, Buntline. Have you got your company yet?" asked Nixon.

"No, sir; but there are plenty of idle theatrical people in town, and I can raise a company in two hours," was his reply.

"You haven't much time to spare, if you open on Monday night," said Nixon. "If you will allow me to look at your drama, to see what kind of people you want, I'll assist you in organizing your company."

"I have not yet written the drama," said Buntline.

"What the deuce do you mean? This is Wednesday, and you propose to open on next Monday night. The idea is ridiculous. Here you are at this late hour without a company and without a drama. This will never do, Buntline. I shall have to break my contract with you, for you can't possibly write a drama, cast it, and rehearse it properly for Monday night. Furthermore, you have no pictorial printing as yet. These two gentlemen, whom you have with you, have never been on the stage, and they certainly must have time to study their parts. It is preposterous to think of opening on Monday night, and I'll cancel the engagement."

This little speech was delivered in rather an excited manner by Mr. Nixon. Buntline said that he would write the drama that day and also select his company and have them at the theater for rehearsal next morning. Nixon laughed at him, and said that there was no use of trying to undertake anything of the kind in so short a time—it was utterly impossible to do it. Buntline, whose ire was rising, said to Nixon:

"What rent will you ask for your theater for next week?"

"Six hundred dollars," was the reply.

"Well, sir, I'll take your theater for next week at that price, and here is half of the amount in advance," said Buntline, as he threw down three hundred dollars on the stand.

Nixon took the money, gave a receipt for it, and had nothing more to say.

"Now, come with me boys," said Buntline; and away we went to the hotel. Buntline immediately obtained a supply of pens, ink and paper, and then engaged all the hotel clerks as penmen. In less than an hour after he had rented the theater, he was dashing off page after page of his proposed drama—the work being done in his room at the hotel. He then set his clerks at copying for him, and at the end of four hours, he jumped up from the table, and enthusiastically shouted:

"Hurrah for 'The Scouts of the Plains!' That's the name of the play. The work is done. Hurrah!"

The parts were then all copied off separately by the clerks, and handing us our respective portions Buntline said:

"Now, boys, go to work, and do your level best to have this dead-letter perfect for the rehearsal, which takes place to-morrow morning at ten o'clock, prompt. I want to show Nixon that we'll be ready on time."

I looked at my part and then at Jack; and Jack looked at his part and then at me. Then we looked at each other, and then at Buntline. We did not know what to make of the man.

"How long will it take you to commit your part to memory, Bill?" asked Jack.

"About six months, as near as I can calculate. How long will it take you?" answered I.

78. Studying the Parts

"It will take me about that length of time to learn the first line," said Jack. Nevertheless we went to our room and commenced studying. I thought it was the hardest work I had ever done.

"This is dry business," finally remarked Jack.

"That's just what it is," I answered; "jerk the bell, Jack." The bell-boy soon appeared. We ordered refreshments; after partaking thereof we resumed our task. We studied hard for an hour or two, but finally gave it up as a bad job, although we had succeeded in committing a small portion to memory. Buntline now came into the room and said:

"Boys, how are you getting along?"

"I guess we'll have to go back on this studying business as it isn't our *forte*," said I.

"Don't weaken now, Bill; you'll come out on the top of the heap yet. Let me hear you recite your part," said Buntline. I began "spouting" what I had learned, but was interrupted by Buntline:

"Tut! tut! you're not saying it right. You must stop at the cue."

"Cue! What the mischief do you mean by the cue? I never saw any cue except in a billiard room," said I. Buntline thereupon explained it to me, as well as to Jack, who was ignorant as myself concerning the "cue" business.

"Jack, I think we had better back out and go to hunting again," said I.

"See here, boys; it won't do to go back on me at this stage of the game. Stick to it, and it may be the turning point in your lives and lead you on to fortune and to fame."

"A fortune is what we are after, and we'll at least give the wheel a turn or two and see what luck we have," said I.

79. Behind the Footlights

This satisfied Buntline, but we didn't study any more after he left us. The next morning we appeared at rehearsal and were introduced to the company. The first rehearsal was hardly a success; and the succeeding ones were not much better. The stage manager did his best to teach Jack and myself what to do, but when Monday night came we didn't know much more about it than when we began.

The clock struck seven, and then we put on our buckskin suits, which were the costumes we were to appear in. The theater was being rapidly filled, and it was evident that we were going to make our *début* before a packed house. As the minutes passed by, Jack and I became more and more nervous. We occasionally looked through the holes in the curtain, and saw that the people were continuing to crowd into the theatre; our nervousness increased to an uncomfortable degree.

When at length the curtain arose, our courage had returned, so that we thought we could face the immense crowd; yet when the time came for us to go on, we were rather slow in making our appearance. As we stepped forth we were received with a storm of applause, which we acknowledged with a bow.

Buntline, who was taking the part of "Cale Durg," appeared, and gave me the "cue" to speak "my little piece," but for the life of me I could not remember a single word. Buntline saw I was "stuck," and a happy thought occurred to him. He said—as if it were in the play:

"Where have you been, Bill? What has kept you so long?"

Just then my eye happened to fall on Mr. Milligan, who was surrounded by his friends, the newspaper reporters, and several military officers, all of whom had heard of his hunt and "Indian fight"—he being a very popular man, and widely known in Chicago. So I said:

"I have been out on a hunt with Milligan."

This proved to be a big hit. The audience cheered and applauded; which gave me greater confidence in my ability to get through the performance all right. Buntline, who is a very versatile man, saw that it would be a good plan to follow this up, and he said:

"Well, Bill, tell us all about the hunt."

I thereupon proceeded to relate in detail the particulars of the affair. I succeeded in making it rather funny, and I was frequently interrupted by rounds of applause. Whenever I began to "weaken," Buntline would give me a fresh start, by asking some question. In this way I took up fifteen minutes, without once speaking a word of my part; nor did I speak a word of it during the whole evening. The prompter, who was standing between the wings, attempted to prompt me, but it did no good; for while I was on the stage I "chipped in" anything I thought of.

"The Scouts of the Plains" was an Indian drama, of course; and there were between forty and fifty "supers"[2] dressed as Indians. In the fight with them, Jack and I were at home. We blazed away at each other with blank cartridges; and when the scene ended in a hand-to-hand encounter—a general knock-down and drag-out—the way Jack and I killed Indians was "a caution." We would kill them all off in one act, but they would come up again ready for business in the next. Finally the curtain dropped; the play was ended; and I congratulated Jack and myself on having made such a brilliant and successful *début*. There was no backing out after that.

The next morning there appeared in the Chicago papers some very funny criticisms on our first performance. The papers gave us a better send-off than I expected, for they did not criticise us as actors. The *Chicago Times* said that if Buntline had actually spent four hours in writing that play, it was difficult for any one to see what he had been doing all the time. Buntline, as "Cale Durg," was killed in the second act, after a long temperance speech; and the *Inter-Ocean* said that it was to be regretted that he had not been killed in the first act. The company, however, was very good, and Mdlle. Morlacchi, as "Pale Dove," particularly fine; while Miss Cafarno "spouted" a poem of some seven hundred and three verses, more or less, of which the reader will be glad to know that I only recall the words "I was born in March."

Our engagement proved a decided success financially, if not artistically. Nixon was greatly surprised at the result, and at the end of the week he induced Buntline to take him in as a partner in the company.

The next week we played at DeBar's Opera House, in St. Louis, doing an immense business. The following week we were at Cincinnati, where the theater was so crowded every night that hundreds were unable to obtain admission. We met with equal success all over the country. Theatrical managers, upon hearing of this new and novel combination; which was drawing such tremendous houses, were all anxious to secure us; and we received offers of engagements at all the leading theaters. We played one week at the Boston Theater, and the gross receipts amounted to $16,200. We also appeared at Niblo's Garden, New York, the theater being crowded to its utmost capacity every night of the engagement.[3] At the Arch Street Theater, Philadelphia, it was the same way. There was not a single city where we did not have crowded houses.

We closed our tour on the 16th of June, 1873, at Port Jervis, New York, and when I counted up my share of the profits I found that I was only about $6,000 ahead. I was somewhat disappointed, for, judging from our large business, I certainly had expected a greater sum.

Texas Jack and myself longed for a hunt on the Western prairies once more; and on meeting in New York a party of gentlemen who were desirous of going with us, we all started Westward, and after a pleasant trip arrived at Fort McPherson.

CHAPTER XXIX

Starring

Texas Jack and I spent several weeks in hunting in the western part of Nebraska, and at the end of our vacation we felt greatly re-invigorated and ready for another theatrical campaign. We accordingly proceeded to New York and organized a company for the season of 1873–74. Thinking that Wild Bill would be quite an acquisition to the troupe, we wrote to him at Springfield, Missouri, offering him a large salary if he would play with us that winter. He was doing nothing at the time, and we thought that he would like to take a trip through the States, as he had never been East.

Wild Bill accepted our offer, and came on to New York; though he told us from the start that we could never make an actor out of him. Although he had a fine stage appearance and was a handsome fellow, and possessed a good strong voice, yet when he went upon the stage before an audience, it was almost impossible for him to utter a word. He insisted that we were making a set of fools of ourselves, and that we were the laughing-stock of the people. I replied that I did not care for that, as long as they came and bought tickets to see us.

Wild Bill was continually playing tricks upon the members of the company, and it was his especial delight to torment the "supers." Quite frequently in our sham Indian battles he would run up to the "Indians" (the supers), and putting his pistol close to their legs, would fire at them and burn them with the powder, instead of shooting over their heads. This would make them dance and jump, so that it was difficult to make them fall and die—although they were paid twenty-five cents each for performing the "dying business." The poor "supers" often complained to me about this, and threatened not to go on the stage and be killed again if that man Wild Bill did not stop shooting and burning their legs. I would order Wild Bill to stop his mischief; he would laugh and then promise not to do it any more. But it would not be long before he was at his old tricks again.

My company, known as the "Buffalo Bill Combination," did a fine business, all through the East. Wild Bill continued his pranks, which caused us considerable annoyance, but at the same time greatly amused us.

One day at Titusville, Pennsylvania, while Burke, the business agent,[1] was registering our names and making arrangements for our accommodation, several of us started for the billiard room; but were met by the landlord, who stopped me and said that there was a party of roughs from the lower oil region who were spreeing, and had boasted that they were staying in town to meet the Buffalo Bill gang and clean them out. The landlord begged of me not to allow the members of the troupe to enter the billiard room, as he did not wish any fight in his house. To please the landlord, and at his suggestion, I called the boys up into the parlor and explained to them the situation. Wild Bill wanted to go at once and fight the whole mob, but I persuaded him to keep away from them during the day.

In order to entirely avoid the roughs, the members of the company entered the theater through a private door from the hotel, as the two buildings joined each other. While I was standing at the door of the theater taking the tickets, the landlord of the hotel came rushing up and said that Wild Bill was having a fight with the roughs in the bar-room. It seemed that Bill had not been able to resist the temptation of going to see what kind of a mob it was that wanted to test the pluck of the Buffalo Bill party; and just as he stepped into the room, one of the bruisers put his hand on his shoulder and said:

"Hello, Buffalo Bill! we have been looking for you all day."

"My name is not Buffalo Bill; you are mistaken in the man," was the reply.

"You are a liar!" said the bruiser.

Bill instantly knocked him down, and then seizing a chair he laid out four or five of the crowd on the floor, and drove the rest out of the room. All this was done in a minute or two, and by the time I got down stairs, Bill was coming out of the bar-room, whistling a lively tune.

"Well!" said he, "I have been interviewing that party who wanted to clean us out."

"I thought you promised to come into the Opera House by the private entrance?"

"I did try to follow that trail, but I got lost among the cañons, and then I ran in among the hostiles," said he; "but it is all right now. They won't bother us any more. I guess those fellows have found us." And sure enough they had. We heard no more of them after that.

80. Learning the Game

Another incident occurred, one night, at Portland, Maine. Bill found it impossible to go to sleep at the hotel on account of the continued talking of some parties who were engaged in a game of cards in an adjoining room. He called to them several times to make less noise, but they paid little or no attention to him. He finally got up and went to the room with the intention of cleaning out the whole crowd. He knocked and was admitted; greatly to his surprise, he found the party to be some merchants of the city, whom he had met the previous day. They were playing poker, and invited him to take a hand. Bill sat down at the table, and said that, inasmuch as they would not let him sleep, he wouldn't mind playing for a while, provided they would post him a little in the game, for he didn't know much about it. At first he didn't play very well, intentionally making many blunders and asking numerous questions; but when morning came, he was about seven hundred dollars ahead. Bill put the money in his pocket, and just as he was leaving the room he advised them never to wake a man up and invite him to play poker.

Wild Bill remained with me until we reached Rochester. I met my family there, and having bought some property in that city, with the intention of making the place my home, I asked Bill not to cut up any of his capers, for I wanted the performance to go off smoothly, as I expected a large audience that evening. He, of course, promised to behave himself. When the curtain rose the house was crowded. The play proceeded finely until the Indian fight in the second act, when Bill amused himself by his old trick of singeing the legs of the "supers."

After the curtain dropped, the "supers" complained to me about it. Bill's conduct made me angry, and I told him that he must either stop shooting the "supers," or leave the company. He made no reply, but went to the dressing-room and changed his buckskin suit for his citizen's dress, and during one of my scenes I looked down in front and saw him elbowing his way through the audience and out of the theater. When I had finished the scene, and had retired from the stage, the stage-carpenter came up and said:

"That long-haired gentleman, who passed out a few minutes ago, requested me to tell you that you could go to thunder with your old show."

That was the last time that Wild Bill and I ever performed together on the stage. After the evening's entertainment I met him at the Osborn House. By this time he had

81. Getting Satisfaction

recovered from his mad fit and was in as good humor as ever. He had made up his mind to leave for the West the next day. I endeavored to persuade him to remain with me till spring, and then we would go together; but it was of no use. I then paid him the money due him, and Jack and myself made him a present of $1,000 besides.

Bill went to New York the next day, intending to start west from there. Several days afterwards I learned that he had lost all his money in New York by playing faro;[2] also that a theatrical manager had engaged him to play. A company was organized and started out, but as a "star" Wild Bill was not a success; the further he went the poorer he got. This didn't suit Bill by any means, and he accordingly retired from the stage. The company, however, kept on the road, using Bill's name, and employing an actor to represent him not only on the stage but on the street and elsewhere. Bill heard of this deception and sent word to the manager to stop it, but no attention was paid to his message.

Finally, Bill resolved to have satisfaction and he proceeded to a town where the company was to play; he entered the theater and took a seat near the stage, and watched the performance until the bogus Wild Bill appeared. He then sprang upon the stage, knocked the actor clear through one of the scenes, and grabbing the manager by the shoulders he threw him over the foot-lights into the orchestra.

The other actors screamed and yelled "Police!" The audience could not at first understand what it all meant, some of them supposing the affair to be a part of the play.

Wild Bill retired from the stage in good order, resumed his seat, and told them to go on with their show. A policeman now appearing, Bill was pointed out as the disturber of the peace; the officer tapping him on the shoulder, said:

"I'll have to arrest you, sir."

"How many of you are there?" asked Bill.

"Only myself," said the policeman.

"You had better get some help," said Bill. The officer then called up another policeman, and Bill again asked:

"How many of you are there now?"

"Two," was the reply.

"Then I advise you to go out and get some more reinforcements," said Bill, very coolly.

The policemen thereupon spoke to the sheriff, who was dressed in citizen's clothes. The sheriff came up and said he would have to take him into custody.

"All right, sir," replied Bill, "I have no objections to walking out with you, but I won't go with any two police-men." At the court next morning Bill stated his reasons for having acted as he had done, and the judge fined him only three dollars and costs.

This was the last time that Wild Bill appeared on the stage. He shortly afterwards returned to the West, and on arriving at Cheyenne, he visited Boulder's gambling room and sat down at a faro table. No one in the room recognized him, as he had not been in Cheyenne for sev-eral years. After losing two or three bets he threw down a fifty dollar bill and lost that also. Boulder quietly raked in the money. Bill placed a second fifty dollar note on another card, when Boulder informed him that the limit was twenty-five dollars.

"You have just taken in a fifty dollar bill which I lost," said Bill.

"Well you needn't make any more such bets, as I will not go above my limit," replied Boulder.

"I'll just play that fifty dollar bill as it lays. If it loses, it's yours; if it wins, you'll pay me fifty dollars, or I'll know the reason why."

"I am running this game, and I want no talk from you, sir," said Boulder.

One word brought on another, until Boulder threat-ened to have Bill put out of the house. Bill was carrying the butt end of a billiard cue for a cane, and bending over the table, he said: "You'd rob a blind man." Then he sud-denly tapped Boulder on the head with the cane, with such force as to knock him over. With another sweep of the cane he tumbled the "look-out" from his chair, and then reaching over into the money drawer he grabbed a handful of greenbacks and stuck them in his pocket.

At this stage of the game four or five men—who were employed as "bouncers" for the establishment to throw out the noisy persons—rushed up to capture Bill, but he knocked them right and left with his cane, and seeing the whole crowd was now closing in on him, he jumped into a corner, and with each hand drew a revolver and faced the enemy. At this moment the bar-keeper recognized him, and sang out in a loud voice:

"Look out boys—that's Wild Bill you've run against."

That settled the matter; for when they heard the name of Wild Bill they turned and beat a hasty retreat out of the doors and windows, and in less time than it takes to tell it, Wild Bill was the only man in the room. He coolly walked over to Dyer's hotel, and retired for the night. Boulder claimed that he had taken $500, but he really got only $200. Boulder, upon learning that it was Wild Bill who had cleaned him out, said nothing more about the money. The next day the two men met over a bottle of wine, and settled their differences in an amicable manner.

Poor Bill was afterwards killed at Deadwood, in the Black Hills, in a cowardly manner, by a desperado who sneaked up behind him while he was playing a game of cards in a saloon, and shot him through the back of the head, without the least provocation. The murderer, Jack McCall, was tried and hung at Yankton, Dakotah, for the crime. Thus ended the career of a life-long friend of mine who, in spite of his many faults, was a noble man, ever brave and generous hearted.[3]

Jack and myself continued playing through the country

after Wild Bill left us, and we finally closed our season in Boston on the 13th of May, 1874.

Business called me from Boston to New York, and after I had been there a few days, I met an English gentleman, Thomas P. Medley, of London, who had come to America for a hunt on the Plains. He had often heard of me, and was anxious to engage me as his guide and companion, and he offered to pay the liberal salary of one thousand dollars a month while I was with him. He was a very wealthy man, as I learned upon inquiry, and was a relative of Mr. Lord, of the firm of Lord & Taylor, of New York. Of course I accepted his offer.

When we reached the hunting ground in Nebraska, he informed me, somewhat to my surprise, that he did not want to go out as Alexis did, with carriages, servants, and other luxuries, but that he wished to rough it just as I would do—to sleep on the ground in the open air, and kill and cook his own meat. We started out from North Platte, and spent several weeks in hunting all over the county. Dr. W. F. Carver,[4] who then resided at North Platte, and who has recently acquired considerable notoriety as a rifle-shot, hunted with us for a few days.

Mr. Medley proved to be a very agreeable gentleman and an excellent hunter. While in camp he busied himself in carrying wood and water, attending to the fire, and preparing and cooking the meals, never asking me to do a thing. He did not do this to save expenses, but because he wanted to do as the other hunters in the party were doing. After spending as much time as he wished, we returned to the railroad, and he took the train for the East. Everything that was required on this hunt was paid for in the most liberal manner by Mr. Medley, who also gave the members of the party several handsome presents.

About this time an expedition consisting of seven companies of cavalry and two companies of infantry—to be commanded by Colonel Mills of the Third Cavalry, was being organized to scout the Powder River and Big Horn country, and I was employed as guide for the command. Proceeding to Rawlins, Wyoming, we "outfitted," and other guides were engaged—among them Tom Sun and Bony Ernest, two noted Rocky Mountain scouts. We there left the railroad, and passing through the Seminole range of the Rocky Mountains we established our supply camp at the foot of Independence Rock on the Sweetwater. I was now on my old familiar stamping ground, and it seemed like home to me. Fifteen years before, I had ridden the pony express and driven the overland stages through this region, and the command was going into the same section of country where Wild Bill's expedition of stage-drivers and express-riders had recaptured from the Indians a large number of stolen stage-horses.

Leaving the infantry to guard the supply camp, Colonel Mills struck out for the north with the seven companies of cavalry. One day while we were resting on a prairie near the head of Powder river, a horseman was seen in the distance approaching us. At first it was thought he was an Indian, but as he came near we saw that he was a white man, and finally when he rode up to us, I recognized him as "California Joe,"[5] a noted scout and frontiersman who had spent many years in California, on the plains and in the mountains. He was armed with a heavy old Sharps rifle,[6] a revolver and a knife. I introduced him to Colonel

Mills and the other officers and asked him where he was going. He replied that he was out for a morning ride only; but the fact was that he had been out prospecting alone for weeks along the foot of the Big Horn mountains.

Having no permanent occupation just at that time, Joe accompanied us for two or three days, when Colonel Mills suggested that I had better employ him as a scout, so that he could make a little money for himself. Joe didn't seem to care whether I hired him or not; but I put him on the pay-roll, and while he was with us he drew his five dollars a day. It was worth the money to have him along for company's sake, for he was a droll character in his way, and afforded us considerable amusement. We finally surprised Little Wolf's[7] band of Arapahoes[8] and drove them into the agencies. We then scouted the Powder river, Crazy Woman's Fork, and Clear Fork, and then pushed westward through the mountains to the Wind river. After having been out for a month or two we were ordered to return.

I immediately went East and organized another Dramatic company for the season of 1874–75, Texas Jack being absent in the Yellowstone country hunting with the Earl of Dunraven. I played my company in all the principal cities of the country, doing a good business wherever I went. The summer of 1875 I spent at Rochester with my family.

For the season of 1875–6, Texas Jack and I reorganized our old Combination, and made a very successful tour. While we were playing at Springfield, Massachusetts, April 20th and 21st 1876, a telegram was handed me just as I was going on the stage. I opened it and found it to be from Colonel G. W. Torrence, of Rochester, an intimate friend of the family, who stated that my little boy Kit was dangerously ill with the scarlet fever. This was indeed sad news, for little Kit had always been my greatest pride. I sent for John Burke, our business manager, and showing him the telegram, told him that I would play the first act, and making a proper excuse to the audience, I would then take the nine o'clock train that same evening for Rochester, leaving him to play out my part. This I did, and at ten o'clock the next morning I arrived in Rochester, and was met at the dépôt by my intimate friend Moses Kerngood who at once drove me to my home. I found my little boy unable to speak but he seemed to recognize me and putting his little arms around my neck he tried to kiss me. We did everything in our power to save him, but it was of no avail. The Lord claimed his own, and that evening at six o'clock my beloved little Kit died in my arms. We laid him away to rest in the beautiful cemetery of Mount Hope amid sorrow and tears.

CHAPTER XXX

A Return to the Plains

We closed our theatrical season earlier than usual in the spring of 1876, because I was anxious to take part in the Sioux war which was then breaking out. Colonel Hills had written me several letters saying that General Crook[1] was anxious to have me accompany his command, and I promised to do so, intending to overtake him in the Powder river country. But when I arrived at Chicago, on my way West, I learned that my old regiment, the gallant Fifth Cavalry, was on its way back from Arizona to join General Crook, and that my old commander, General Carr, was in command. He had written to military headquarters at Chicago to learn my whereabouts, as he wished to secure me as his guide and chief of scouts. I then gave up the idea of overtaking General Crook, and hastening on to Cheyenne, where the Fifth Cavalry had already arrived, I was met at the dépôt by Lieutenant King, adjutant of the regiment, he having been sent down from Fort D. A. Russell for that purpose by General Carr, who had learned by a telegram from military headquarters at Chicago that I was on the way. I accompanied the Lieutenant on horseback to the camp, and as we rode up, one of the boys shouted, "Here's Buffalo Bill!" Soon after there came three hearty cheers from the regiment. Officers and men all were glad to see me, and I was equally delighted to meet them once more. The General at once appointed me his guide and chief of scouts.

The next morning the command pulled out for Fort Laramie, and on reaching that post we found General Sheridan there, accompanied by General Frye and General Forsyth, *en route* to Red Cloud Agency.[2] As the command was to remain here a few days, I accompanied General Sheridan to Red Cloud and back, taking a company of cavalry as escort.

The Indians having recently committed a great many depredations on the Black Hills road, the Fifth Cavalry was sent out to scout the country between the Indian agencies and the hills. The command operated on the South Fork of the Cheyenne and at the foot of the Black Hills for about two weeks, having several small engagements with roving bands of Indians during the time. General Wesley Merritt[3]—who had lately received his promotion to the Colonelcy of the Fifth Cavalry—now came out and took control of the regiment.

I was sorry that the command was taken from General Carr, because under him it had made its fighting reputation. However, upon becoming acquainted with General Merritt, I found him to be an excellent officer.

The regiment, by continued scouting, soon drove the Indians out of that section of the country, as we supposed, and we had started on our way back to Fort Laramie, when a scout arrived at the camp and reported the massacre of General Custer and his band of heroes on the Little Big Horn, on the 25th of June, 1876;[4] and he also brought orders to General Merritt to proceed at once to Fort Fetterman and join General Crook in the Big Horn country.

Colonel Stanton, who was with the Fifth Cavalry on this scout, had been sent to Red Cloud agency two days before, and that same evening a scout arrived bringing a message from him that eight hundred Cheyenne warriors had that day left the Red Cloud Agency to join Sitting Bull's hostile forces in the Big Horn region. Notwithstanding the instructions to proceed immediately to join General Crook by the Way of Fort Fetterman, Colonel Merritt took the responsibility of endeavoring to intercept the Cheyennes, and as the sequel shows he performed a very important service.

He selected five hundred men and horses, and in two hours we were making a forced march back to Hat, or War-Bonnet Creek—the intention being to reach the main Indian trail running to the north across that creek before the Cheyennes could get there. We arrived there the next night, and at daylight the following morning, July 17th, 1876, I went out on a scout, and found that the Indians had not yet crossed the creek. On my way back to the command I discovered a large party of Indians, which proved to be the Cheyennes, coming up from the south, and I hurried to the camp with this important information.

The cavalrymen quietly mounted their horses, and were ordered to remain out of sight, while General Merritt, accompanied by two or three *aides*[5] and myself, went out on a little tour of observation to a neighboring hill, from the summit of which we saw that the Indians were approaching almost directly towards us. Presently fifteen or twenty of them dashed off to the west in the direction from which we had come the night before; and upon closer observation with our field glasses, we discovered two mounted soldiers, evidently carrying dispatches for us, pushing forward on our trail.

The Indians were evidently endeavoring to intercept these two men, and General Merritt feared that they would accomplish their object. He did not think it advisable to send out any soldiers to the assistance of the couriers, for fear that would show to the Indians that there were troops in the vicinity who were waiting for them. I finally suggested that the best plan was to wait until the couriers came closer to the command, and then, just as the Indians were about to charge, to let me take the scouts and cut them off from the main body of the Cheyennes, who were coming over the divide.

"All right, Cody," said the General, "if you can do that, go ahead."

I rushed back to the command, jumped on my horse, picked out fifteen men, and returned with them to the point of observation. I told General Merritt to give us the word to start out at the proper time, and presently he sang out:

"Go in now, Cody, and be quick about it. They are going to charge on the couriers."

The two messengers were not over four hundred yards from us, and the Indians were only about two hundred yards behind them. We instantly dashed over the bluffs, and advanced on a gallop towards the Indians. A running fight lasted several minutes, during which we drove the enemy some little distance and killed three of their number. The rest of them rode off towards the main body, which had come into plain sight, and halted, upon seeing the skirmish that was going on. We were about half a mile from General Merritt, and the Indians whom we were chasing suddenly turned upon us, and another lively skirmish took place. One of the Indians, who was handsomely decorated with all the ornaments usually worn by a war chief when engaged in a fight, sang out to me, in his own tongue:

"I know you, Pa-he-haska; if you want to fight, come ahead and fight me."

The chief was riding his horse back and forth in front of his men, as if to banter me, and I concluded to accept the challenge. I galloped towards him for fifty yards and he advanced towards me about the same distance, both of us riding at full speed, and then, when we were only about thirty yards apart, I raised my rifle and fired; his horse fell to the ground, having been killed by my bullet.

Almost at the same instant my own horse went down, he having stepped into a hole. The fall did not hurt me much, and I instantly sprang to my feet. The Indian had also recovered himself, and we were now both on foot, and not more than twenty paces apart. We fired at each other simultaneously. My usual luck did not desert me on this occasion, for his bullet missed me, while mine struck him in the breast. He reeled and fell, but before he had fairly touched the ground I was upon him, knife in hand, and had driven the keen-edged weapon to its hilt in his heart. Jerking his war-bonnet off, I scientifically scalped him in about five seconds.

The whole affair from beginning to end occupied but little time, and the Indians, seeing that I was some little distance from my company, now came charging down upon me from a hill, in hopes of cutting me off. General Merritt had witnessed the duel, and realizing the danger I

82. A Duel with Chief Yellow Hand

was in, ordered Colonel Mason with Company K to hurry to my rescue. The order came none too soon, for had it been given one minute later I would have had not less than two hundred Indians upon me. As the soldiers came up I swung the Indian chieftain's top-knot and bonnet in the air, and shouted: *"The first scalp for Custer."*

General Merritt, seeing that he could not now ambush the Indians, ordered the whole regiment to charge upon them. They made a stubborn resistance for a little while, but it was of no use for any eight hundred, or even sixteen hundred Indians to try and check a charge of the gallant old Fifth Cavalry, and they soon came to that conclusion and began a running retreat towards Red Cloud Agency. For thirty-five miles we drove them; pushing them so hard that they were obliged to abandon their loose horses, their camp equipage and everything else. We drove them into the agency, and followed in ourselves, notwithstanding the possibility of our having to encounter the thousands of Indians at that point. We were uncertain whether or not the other agency Indians had determined to follow the example of the Cheyennes and strike out upon the warpath; but that made no difference with the Fifth Cavalry, for they would have fought them all if necessary. It was dark when we rode into the agency, where we found thousands of Indians collected together; but they manifested no disposition to fight.

While at the agency I learned the name of the Indian Chief whom I had killed in the morning; it was Yellow Hand;[6] a son of old Cut-nose—a leading chief of the Cheyennes. Cut-nose, having learned that I had killed his son sent a white interpreter to me with a message to the effect that he would give me four mules if I would turn over to him Yellow Hand's war-bonnet, guns, pistols, ornaments, and other paraphernalia which I had captured. I sent back word to the old gentleman that it would give me pleasure to accommodate him, but I could not do it this time.

The next morning we started to join General Crook, who was camped near the foot of Cloud Peak in the Big Horn mountains; awaiting the arrival of the Fifth Cavalry, before proceeding against the Sioux, who were somewhere near the head of the Little Big Horn,—as his scouts informed him. We made rapid marches and reached General Crook's camp on Goose Creek about the 3d of August.

At this camp I met many old friends, among whom was Colonel Royall, who had received his promotion to the Lieutenant Colonelcy of the Third Cavalry. He introduced me to General Crook, whom I had never met before, but of whom I had often heard. He also introduced me to the General's chief guide, Frank Grouard, a half breed, who had lived six years with Sitting Bull, and knew the country thoroughly.

We remained in this camp only one day, and then the whole troop pulled out for the Tongue river, leaving our wagons behind, but taking with us a large pack train. We marched down the Tongue river for two days, thence in a westerly direction over to the Rosebud, where we struck the main Indian trail, leading down this stream. From the size of the trail, which appeared to be about four days old, we estimated that there must have been in the neighborhood of seven thousand Indians who had made the broad trail.

At this point we were overtaken by Jack Crawford,[7]

familiarly known as "Captain Jack, the Poet Scout of the Black Hills," and right here I will insert the following lines, written by him, just after the "Custer Massacre," upon receiving from me the following dispatch:

"Jack, old boy, have you heard of the death of Custer?"

Custer's Death

Did I hear the news from Custer?
Well, I reckon I did, old pard;
It came like a streak of lightnin',
And, you bet, it hit me hard.
I ain't no hand to blubber,
And the briny ain't run for years;
But chalk me down for a lubber,
If I didn't shed regular tears.

What for? Now look you here, Bill,
You're a bully boy, that's true;
As good as e'er wore buckskin,
Or fought with the boys in blue;
But I'll bet my bottom dollar
Ye had no trouble to muster
A tear, or perhaps a hundred,
At the news of the death of Custer.

He always thought well of you, pard,
And had it been heaven's will,
In a few more days you'd met him,
And he'd welcome his old scout Bill.
For if ye remember at Hat Creek,
I met ye with General Carr;
We talked of the brave young Custer,
And recounted his deeds of war.

But little we knew even then, pard,
(And that's just two weeks ago),
How little we dreamed of disaster,
Or that he had met the foe—
That the fearless, reckless hero,
So loved by the whole frontier,
Had died on the field of battle
In this, our centennial year.

I served with him in the army,
In the darkest days of the war:
And I reckon ye know his record,
For he was our guiding star;
And the boys who gathered round him
To charge in the early morn,
War just like the brave who perished
With him on the Little Horn.

And where is the satisfaction,
And how will the boys get square?
By giving the reds more rifles?
Invite them to take more hair?
We want no scouts, no trappers,
Nor men who know the frontier;
Phil, old boy, you're mistaken,
We must have the volunteer.

Never mind that two hundred thousand
But give us a hundred instead;
Send five thousand men towards Reno,
And soon we won't leave a red.
It will save Uncle Sam lots of money,

In fortress we need not invest,
Jest wollup the devils this summer,
And the miners will do all the rest.

The Black Hills are filled with miners,
The Big Horn will soon be as full,
And which will show the most danger
To Crazy Horse and old Sitting Bull
A band of ten thousand frontier men,
Or a couple of forts with a few
Of the boys in the East now enlisting—
Friend Cody, I leave it with you.

They talk of peace with these demons
By feeding and clothing them well:
I'd as soon think an angel from Heaven
Would reign with contentment in H—l
And one day the Quakers will answer
Before the great Judge of us all,
For the death of daring young Custer
And the boys who round him did fall.

Perhaps I am judging them harshly,
But I mean what I'm telling ye, pard;
I'm letting them down mighty easy,
Perhaps they may think it is hard.
But I tell you the day is approaching—
The boys are beginning to muster—
That day of the great retribution,
The day of revenge for our Custer.

And I will be with you, friend Cody,
My weight will go in with the boys;

I shared all their hardships last winter,
I shared all their sorrows and joys;
Tell them I'm coming, friend William,
I trust I will meet you ere long;
Regards to the boys in the mountains;
Yours, ever; in friendship still strong.

Jack was a new man in the country, but evidently had plenty of nerve and pluck, as he had brought dispatches from Fort Fetterman, a distance of 300 miles through a dangerous Indian country. The dispatches were for General Crook, and notified him that General Terry was to operate with a large command south of the Yellowstone, and that the two commands would probably consolidate somewhere on the Rosebud.

Jack at once hunted me up and gave me a letter from General Sheridan, informing me that he had appointed him (Jack) as one of the scouts.

While we were conversing, Jack informed me that he had brought me a present from Colonel Jones of Cheyenne, and that he had it in his saddle-pockets. Asking the nature of the gift, he replied that it was only a bottle of good whiskey.

I placed my hand over his mouth and told him to keep still, and not to whisper it even to the winds, for there were too many dry men around us; and only when alone with him did I dare to have him take the treasure from his saddle-pockets.

In this connection I may remark that Jack Crawford is the only man I have ever known that could have brought that bottle of whiskey through without *accident* befalling it, for he is one of the very few teetotal[8] scouts I ever met.

Not wishing to have a game of "whiskey *solitaire*," I invited General Carr to sample the bottle with me. We soon found a secluded spot, and dismounting, we thought we were going to have a nice little drink all by ourselves, when who should ride up but Mr. Lathrop, the reporter of the Associated Press of the Pacific slope—to whom we had given the name of the "Death Rattler,"—and who was also known in San Francisco as "the man with the iron jaw," he having, with the true nose of a reporter, smelt the whiskey from afar off, and had come to "interview" it. He was a good fellow withal, and we were glad to have him join us.

Now to resume: For two or three days we pushed on, but we did not seem to gain much on the Indians, as they were evidently making about the same marches that we were. On the fourth or fifth morning of our pursuit, I rode ahead of the command about ten miles, and mounting a hill I scanned the country far and wide with my field glass, and discovered an immense column of dust rising about ten miles further down the creek, and soon I noticed a body of men marching towards me, that at first I believed to be the Indians of whom we were in pursuit; but subsequently they proved to be General Terry's command. I sent back word to that effect to General Crook, by a scout who had accompanied me, but after he had departed I observed a band of Indians on the opposite side of the creek, and also another party directly in front of me. This led me to believe that I had made a mistake.

But shortly afterwards my attention was attracted by the appearance of a body of soldiers, who were forming into a skirmish line, and then I became convinced that it was General Terry's command after all, and that the red-skins whom I had seen were some of his friendly Indian scouts, who had mistaken me for a Sioux, and fled back to their command terribly excited, shouting, "The Sioux are coming!"

General Terry at once came to the post, and ordered the Seventh Cavalry to form line of battle across the Rosebud; he also ordered up his artillery and had them prepare for action, doubtless dreading another "Custer massacre." I afterwards learned the Indians had seen the dust raised by General Crook's forces, and had reported that the Sioux were coming.

These manoeuvres I witnessed from my position with considerable amusement, thinking the command must be badly demoralized, when one man could cause a whole army to form line of battle and prepare for action. Having enjoyed the situation to my heart's content, I galloped down towards the skirmish line, waving my hat and when within about one hundred yards of the troops, Colonel Weir, of the Seventh Cavalry, galloped out and met me. He recognized me at once, and accompanied me inside the line; then he sang out, "Boys, here's Buffalo Bill. Some of you old soldiers know him; give him a cheer!" Thereupon the regiment gave three rousing cheers, and it was followed up all along the line.

Colonel Weir presented me to General Terry, and in answer to his questions I informed him that the alarm of Indians which had been given was a false one, as the dust seen by his scouts was caused by General Crook's troops. General Terry thereupon rode forward to meet General Crook, and I accompanied him at his request. That night both commands went into camp on the Rosebud. General Terry had his wagon train with him, and everything to make life comfortable on an Indian campaign. He had large wall tents and portable beds to sleep in, and large hospital tents for dining-rooms. His camp looked very comfortable and attractive, and presented a great contrast to that of General Crook, who had for his headquarters only one small fly tent; and whose cooking utensils consisted of a quart cup—in which he made his coffee himself—and a stick, upon which he broiled his bacon. When I compared the two camps, I came to the conclusion that General Crook was an Indian fighter; for it was evident that he had learned that, to follow and fight Indians, a body of men must travel lightly and not be detained by a wagon train or heavy luggage of any kind.

That evening General Terry ordered General Miles[9] to take his regiment, the Fifth Infantry, and return by a forced march to the Yellowstone, and proceed down that river by steamboat to the mouth of Powder river, to intercept the Indians, in case they attempted to cross the Yellowstone. General Miles made a forced march that night of thirty-five miles, which was splendid traveling for an infantry regiment through a mountainous country.

Generals Crook and Terry spent that evening and the next day in council, and on the following morning both commands moved out on the Indian trail. Although General Terry was the senior officer, he did not assume command of both expeditions, but left General Crook in command of his own troops, although they operated together. We crossed the Tongue river to Powder river, and proceeded down the latter stream to a point twenty miles from its junction with the Yellowstone, where the Indian trail turned to the southeast in the direction of the Black Hills. The two commands now being nearly out of supplies, the trail was abandoned, and the troops kept on down Powder river to its confluence with the Yellowstone, and remained there several days. Here we met General Miles, who reported that no Indians had as yet crossed the Yellowstone. Several steamboats soon arrived with a large quantity of supplies, and once more the "Boys in Blue" were made happy.

CHAPTER XXXI

Dangerous Work

One evening while we were in camp on the Yellowstone at the mouth of Powder river, I was informed that the commanding officers had selected Louis Richard, a half breed, and myself to accompany General Miles on a scouting expedition on the steamer Far West, down the Yellowstone as far as Glendive Creek. We were to ride on the pilot house and keep a sharp lookout on both sides of the river for Indian trails that might have crossed the stream. The idea of scouting on a steamboat was indeed a novel one to me, and I anticipated a pleasant trip.

At daylight next morning we reported on board the steamer to General Miles, who had with him four or five companies of his regiment. We were somewhat surprised when he asked us where our horses were, as we had not supposed that horses would be needed if the scouting was to be done on the steamer. He said we might need them before we got back, and thereupon we had the animals brought on board. In a few minutes we were booming down the river, at the rate of about twenty miles an hour.

The steamer Far West was commanded by Captain Grant Marsh, whom I found to be a "brick."[1] I had often heard of him, for he was and is yet one of the best known river captains in the country. He it was who, with his

83. Scouting on a Steamboat

steamer the Far West, transported the wounded men from the battle of the Little Big Horn to Fort Abraham Lincoln on the Missouri river, and on that trip he made the fastest steamboat time on record. He was a skillful and experienced pilot, handling his boat with remarkable dexterity.

While Richard and myself were at our stations on the pilot house, the steamer with a full head of steam went flying past islands, around bends, over sand-bars, at a rate that was exhilarating. Presently I thought I could see horses grazing in a distant bend of the river and I reported the fact to General Miles, who asked Captain Marsh if he could land the boat near a large tree which he pointed out to him.

"Yes, sir; I can land her there, and make her climb the tree if necessary," said he.

On reaching the spot designated, General Miles ordered two companies ashore, while Richard and myself were ordered to take our horses off the boat and push out as rapidly as possible to see if there were Indians in the vicinity. While we were getting ashore, Captain Marsh remarked that if there was only a good heavy dew on the grass he would shoot the steamer ashore and take us on the scout without the trouble of leaving the boat.

It was a false alarm, however, as the objects we had seen proved to be Indian graves. Quite a large number of braves who had probably been killed in some battle, had been buried on scaffolds, according to the Indian custom, and some of their clothing had been torn loose from the bodies by the wolves and was waving in the air.

On arriving at Glendive Creek we found that Colonel Rice and his company of the Fifth Infantry, who had been sent there by General Miles, had built quite a good little fort with their trowel-bayonets—a weapon which Colonel Rice was the inventor of, and which is, by the way, a very useful implement of war, as it can be used for a shovel in throwing up intrenchments and can be profitably utilized in several other ways. On the day previous to our arrival, Colonel Rice had a fight with a party of Indians, and had killed two or three of them at long range with his Rodman cannon.

The Far West was to remain at Glendive over night, and General Miles wished to send dispatches back to General Terry at once. At his request I took the dispatches and rode seventy-five miles that night through the bad lands of the Yellowstone, and reached General Terry's camp next morning, after having nearly broken my neck a dozen times or more.

There being but little prospect of any more fighting, I determined to go East as soon as possible to organize a new "Dramatic Combination," and have a new drama written for me, based upon the Sioux war. This I knew would be a paying investment as the Sioux campaign had excited considerable interest. So I started down the river on the steamer Yellowstone *en route* to Fort Beauford. On the same morning Generals Terry and Crook pulled out for Powder river, to take up the old Indian trail which we had recently left.

The steamer had proceeded down the stream about twenty miles when it was met by another boat on its way up the river, having on board General Whistler and some fresh troops for General Terry's command. Both boats landed, and almost the first person I met was my old friend and partner, Texas Jack, who had been sent out as a dispatch carrier for the *New York Herald*.

General Whistler, upon learning that General Terry had left the Yellowstone, asked me to carry to him some important dispatches from General Sheridan, and although I objected, he insisted upon my performing this duty, saying that it would only detain me a few hours longer; as an extra inducement he offered me the use of his own thorough-bred horse, which was on the boat. I finally consented to go, and was soon speeding over the rough and hilly country towards Powder river; and I delivered the dispatches to General Terry that same evening. General Whistler's horse, although a good animal, was not used to such hard riding, and was far more exhausted by the journey than I was.

After I had taken a lunch, General Terry asked me if I would carry some dispatches back to General Whistler, and I replied that I would. Captain Smith, General Terry's aid-de-camp, offered me his horse for the trip, and it proved to be an excellent animal; for I rode him that same night forty miles over the bad lands in four hours, and reached General Whistler's steamboat at one o'clock. During my absence the Indians had made their appearance on the different hills in the vicinity, and the troops from the boat had had several skirmishes with them. When General Whistler had finished reading the dispatches, he said:

"Cody, I want to send information to General Terry concerning the Indians who have been skirmishing around here all day. I have been trying all the evening long to induce some one to carry my dispatches to him, but no one seems willing to undertake the trip, and I have got to

84. Close Quarters

fall back on you. It is asking a great deal, I know, as you have just ridden eighty miles; but it is a case of necessity, and if you'll go, Cody, I'll see that you are well paid for it."

"Never mind about the pay," said I, "but get your dispatches ready, and I'll start at once."

In a few minutes he handed me the package, and mounting the same horse which I had ridden from General Terry's camp, I struck out for my destination. It was two o'clock in the morning when I left the boat, and at eight o'clock I rode into General Terry's camp, just as he was about to march—having made one hundred and twenty miles in twenty-two hours.

General Terry, after reading the dispatches, halted his command, and then rode on and overtook General Crook, with whom he held a council; the result was that Crook's command moved on in the direction which they had been pursuing, while Terry's forces marched back to the Yellowstone and crossed the river on steamboats. At the urgent request of General Terry I accompanied the command on a scout in the direction of the Dry Fork of the Missouri, where it was expected we would strike some Indians.

The first march out from the Yellowstone was made in the night, as we wished to get into the hills without being discovered by the Sioux scouts. After marching three days, a little to the east of north, we reached the buffalo range, and discovered fresh signs of Indians, who had evidently been killing buffaloes. General Terry now called on me to carry dispatches to Colonel Rice, who was still camped at the mouth of Glendive Creek, on the Yellowstone—distant about eighty miles from us.

Night had set in with a storm, and a drizzling rain was falling when, at ten o'clock, I started on this ride through a section of country with which I was entirely unacquainted. I traveled through the darkness a distance of about thirty-five miles, and at daylight I rode into a secluded spot at the head of a ravine where stood a bunch of ash trees, and there I concluded to remain till night; for I considered it a dangerous undertaking to cross the wide prairies in broad daylight—especially as my horse was a poor one.

I accordingly unsaddled my animal, and ate a hearty breakfast of bacon and hard tack which I had stored in the saddle-pockets; then, after taking a smoke, I lay down to sleep, with my saddle for a pillow. In a few minutes I was in the land of dreams.

After sleeping some time—I can't tell how long—I

was suddenly awakened by a roaring, rumbling sound. I instantly seized my gun, sprang to my horse, and hurriedly secreted him in the brush. Then I climbed up the steep side of the bank and cautiously looked over the summit; in the distance I saw a large herd of buffaloes which were being chased and fired at by twenty or thirty Indians. Occasionally a buffalo would drop out of the herd, but the Indians kept on until they had killed ten or fifteen. They then turned back, and began to cut up their game.

I saddled my horse and tied him to a small tree where I could reach him conveniently in case the Indians should discover me by finding my trail and following it. I then crawled carefully back to the summit of the bluff, and in a concealed position watched the Indians for two hours, during which time they were occupied in cutting up the buffaloes and packing the meat on their ponies. When they had finished this work they rode off in the direction whence they had come and on the line which I had proposed to travel. It appeared evident to me that their camp was located somewhere between me and Glendive Creek, but I had no idea of abandoning the trip on that account.

I waited till nightfall before resuming my journey, and then I bore off to the east for several miles, and by making a semi-circle to avoid the Indians, I got back on my original course, and then pushed on rapidly to Colonel Rice's camp, which I reached just at daylight.

Colonel Rice had been fighting Indians almost every day since he had been encamped at this point, and he was very anxious to notify General Terry of the fact. Of course I was requested to carry his dispatches. After remaining at Glendive a single day I started back to find General Terry, and on the third day out I overhauled him at the head of Deer Creek while on his way to Colonel Rice's camp. He was not, however, going in the right direction, but bearing too far to the east, and I so informed him. He then asked me to guide the command and I did so.

On arriving at Glendive I bade good-bye to the General and his officers and took passage on the steamer Far West, which was on her way down the Missouri. At Bismarck I left the steamer, and proceeded by rail to Rochester, New York, where I met my family.

Mr. J. Clinton Hall, manager of the Rochester Opera House, was very anxious to have me play an engagement at his theatre. I agreed to open the season with him as soon as I had got my drama written; and I did so, meeting with an enthusiastic reception.

My new drama was arranged for the stage by J. V. Arlington, the actor. It was a five-act play, without head or tail, and it made no difference at which act we commenced the performance. Before we had finished the season several newspaper critics, I have been told, went crazy in trying to follow the plot. It afforded us, however, ample opportunity to give a noisy, rattling, gunpowder entertainment, and to present a succession of scenes in the late Indian war, all of which seemed to give general satisfaction.

From Rochester I went to New York and played a very successful engagement at the Grand Opera House under the management of Messrs. Poole and Donnelly. Thence my route took me to all the principal cities in the Eastern, Western and Middle States, and I everywhere met with crowded houses. I then went to the Pacific Coast, against the advice of friends who gave it as their opinion that my style of plays would not take very well in California. I opened for an engagement of two weeks at the Bush Street Theatre, in San Francisco, at a season when the theatrical business was dull, and Ben DeBar and the Lingards were playing there to empty seats. I expected to play to a slim audience on the opening night, but instead of that I had a fourteen hundred dollar house. Such was my success that I continued my engagement for five weeks, and the theatre was crowded at every performance. Upon leaving San Francisco I made a circuit of the interior towns and closed the season at Virginia City, Nevada.

On my way East, I met my family at Denver, where they were visiting my sisters Nellie and May who were then residing there.

Some time previously I had made arrangements to go into the cattle business in company with my old friend, Major Frank North, and while I was in California he had built our ranches on the South Fork of the Dismal river, sixty-five miles north of North Platte, in Nebraska. Proceeding to Ogalalla, the headquarters of the Texas cattle drovers, I found Major North there awaiting me, and together we bought, branded and drove to our ranches, our first installment of cattle. This occupied us during the remainder of the summer.

Leaving the cattle in charge of Major North, I visited Red Cloud Agency early in the fall, and secured some Sioux Indians to accompany me on my theatrical tour of 1877–78. Taking my family and the Indians with me, I went directly to Rochester. There I left my oldest daughter, Arta, at a young ladies' seminary, while my wife and youngest child traveled with me during the season.

I opened at the Bowery Theatre, New York, September 3d, 1877, with a new Border Drama entitled, "May Cody, or Lost and Won," from the pen of Major A. S. Burt, of the United States army. It was founded on the incidents of the "Mountain Meadow Massacre,"[2] and life among the Mormons. It was the best drama I had yet produced, and proved a grand success both financially and artistically. The season of 1877–78 proved to be the most profitable one I had ever had.

In February, 1878, my wife became tired of traveling, and proceeded to North Platte, Nebraska, where, on our farm adjoining the town, she personally superintended the erection of a comfortable family residence, and had it all completed when I reached there, early in May. In this house we are now living, and we hope to make it our home for many years to come.

CHAPTER XXXII

Conclusion

After my arrival at North Platte, I found that the ranchmen or cattle-men, had organized a regular annual "round-up," to take place in the spring of the year.

The word "round-up" is derived from the fact that during the winter months the cattle become scattered over a vast tract of land, and the ranchmen assemble together in the spring to sort out and each secure his own stock. They form a large circle, often of a circumference of two hundred miles, and drive the cattle towards a common centre, where, all the stock being branded, each owner can readily separate his own from the general herd, and then he drives them to his own ranch.

In this cattle driving business is exhibited some most magnificent horsemanship, for the "cow-boys," as they are called, are invariably skillful and fearless horsemen—in fact only a most expert rider could be a cow-boy, as it requires the greatest dexterity and daring in the saddle to cut a wild steer out of the herd.

Major North was awaiting me, upon my arrival at North Platte, having with him our own horses and men. Other cattle owners, such as Keith and Barton, Coe and Carter, Jack Pratt, the Walker brothers, Guy and Sim Lang, Arnold and Ritchie and a great many others with their outfits, were assembled and were ready to start on the round-up.

My old friend Dave Perry, who had presented Buckskin Joe to me, and who resided at North Platte, was most anxious to go with us for pleasure, and Frank North told him he could, and have plenty of fun, provided he would furnish his own horses, provisions and bedding, and do the usual work required of a cow-boy. This, Dave was willing to undertake. We found him to be a good fellow in camp, and excellent company.

As there is nothing but hard work on these round-ups, having to be in the saddle all day, and standing guard over the cattle at night, rain or shine, I could not possibly find out where the fun came in, that North had promised me. But it was an exciting life, and the days sped rapidly by; in six weeks we found ourselves at our own ranch on Dismal river, the round-up having proved a great success, as we had found all our cattle and driven them home.

This work being over, I proposed to spend a few weeks with my family at North Platte, for the purpose of making their better acquaintance, for my long and continued absence from home made me a comparative stranger under my own roof-tree. One great source of pleasure to me was that my wife was delighted with the home I had given her amid the prairies of the far west. Soon after my arrival, my sisters Nellie and May, came to make us a visit, and a delightful time we all had during their stay. When they left us, I accompanied them to their home in Denver, Colorado, where I passed several days visiting old friends and scenes.

Returning to Ogallala I purchased from Bill Phant, an extensive cattle drover from Texas, a herd of cattle, which

I drove to my ranch on the Dismal river, after which I bade my partner and the boys good-bye, and started for the Indian Territory to procure Indians for my Dramatic Combination for the season of 1878–79.

En route to the Territory, I paid a long promised visit to my sisters, Julia—Mrs. J. A. Goodman—and Eliza—Mrs. George M. Myers—who reside in Kansas, the state which the reader will remember was my boyhood home.

Having secured my Indian actors, and along with them Mr. C. A. Burgess, a government interpreter, and Ed. A. Burgess, known as the "Boy Chief of the Pawnees," I started for Baltimore, where I organized my combination, and which was the largest troupe I had yet had on the road; opening in that city at the Opera House, under the management of Hon. John T. Ford,[1] and then started on a southern tour, playing in Washington, Richmond and as far south as Savannah, Georgia, where we were brought to a sudden halt, owing to the yellow fever which was then cruelly raging in the beautiful cities of the "Land of the cotton and the cane."

While playing in Washington, I suddenly learned from a reporter—Washington newspaper men know everything—that my Indians were to be seized by the Government and sent back to their agency. Finding that there was foundation for the rumor, I at once sought General Carl Shurz,[2] Secretary of the Interior, and asked him if he intended depriving me of my Indian actors. He said that he did, as the Indians were away from their reservation without leave. I answered that I had had Indians with me the year before and nothing had been said about it; but Commissioner Haight replied that the Indians were the

85. One of the Troupe

"wards of the government," and were not allowed off of their reservation.

I told the Commissioner that the Indians were frequently off of their reservations out west, as I had a distinct remembrance of meeting them upon several occasions "on the war path," and furthermore I thought I was benefitting the Indians as well as the government, by taking them all over the United States, and giving them a correct idea of the customs, life, etc., of the pale faces, so that when they returned to their people they could make known all they had seen.

After a conversation with the Secretary of the Interior, the Commissioner concluded to allow me to retain the Indians, by appointing me Indian Agent, provided I would give the necessary bonds, and pledge myself to return them in safety to their agency—which terms I agreed to.

From Savannah, Georgia, having changed my route on account of the yellow fever, I jumped my entire company to Philadelphia, and at once continued on a north-eastern tour, having arranged with the well-known author and dramatist, Colonel Prentiss Ingraham,[3] to write a play for me.

The drama entitled "The Knight of the Plains, or Buffalo Bill's Best Trail," was first produced at New Haven, Conn.; it has proved a great success, and I expect to play it in England, where I purpose to go next season on a theatrical tour, having been urged to do so by my many friends abroad.

After a successful tour of six weeks on the Pacific Slope, thus ending the season of 1878–79, I am at my home at North Platte, Nebraska, for the summer; and thus ends the account of my career as far as it has gone.

THE END.

APPENDIX 1

Cody and Visual Culture

The emergence of William F. "Buffalo Bill" Cody as an American icon corresponds with the proliferation of the photographic image. Indeed, the photograph was a primary vehicle for creating an iconography of Buffalo Bill. Beginning in the 1860s with advancements in photographic technologies, Americans found themselves confronted with a steadily increasing volume of black and white images. First, with the popular card-mounted 2 x 3½ inch photographs called cartes de visite and, later, with the slightly larger cabinet cards, Americans were inundated with mass-mediated images that transformed the way they saw themselves and the world around them. As one of the most photographed men of his era, Cody, in a sense, presided over the transition to a visual culture. The portraits included here capture the intimate faces of Cody's youth and the private life of his family, as well as the phases of his early celebrity. They chronicle the development of Buffalo Bill as a frontier type and suggest why Cody made such a compelling visual subject.

86. Portrait of Cody at 11, ca. 1857. Courtesy of Buffalo Bill
Museum and Grave, Golden, Colorado.

87. Portrait of Cody at 18, ca. 1863. Courtesy of Buffalo Bill
Museum and Grave, Golden, Colorado.

88. Round tintype photograph of Cody in dress clothing, ca. 1864.
Buffalo Bill Historical Center, Cody, Wyoming. P.69.2078.

89. Louisa Frederici Cody, ca. 1876, posed sitting at a table. Date uncertain. Courtesy of Buffalo Bill Museum and Grave, Golden, Colorado.

90. Portrait of Cody in scout costume, 1871. Denver Public Library,
Western History Collection, Denver, Colorado.

91. Lt. Francis Michler, Lt. Walter Scribner Schuyler, Windham
Thomas Wyndham-Quin, Lord Adare, and William F. Cody.
Cody holds his rifle, "Lucretia Borgia." 1871. Buffalo Bill
Historical Center, Cody, Wyoming. P.6.906.

92. Cody carte de visite, 1872. Buffalo Bill Historical Center, Cody, Wyoming. William Cody Bradford Collection, P.69.269.

93. Flamboyant Fraternity: Eugene Overton, Wild Bill Hickok, Buffalo Bill Cody, Texas Jack Omohundro, and Elisha Green, ca. 1874. Buffalo Bill Historical Center, Cody, Wyoming. Garlow Collection, P.6.908.

94. Cody carte de visite in fur-fringed overcoat with horseshoe
pendant, ca. 1875. Buffalo Bill Historical Center,
Cody, Wyoming. P.69.31.

95. Cody carte de visite, ca.1875. Robert G. McCubbin Collection.

96. Portrait of Kit Carson Cody, ca. 1875. Buffalo Bill
Museum, Golden, Colorado. 331.

97. Portrait of Cody ¾ length, ca. 1875. Buffalo Bill
Historical Center, Cody, Wyoming. P.69.189.

98. Cody carte de visite in faux Western setting, ca. 1878.
Buffalo Bill Historical Center, Cody, Wyoming. P.69.1541.

99. Cody carte de visite in outfit worn during the Skirmish at
Warbonnet Creek and in the stage production of *Red Right Hand,
or Buffalo Bill's First Scalp for Custer*, ca. 1878. Buffalo Bill
Historical Center, Cody, Wyoming. P.69.30.

100. Portrait of Orra Maude Cody, ca. 1877. Courtesy of
Buffalo Bill Museum and Grave, Golden, Colorado.

101. William, Louisa, and Orra Cody, ca. 1878. Buffalo Bill
Historical Center, Cody, Wyoming. P.69.756.

102. Portrait of Arta L. Cody , ca. 1879. Courtesy of Buffalo
Bill Museum and Grave, Golden, Colorado.

APPENDIX 2

Letters

Although William Cody became an active letter writer in his later years, the hand-written record prior to 1879 is sparse. The two letters he wrote to his sister Julia,[1] included here in addition to a letter written to Louisa, his wife, were written during one of the most defining years of his life: the first letter came two days after the death of his son, Kit. The syntax and punctuation may suggest something of his emotional state. It reveals his sense of family attachment and the intense grief of this loss. The second letter to Julia and the letter to Louisa, written in July and September, respectively, put Cody in a very different context and reflect his mind-set as chief of scouts for General Crook during the Sioux War. They suggest the degree to which Cody's stage career had become inextricably connected to his life offstage.

Rochester N. Y.
June 22nd 1876

To my Oldest Sister
Julia.

You are
the first to write
to after our sad sad
loss. Julia. God has
taken from us our only
little boy. He was to
good for this world. we
loved him to dearly
he could not stay.
God wanted him where
he could live in a
better world. So he

103. Letter to Julia Cody Goodman, 1876. Buffalo Bill Historical Center,
Cody, Wyoming. MS6.1.B.1.5.01-04.

he sent the angel
of death. to take <s>who</s>
the treasure that he
had given us five
Years and five months
ago. and how dear he
had grown to us in
that time. and when
we seen that there
was danger of him
leaving us how we all
clung to him. And prayed
God not to take from
us our little boy. But
when he sent that
hasty. cruel messenger
the Scarlet fever. there
was no hope from the
start. death claimed him
as their own at once.
And only gave us

two short days. to say
farewell and bid
him good bye. then
he was gone. and now
his place is vacant.
and can never never
be filled. for he has
gone to be a beautiful
Angel in that better
world. where he will
wait for us. every
one will know him
there. as they did here
on earth. (For every one
knew our little Kitty)
So if we only live. that
we may be permitted
to go where he has
gone. We will have
no trouble in finding

him when we are
there. for every one
will know our Kitty,
The Messenger seems not
to have been satisfied
by plucking the brightest
brightest flower. and
is still hovering near
by. thinking whether
he shall take the
others or not. for the
same fever. has taken
hold of our little girls
but so far only lightly.
But ... him from the first. Lulu
is worn out and sick. ...
it is now three o'lock
in the morning. I am sitting
by the bed side of our sick
babys. Jues hundreds of miles
away when Lulu telegraphed
me. and I only got here a
few hours before Kitty died

To Julia Cody Goodman

April 22nd 1876

Rochester. N. Y.[2]

To My Oldest Sister Julia

You are the first to write to after our sad sad loss. Julia.
God has taken from us our only little Boy.[3] He was to
good for this world. We loved him to dearly he could not
stay. God wanted him where he could live in a better
world. So he[4] sent the angel of death. to take ~~whe~~ the
treasure that he had given us five years and five months
ago. And how dear he had grown to us in that time.
And when we seen that there was danger of him leaving
us how we all clung to him. And pray God not to take
from us our little boy. But when he sent that hasty cruel
messenger the Scarlet fever. there was no hope from
the start. death claimed him as their own at once. And
only gave us two short days. to say farewell and bid
him good bye. then he was gone. And now his place is
vacant and can never never be filled. for he has gone to
be a beautiful angel in that better world. where he will
wait for us. every one will know him there. As they did
here on earth. (For every one knew our little Kitty.) So
if we only live ^good^ that we may be permitted to go
where he has gone. We will have no trouble in finding
him when we are theare for every one will know our
Kitty. The messenger seems not to have been satisfied
by plucking the brightest brightest flower. and is still
hovering near by. thinking whether he shall take the
others or not. for the same fever has taken hold of

our little Girl[5] but so far only lightly. But with Kitty it claimed him from the first. Lulu[6] is worn out and sick. ~~I am~~ it is now three oclock in the morning. I am sitting by the bedside of our sick babys. I was hundreds of miles away when Lulu telegraphed me. and I only got here a few hours before Kitty died. He could not speak. but he put his little arms around my neck. as much as to say. Papa has come. I must now write to Lida, Nellie & May.[7] Good bye from

Brother Will

To Louisa Frederici Cody

July 18th 76

Red Cloud Agency[8]

My Darling Lulu

We have come in here for rations we have had a fight I killed Yellow Hand A Cheyenne Chief. in a single handed fight You will no doupt hear of it through the papers. I ~~will~~ am going as soon as I reach Fort Laramie the place we are heading for now, Send the War Bonnet Shield bride whip arms and his *Scalp* to Kerngood[9] to put up in his window I will write Kerngood to bring it up to the house so that you can show it to the neighbors we are now ordered to join Gen Crook and will be there in two weeks write Me at once to Fort ~~Laramie~~ Fetterman Wyoming. My health is not very good I have worked my self to death. although I have shot at lots of Indians I have. only one scalp I can call my one that fellow I fought single handed in sight of our command and the cheerss that ~~wh~~ went up when he fell was deafening. Well Lulu I have no more time to write now will write from Laramie to every body and long letters

Good bye my Lulu a thousand Kisses to all
from you Hubby
Willie

Lulu
We have lost Gen Carr Gen Merritt has taken command as he ranks. Carr.[10]

To Julia Cody Goodman

Sep. 4th [1876]

On Board
Steamer Far West
Yellow Stone River

My Dear Sister

You no doubt will be surprised to hear from me away up in this country. I presume you heard I had gone back to my old life that of a Scout. Well so I did I could not remain East. while this Indian War was going on without takeing a hand. I went to Cheyenne the first of June. I would have come by and seen you but the Government was hurrying me up so I could not find time. I did not have time to go to Denver and see Nellie & May. So Ed brought them over to Cheyenne. **that** since then I have been continually in the saddle I have been in several fights. And killed three Indians during the summer. I call my own. That is I never say that I kill an Indian without I get his scalp. I sent two scalps east to the Sentennial and have one on the boat with me that I killed one week ago yesterday. But it came near being my last. for the

Indians had the first shot and tore a small piece out of my side. but it was his *last shot*. I am now carrying his *scalp* home My wound is but a slight one. two weeks at home will fix me all right. then I expect to return to my command. I was Chief of Scouts for *General* Crook.[11] But got separated from him in carrying dispatches to General Terry and got wounded on my way to Gen Terry and could not get back to Crook I have no time to write you all so good bye will write you from home. Love to all from your Brother

Will

APPENDIX 3

Cody and Celebrity

Cody traces the roots of his public life to a newspaper account of his exploits—an article about his first Indian slaying as an eleven year old boy. His autobiography reflects the media savvy that would later make him one of the most famous men in the world including an acute awareness of press coverage and the role of audience at every stage of his career. The material included here represents the primary components of Cody's early celebrity, including representations of Cody in the press, dime novels, and on stage. Foundational to an understanding of Cody's legacy, all of these popular culture elements would eventually inform the making of Buffalo Bill's Wild West.

104. Poster for the Buffalo Bill combination's *May Cody; or, Lost and Won*, 1877. Yale Collection of Western Americana, Beinecke Rare Book and Manuscript Library.

Press Coverage

A sampling of Cody's press coverage in the 1870s suggests how the public perceived him during the early stages of his celebrity. In addition to notices and reviews of his stage performances, Cody found himself in the newspapers for his exploits on the plains as well as for his public appearances, exhibitions, and product endorsements. He was interviewed for his views on Indian policy and his dime novels were debated for their moral influence on America's youth.

Sheridan's Buffalo Hunt

Return with His Party to Chicago Laden with Spoils of the Chase—
Buffalo, Elk and Antelope, Deer, Coyotes and Wild Turkeys.

Gen. SHERIDAN and party reached Chicago in return from a very successful buffalo hunt on the Western plains, on Wednesday morning, in fine health and spirits. Some incidents of the trip are thus given by the Chicago *Evening Journal:*

"The party left Chicago on the 20th ultimo, by the Chicago and North-western Road, JOHN C. GAULT, Esq., Superintendent, tendering the Director's car to the General for his party. At Omaha a like courtesy was shown by Mr. SICKLES, Superintendent of the Union Pacific, and L. M. BENNETT, Superintendent of the Pullman Car Company on that road. The trip was most delightful. On arriving at North Platte, Major-Gen. EMORY and Major J. H. BROWN, the commander of the expedition, met the party, which was escorted by them to Fort McPherson, a pleasant ride of seventeen miles over the plains. About two miles from the post several companies of cavalry, with a regimental band, were drawn up, and received Gen. SHERIDAN, and were reviewed by him, after which the party were presented to the officers of the post and their ladies, who also had come out in carriages and on horseback. The party were escorted to Camp Rucker, where quarters were assigned, and the day spent in choosing horses, target practice, &c., concluding with a grand hop at the post.

At 8 o'clock next morning tents were struck, and the grand march begun. Lieut. E. M. HAYES, Quartermaster, and "Buffalo Bill," the observed of all observers,"—splendid in form, the beau ideal of the rough rider that he is—as scout and guide. The advance was lead by Gen. SHERIDAN and Major BROWN; eighty-five mounted men, fourteen wagons, three ambulances, and led horses for the party, constituted the outfit. Twelves miles out leave was taken of the ladies and officers who thus far accompanied the party, and the first camp was reached on Plum Creek, eighteen miles, which, in honor of the commander, was named 'Camp Brown, my Boy.'

The march was commenced for the grand hunt at an early hour next morning. A cup was voted to the slayer of the first buffalo, and one also for the first elk. About ten miles out, seven buffalo were seen on a distant hill; the command was halted, and seven 'solitary horsemen might have been seen,' led by Buffalo Bill, and all eager for the chase. Gen. FITZHUGH secured the first tongue and brush, and became winner of the cup. CROSBY made a good second, and LIVINGSTON third, while JEROME, the younger, brought in the trophies from the fourth. Camp was reached at about 2 o'clock, which, in honor of one of the most gallant soldiers in the service, was named 'Camp Jack Hayes.' Before the camp-fires were lighted, WILSON brought in an elk of about 600 pounds avoirdupois, and become the winner of the cup.

The next was a regular field-day. The party camped on the Beaver, and "Camp Cody," named in honor of Buffalo Bill, was filled with trophies taken from forty buffalo. Gen. STAGER brought in six, LAWRENCE JEROME four, and every one of the party two or three.

All having now killed buffaloes, but little interest was taken in the numerous herds seen on the adjacent hillsides, except to secure enough for use in the camp.

Elk, antelope, black-tailed deer, coyotes, jack rabbits, skunks, porcupines, prairie dogs, rattlesnakes, wild turkeys, mallard, teal and wood-duck, and three or four kinds of fish, embraced the game found and secured— FITZHUGH shooting the first buffalo, WILSON the first elk, CROSBY the first antelope, RUCKER the first coyote, SHERIDAN the first rabbit, and LEONARD JEROME the first wild turkey. The finest elk were killed by Lieut. HAYES, FITZHUGH and JOHNSON, weighing nearly 1,000 pounds.

The first day's march was to Camp Brown, on Plum Creek, 18 miles; the second to Camp Jack Hayes, on the Medicine, 30 miles; the third to Camp Asch, on the Republican, 13 miles; the fourth to Camp Cody, on the Beaver, 15 miles; the fifth to Camp Stager, on the Short Nose, 24 miles; the sixth to Camp Jerome, on the North Solomon, 24 miles; the seventh to Camp Sam Johnston, on the South Solomon, 25 miles; the eighth to Camp Davis, on the Saline, 30 miles, and on the ninth to Camp Hecksher, 15 miles.

On their arrival at Fort Hayes, on the Kansas and Pacific Railroad, a palace car was in waiting, having been placed at the disposal of Gen. SHERIDAN by the Superintendent of that road, in which the party, by the courtesy of the Superintendents of the Hannibal and St. Joseph and the Chicago, Burlington and Quincy roads, were brought safely home, and the grand hunt was successfully completed without an accident, and with thousands of pleasant memories clustering around it."

Buffalo Bill

His Arrival in Denver

We had the pleasure, this morning, of meeting the renowned scout and buffalo hunter, Mr. WILLIAM F. CODY, known to fame as "BUFFALO BILL." He came in from Cheyenne on yesterday evening's Denver Pacific train, and was met at the depot by a few friends. He went immediately to the residence of his sister, Mrs. WILLIAM BRADFORD, where he remained until this morning. He is now "doing" Denver as the guest of a few of his old comrades, who are now residents of this city. "BILL" is here on government business, and intends returning to his headquarters, at Fort McPherson, Nebraska, on Friday.

He expresses great surprise and admiration at the wonderful progress Denver has made since the time of his last visit, four years ago. He was after a band of horsethieves at that time, and of course he got them.

Since his arrival in the city became known, we have heard a thousand stories of his wonderful deeds, replete with evidences of a lion-like courage, and a reckless disregard of personal safety. He is known far and near as the best scout and best buffalo slayer in the country—while those who know him best, speak of him as one of Nature's noblemen. His quiet, modest and unassuming manner impress you favorably, and you feel that he is a fit companion for such men as Alexis, Sheridan and Sherman.

He has just returned from a forty day's trip through the States, where he met with a hearty welcome from all classes. He is employed by the government as chief scout, and has command of the entire scouting force employed by Uncle Sam in the country lying between the "Great Muddy" and the Rockies.

Denver's latch-string is always out to "BUFFALO BILL," and we hope to see him here again as soon as his duties will permit of his leaving them.

SIOUX CITY JOURNAL, MARCH 22, 1873

Buffalo Bill as a Shootist

"Buffalo Bill" was at Hartford, Conn., the other day, and while visiting Colt's Armory, the large number of spectators who had assembled to see the famous scout, desired him to favor them with an exhibition of his skill as a marksman. Bill gave the chew of tobacco in his mouth to a small boy to keep warm; a small piece of white paper was put up on a barn door, fifty rods distant, B. William seized a fine new rifle, spit on his hands, and in the manner so often described by Ned Buntline, raised the weapon until his nose rested on the stock, fired, and a picket was knocked off from a fence ten feet to the left of the barn. "This rifle barrel is crooked," said Bill, so saying he hit it over a stone to straighten it, then shot again, this time barking the shin of an old pie-woman on his right flank. A third trial and he hit the barn fair in the center, and the shout that arose from the assemblage attested the joy of the spectators at his success. Bill is just as good an actor as he is a marksman, which is very remarkable in these days of corruption and bribery.

THE NEW HAMPSHIRE PATRIOT,
DECEMBER 23, 1874

From the Noted Scout "Buffalo Bill"

Holland House, Rockford, Ill, April 20, 1874—
Dr. R. V. Pierce, Buffalo, N.Y.:

Sir—I have now taken four bottles of your Golden Medical Discovery in connection with your Pellets, and must say that nothing I have ever taken for my liver has done me as much good. I feel like a new man. Thanks to your wonderful medicine.

W. F. Cody, ("Buffalo Bill.")

SAN FRANCISCO BULLETIN, AUGUST 11, 1876

Buffalo Bill's Indian Trophies

Since Yellow Hand, The Cheyenne warrior, yielded up his life to the strength and bravery of Buffalo Bill, it was reported that the intrepid scout was to honor this city with the scalp, the arms and the dress of the poor but haughty Indian. The report has become a fact. Yesterday morning they arrived, and now they adorn the window of the Pickwick cigar store, where they have attracted the attention of large numbers of people. The old man with his spectacles and the street gamin with his wonderment gazes in admiration at the following articles: The scalp of the noble Cheyenne, head-dress, shield, blanket, bowie knife, whip, bridle and blanket.

The shield has the ghastly ornament of several Indian scalps, thus showing that his death-dealing band had only been felt by those in whose veins the blood of the red man runs. To the scalp, which is about three inches square, is attached a braided switch of straight, black hair about two feet long. The head-dress is the chief and most attractive part of the warrior's costume. It is five or six inches wide and as many feet long, and made of buffalo skin. The whole thing is closely set with feathers from that noble bird, the American eagle. Each feather is tipped with the hair, attached with some kind of cement. The flowing end of this head-dress is ornamented with scarlet cloth sewed with green thread. Bells are attached to the cloth, no doubt to give warning when the brave was upon the war-path.

Sporting Items

"Buffalo Bill," at a recent glass ball shooting match in Omaha, broke twenty-three out of twenty-five balls thrown in the air, using a rifle without sights.

Buffalo Bill gave an exhibition in Baltimore the other night, and while sloshing around with a pistol, sent a ball into the gallery, which entered the breast of a boy. The lad, however, made no outcry, and his injury was only discovered after the audience had left the hall. The supreme felicity of being shot by Buffalo Bill can only be appreciated by a boy. If anybody else had fired that shot, that boy would have died right in his seat.

Personal

Mr. James T. Fields lectures on "Fiction." At the Brooklyn Athenæum he alluded in the course of his remarks to Pomeroy, the boy-murderer, thus: "I recently paid a visit to the Pomeroy boy, who was sentenced to be hanged for killing three children, but whose sentence was afterward commuted to imprisonment for life. I asked him if he read much. He said that he did. 'What kind of books do you read?' said I. 'Mostly one kind,' he said—'mostly dime novels.' 'What is the best book that you have read?' I asked. 'Well, I like "Buffalo Bill" best,' he replied. 'It was full of murders and pictures about murders.' 'Well,' I asked, 'how did you feel after reading such a book?' 'Oh,' said he, 'I felt as if I wanted to do the same.'"

Review of "The Life of Hon. William F. Cody"
(autobiography of Buffalo Bill)

Buffalo Bill

For once we have in print the history of a scout of the Plains
in his own words and without any of the hideous red glare of
melodrama to read it by. Hon. William F. Cody, better known
by his honestly earned nickname of "Buffalo Bill," has been
well known on the border for twenty years, although not now
thirty-five years of age, and his success in his peculiar line has
been remarkable; but it all came about in the most matter of fact
way in the world, he having been born west of the Mississippi
at a time when men were scarce and boys who could handle a
plough or gun were considered as good as adults. It is hard to
realize that the subject of this volume was a full teamster in a
government train at the age of twelve, killing his first Indian at
the same time; was a hunter at thirteen, prospector for gold and
rider in the dangerous, wearing pony express line at fourteen;
that at fifteen he lay for thirty days alone in a "dug-out," or hole
in the ground, with only his own thoughts and a broken leg
to keep him company, while his companion went back to the
settlements for supplies and a conveyance, and that when the
civil war ended he had been four years a soldier and scout, yet
was not even then of age. Mr. Cody tells his story in a simple,
unaffected style that commands belief, and it is about as full
of incident and adventure as its pages will allow. We doubt
whether the perusal of the book will lure a single boy to run
away from school, steal a revolver and tramp to the border, for
somehow the men who know what frontier life really is always
give the impression that there is a great deal of downright hard
work about the borderer's life. (F. E. Bliss, Hartford.)

The Proper Way to Treat the Indians

From an Interview with "Buffalo Bill"

"What are your ideas on the Indian problem, Mr. Cody? In other words, what would you do to secure a better and more economical management of the Indian tribes by the Government?"

"I think I can sum up my policy in a single sentence. It is this: Never make a single promise to the Indians that is not fulfilled. Agents promise too much. Men of calm, prudent determination must be sent among the Indians as agents. Those who are sent often know nothing of the Indian character, and either through fear, ignorance, or dishonesty are led into making promises which the Government can not or will not fulfill. Every Indian outbreak that I have ever known has resulted from broken promises and broken treaties by the Government."

"What do you think of the peace policy or the policy of encouraging agricultural pursuits by the Indians, Mr. Cody?"

"It has already resulted in good, and will result in still greater good if honestly and intelligently pursued. You can not make an Indian work by standing over him with a shot-gun. He must be taught that it is to his interest to do so, and brought into it by degrees. Too much can not be accomplished all at once. But if a wise, firm policy is pursued the Indians will gradually drift into agricultural pursuits."

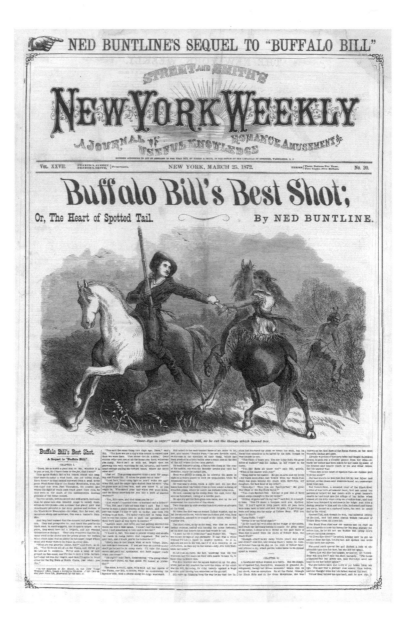

105. *New York Weekly* first installment of *Buffalo Bill's Best Shot*, by Ned Buntline, 1872. Buffalo Bill Historical Center, Cody, Wyoming. MS6.10.Q.MC-D2.1872.01.

Dime Novels

The first Buffalo Bill dime novel was written by Ned Buntline in 1869. It appeared serially in Street & Smith's *New York Weekly*. Though Buntline would write only three more Buffalo Bill stories, the marketplace demand for them would continue into the twentieth century. Over 500 Buffalo Bill dime novels were written by various authors, including Prentiss Ingraham, and were published in countless editions in the U.S. and Europe. They appeared most commonly in story papers such as *New York Weekly* at a nickel cost, but were also published in conventional book form. Stories of the frontier were the most popular subject of this genre and Buffalo Bill the most popular frontier hero. Since the stories were written and published quickly and cheaply, the plots are highly conventional working with standardized incidents and settings as well as stock characters. The following excerpt from Ned Buntline's second Buffalo Bill story, published serially in 1872, contains many of the genre's most characteristic elements.

BUFFALO BILL'S BEST SHOT: OR, THE HEART
OF SPOTTED TAIL BY NED BUNTLINE

CHAPTER I

"Dave, life is worth a good deal to *me*, whether it is to you or not, for I have them to *live for*, that I love!"

Thus spoke Buffalo Bill to his bosom friend and longtime mate in many a wild hunt, and yet wilder scout, Dave Estes,* as they looked eastward from a peak in the great Wind-River Gap of the Rocky Mountain,[1] west, full two days' ride from Fort Thompson,[2] the nearest spot where the sight of white men could greet their eyes, for they were in the heart of the northwestern hunting grounds of the Sioux nation.

The two scouts, well-mounted and well-armed, had come thus far alone into this dreaded range to satisfy themselves on two points—one, a rumor that placer gold was wondrously plentiful in the deep gulches and ravines of the Wind-River Mountains—the other, that for bear, elk, mountain sheep and antelope, this was a hunter's Paradise.

And they had learned that the rumors had good foundation. They had prospected for, and found fine gold in the black sand, in small nuggets, and in quartz ledges. As to game, they could have fed a brigade, and not worried themselves in doing it. They only wondered that the Indians went so far down into the grassy plains for buffalo when other meat was so plenty in this upper range where wood and water were to be found on every side.

"What are you growlin' about, Bill?" said Dave, in reply. "The Reds are all off on the Plains, and we've got the hills all to ourselves. We've seen a heap of new ground on this scout, and I'd like to look a little further. Let's stay out one day longer, and then I'll agree to head either for the Big Horn or North Platte,[3] just which you like,"

"You said the same thing two days ago, Dave," said Bill. "Yet here we are a day's ride nearer to sunset now than we were then. '*You* never tire on a scout.' Good reason why—you are at all the home you have, wherever you camp. But it isn't so with me. Bright eyes are growing dim with watching for me, far away, and there's heart-strings pulling me toward home, where my loved ones are!"

"Just so! This getting married ruins a man for scouting and Plains-life. It takes the game out of him!"

"Look *here*, Dave—step light or you'll wake me up!" cried Bill, and the anger-light flashed from his eyes. "I'm as game now as I ever was, and you know it, or you ought to. Who saved your hair when you were down, and the Sioux crowding for you like a pack of starved wolves?"

"You, Bill—*you*, and God bless you for it!"

"And wasn't I married then—a husband and a father?"

"Yes, Bill, and I take all back that I said. But I was never in such a game country as this before, and there's just one range I'd like to look at to-day, and then I'm willing to go back. I'd rather you'd stay in camp than not to rest the horses and to pack our specimens, and then we'll move at day-dawn to-morrow."

"Agreed, mate—but never say that getting married has made me less a man again. I wasn't half the man I am until I had something to love and to live for."

"I know it, Bill. You used to punish whisky and shuffle the cards in camp before *that* happened. But you've quit that, and I know you're the better for it!"

"*Every* man is that keeps wide of such things, Dave, but *talk* isn't business. If you are bent on a scout to-day don't go far and be in camp early. I'll take the horses down and pack our specimens, and have supper ready when you come!"

"All right!" said Dave, dismounting. "I'm going where horses can't travel, up that gulch we looked at yesterday!"

The scout, a small, agile, wiry man left the Apollo of the Plains, *our* Bill, to return, while he, shouldering his Spencer rifle, took a course along the ridge westward.

Bill called to the well-trained horse of his mate to follow, and turned "Powder Face," his own favorite steed, to the east in the direction of their camp, which had been pitched in a little valley near a small lake at the foot of the hill where the two men parted.

He rode leisurely along, a Henry rifle slung at the rear of

his saddle, but with his favorite needle-gun over his shoulder, ready for instant use.

Meat was plenty in camp, so he allowed the game in sight at a dozen points to feed on unmolested, while he descended the hill.

He was nearly down, when a sight met his eye that made him draw his horses close in cover under a clump of dwarfish pines, where he could see without being seen.

He saw, coming up the valley from the east, three figures on horseback, riding at a terrific pace.

He quickly got his field-glass into focus, and by its aid discovered the character of the riders.

Two rode side by side several hundred yards in advance of the third.

Of these the first was an armed Indian warrior, and he led the second horse, which bore an Indian girl, who, from her position, seemed to be bound to the horse, which the warrior led. The third rider, so far in the rear, was also an armed Indian warrior, and he was lashing his horse furiously, as the first also lashed his and that which he led.

"A race for life it looks like!" said Buffalo Bill. "But I see no see no sign of any pursuers! If that was a white woman I'd take a hand in mighty sudden. As it is, squaws are not in my line, and if it is a runaway or an *abduction*, as they say in the towns—why, it's their business, not mine!"

So he rode on down the hill, knowing that the two warriors had too much on their own hands to look to, to have time to notice him.

The first warrior and the squaw dashed on up the gap, while just as Bill reached the level the horse of the other warrior fell, throwing its rider heavily against a huge boulder and leaving him senseless on the ground.

Bill rode up, thinking from the way he lay that the Indian had fractured his skull or broke his neck, but he found him conscious as he halted by his side, though he was unable to rise.

"Pale-Face—I know you. You are Long Rifle, the great killer of buffalo!" said the Indian, as Bill reined in his horse.

"Yes—the Reds all know *me!*" said Bill, quietly. "What is the matter with you?"

"Heap *bad* is the matter. Me got an arm and leg broke—my horse most dead, and Yellow Bear, the Black-Foot Chief, has gone beyond my reach with Dove-Eye, my daughter, the Red Rose of my tribe!"

"Dove-Eye? Then you are 'Spotted-Tail,' the great War-Chief of the Big-Horn Sioux?"[4]

"Yes—I am Spotted-Tail. Kill me if you like—I have taken scalps enough to line my lodge!"

"Killing cripples isn't in my line!" said Bill, in a haughty tone. "But I'll make a bargain with you, Spotted-Tail. If you'll agree to keep peace with all pale faces who come here to hunt and look for gold, I'll get that gal back and bring you the scalp of Yellow Bear. Will you agree to this?"

"Long-Rifle, I will!"

"Swear it by the Great Spirit!"

"As He hears me who rides on the wings of the storm, and sends the lightning-knives to scathe the great trees of the forest, I swear to be a friend to the pale faces if Dove-Eye is saved from the claws of Yellow Bear, the Black-Foot!"

"Enough—crawl to my camp where you'll find meat and drink!" said Bill, and loosing Dave's horse, he turned Powder Face up the gap on the trail of Yellow Bear, and uttered a cry, which put the noble horse to its utmost speed in second.

A handsome Indian woman is a rarity. But the daughter of Spotted-Tail, DOVE-EYE, womanly in graceful development, though but fifteen summers' bloom was on her cheek, was an exception. On all the Plains, through the Black Hills and in the Great Mountains, she was known as the Red Rose of the Sioux Nation, as the most beautiful Indian girl alive.

Already warriors of her own tribe had fought in jealous rivalry to gain but a friendly glance from her eyes—already her father had been asked for her hand by some of the bravest and richest chiefs of his and other tribes. But his answer was:

"Dove-Eye is the heart of Spotted-Tail—he cannot part with his child!"

She had known no love but that felt for her father and mother, so the chiefs and warriors found no encouragement from her.

But Yellow-Bear, a dreaded chief of the Black-Feet, a tribe at war with all around them, had not asked her parents or herself for her hand—with a great hunter's stealth he had crept into the village of her father when almost all the tribe were away on a buffalo hunt, and that father was detained by sickness in his lodge, and with a daring peculiar to him and his tribe, had seized and borne her away, bound on a captured horse, the best he could find in the corral.

Spotted-Tail, sick though he was, had followed swiftly on the trail, and had come almost within rifle-shot of Yellow-Bear when his horse fell.

The Black-Foot chief saw the mishap and he rode on more leisurely to save his horses for the long journey yet before him, for he did not see Buffalo Bill riding down toward his fallen pursuer.

"Is Dove-Eye tired?" he asked, hoping now to get an answer from her lips, for she had not spoken one word to him since her capture.

The great black eyes of the girl flashed a look of unutterable hate into his face, but she did not speak.

"Dove-Eyes will find her tongue, by- and-by, or Yellow-Bear will help her!" said the chief, savagely. "The horse of Spotted-Fail has given out, and Dove-Eye need not hope to see her father again!"

The girl looked back and a cry of joy broke from her lips. She saw that a pursuer was nearer than before, and she thought none but her father was on the trail.

Yellow-Bear turned his eyes back, and *he* saw that it was not Spotted-Tail, but a well-armed and well-mounted pale-face, who was coming swiftly on his track.

Quickly he lashed his horse and that which bore Dove-Eye into furious speed once more. Dangerous speed, indeed, for the rough route he was passing over—growing rougher and more narrow as they ascended the pass, but there was a danger behind which the Black-Foot could comprehend, for he had battled with pale-faces before, and on—on madly he went.

Nearer and nearer the pursuer came, and a low, scornful laugh broke from the lips of Dove-Eye, for she deemed her rescue sure now.

Yellow-Bear heard it, and his anger flamed up and he resolved that *she* should first die and then he would face his pursuer.

Checking his horse suddenly, he clutched her round arm and raising her form so as to bring her heart full before him, he raised his arm to drive the knife which he held, home in her unprotected bosom.

As he thus raised his arm a terrible yell broke from his lips—a cry of defiance and hate.

Dove-Eye, fearless and full of scorn, looked him defiantly in the face, expecting instant death, but suddenly his arm fell and the knife dropped to the earth, for Buffalo Bill full one hundred yards away, saw her peril, raised his rifle quick as thought, fired and sent the ball through the upraised right-arm.

Yellow-Bear helpless to use knife or rifle now, uttered a scream of baffled rage and pain, then leaping from his horse he plunged off into a thicket where no horseman could follow him, just as Buffalo Bill dashed up on his horse to finish the work begun, by what he has since termed the BEST SHOT he ever made.

"Dove-Eye is safe!" he said, as he reined his horse back to its haunches and cut the thongs which bound her. "Her father is at my camp waiting for her."

"Dove-Eye has no words to thank the brave pale-face with," said she. "Her life has been saved by him and she will be his slave forever."

"Buffalo Bill don't believe in slave-women, and he needs no thanks," said the heroic scout. "But look to his horse. He promised to take your father back a scalp, and he must get it."

Bill threw the reins of his horse into the hands of the liberated maiden and sprung into the thicket after Yellow Bear.

It may be wondered by the reader why he did not send a bullet through the heart of the Black-Foot instead of through his arm, when his rifle could have done either.

Simply because he knew that a shot through the heart would never check that descending arm and that the arm must be struck or its blow would be death to her. And he had pierced it though his horse was at full speed and he full one hundred yards away.

Dove-Eye saw the noble form of her preserver disappear in the chapparal, and her eyes gleamed with a new light.

"He is brave as the bravest and beautiful as a lone pine upon a hill-top," she said. "Dove-Eye will be *his* slave or she will cook meat for no man."

She waited minutes, and they seemed long, for him to return—and then almost an hour passed before Buffalo Bill came back.

When he did return he looked flushed and angry.

"The skulking cuss has got away," he said. "He can outrun a crippled wild-turkey and hid better than a chick-pheasant. I've lost him and his trail, but I'll have his scalp yet and keep my word with Spotted-Tail."

Dove-Eye did not speak. She never dared to speak to her father when *his* brow wore the anger-cloud, and she thought she must be silent when the brave pale-face was angry.

When he said, as he took his bridle-rein from her hand: "We will go to the camp where your father is," she bowed her head and turned her horse, while Bill secured the other horse so that the Black-Foot chief could not find him and remount.

Bill now led the way back down the pass, closely followed by Dove-Eye, whose eyes watched with free admiration every movement of his manly, graceful form.

"There is no warrior like him in all the tribes," she murmured, as she rode on. "Dove-Eye must win his love or die."

106. Portrait of Buffalo Bill Combination, in theater costumes, ca. 1873. *From left:* E. Z. C. Judson (Ned Buntline), Cody, Giuseppina Morlacchi, and John "Texas Jack" Omohundro. Buffalo Bill Historical Center, Cody, Wyoming. P.69.28.

Cody on Stage

Although the reviews of his first drama, *Scouts of the Prairie* (1872), suggest an inauspicious beginning, Cody would go on to professional success as a theater star for over a decade. For most of that time his theatrical troupe toured as the "Buffalo Bill Combination." Their tour would begin in the fall and continue through the spring. Disbanding the group for the summer, Cody would occasionally return to the plains with an eye to finding new dramatic material. Notices and reviews of Combination productions offer a sense of Cody's audience and the appeal of his performances which blended melodrama, sensationalism, and the impression of authentic frontier experience. The program notes for *Red Right Hand or, Buffalo Bill's First Scalp for Custer* provide a sense of how Buffalo Bill plays incorporated elements of Cody's experience—in this case, the killing of Yellow Hair—into conventional plots of the popular theater.

CHICAGO DAILY TRIBUNE, DECEMBER 19, 1872

Amusements

Nixon's Amphitheatre

The long-neglected place of amusement has suddenly loomed up as the most largely patronized of any in the city, the audiences making up the quantity what they lack in quality. The drama entitled "Scouts of the Prairie," written in Chicago by Ned Buntline, and introducing two frontier celebrities, is the immediate occasion of the large attendance. It purports to be a vivid picture of life in the Western wilds, and is such to a certain extent,—as much so as are the average sensational novels on the same subject, and, like the latter, full of inconsistencies. The original plan was to concoct a play to suit the material at command, and it is apparent that the design was carried out. "Buffalo Bill" (William F. Cody), now a member of the Nebraska Legislature, and Texas Jack, both widely-known scouts, and a half-dozen genuine Pawnee Indians, having nothing in particular to do, stood ready to accept a histrionic engagement. They had never been on any but the overland stage, and the copper-colored portion of the troupe had generally been accredited with a greater capacity for robbing than ranting. It occurred to Colonel Judson ("Ned Buntline") that here was a chance for a sensation. The "Scouts of the Prairie" was the result, and it proves to be a sensation. The Pawnees, however, failed to keep their engagement, probably on account of pressing duties with reference to a projected horse-stealing expedition, and in their places there have been substituted a collection of talented supers in tan-colored frocks and cambric pantalettes. Buffalo Bill and Texas Jack are on hand, however, completely equipped in buckskin shirts and leggings, and fairly bristling with revolvers, knives, rifles, etc. Of course, they look like "Scouts of the Prairie," but they seem to labor under a distressing uncertain[t]y as to what they ought to do with their hands, fidgeting uneasily when silent, and when in dialogue poking out the right and then the left at regular intervals, with an evident determination to show no favor between the two. Their elocution differs somewhat from Booth's and Barrett's, but then Edwin and Lawrence are not scouts, and cannot be expected to stand as examplars under the circumstances. The fact that Bill and Jack [s]peak their pieces after the manner a diffident school-boy in his maiden effort must not be taken as an evidence of meagre dramatic talent or training; all this weakness of voi[ce] and nervousness of deportment is but an [ar]tful assumption, designed to show that bene[at]h the rough exterior of the daring scout th[e]re beats a heart as [t]ender as a chicken's, while his reckless bravado is merely put on to conceal a delicate, shrinking nature. The illusion is so complete, however, that one would be almost ready to swear that these gentlemen are not great actors. What with the aid of numerous bloody conflicts, wherein persons who, a minute before, were twenty miles away, are telegraphed back, and get there just in time; the beautiful Indian maiden with the Italian accent and weakness for scouts; the lovely white girl held in captivity by the aborigines; the poetical trapper and his felicitous homilies on the beauties of nature and the superiority of water to rotgut as a beverage; the cambric-clad Pawnees from Blue Island avenue;

the inexplicable inebriate who manages to keep drunk for several days without a drop of anything; the prairie fire, the fight for life, the vengeance wreaked on the murderous redskins, and the grand tableau at the close—all these put together furnish rare entertainment for the toiling masses who patronize the show. There is a plentiful lack of ventilation at the amphitheatre, where, in the presence of 2,000 bad breaths and twice as many unclean feet, it is well to adopt the tactics of *Casca*, who "darst not laugh, for fear of opening his lips and receiving the bad air." These defects are easily remedied, and should be looked to at once, unless Mr. Nixon courts an indictment for manslaughter by slow poison.

THE WASHINGTON POST, APRIL 24, 1878

Buffalo Bill's New Play

"May Cody," the new play at the Bowery Theatre, in which Buffalo Bill takes the principal role, is a remarkable production. It includes a little of everything, from a haughty dame in a Fifth avenue drawing-room, to a roaring, howling, scalping savage on the plains. Mormons, emigrants, soldiers, negroes, Irishmen and jackasses move through its scenes in a medley which defies explanation or unravelment. The second act introduces a shooting scene, in which Bill snuffs candles, shoots the fire from a cigar and punctures an apple placed on May's head. In a subsequent scene Brigham Young appears, in appearance remarkably like Senator Blaine, with the addition of chin-whiskers. The two bears advertised to appear did not come on time and the audience had to put up with a weak imitation in a buffalo robe.

The Indian Actors

An Attempt by the Interior Department to take them from Buffalo Bill

The commissioner of Indian affairs, having found that the Pawnees with the Buffalo Bill combination are off their reservation without permission, issued an order that they should return immediately. When this fact became known to the Indians they executed a terrific war dance, held an excited pow-wow, and finally concluded not to go. Mr. Cody then took the matter in hand, and called upon the commissioner, stating that if the order was carried into effect, it would cause considerable pecuniary loss to him, as the combination had been advertised for appearance for twenty days ahead. He also assured the commissioner that the Indians were well treated. The commissioner then revoked his order, on condition that Mr. Cody enter into $5,000 bonds to return the Indians after a specified time (within which it is agreed the Indians shall be kept sober) to their agency at his own expense. This arrangement was satisfactory, and Mr. Cody departed happy. The dusky chiefs of the forest sang "O-be-joyful!" and will indulge in deeds of daring and blood-curdling horror upon the stage, instead of living on Government rations at their agency.

Amusements

National Theatre. Buffalo Bill

In keeping with the policy of this house in presenting all the first-class artists in their respective lines, the entertainment for this week is announced with confident anticipations of a great success. Mr. Cody, as a scout and Indian fighter, has a national reputation. He is appreciated by the military authorities as the first and foremost of frontier heroes.

As a Buffalo Hunter he was selected by the State Department being the most daring and skillful, as companion and guide to Duke Alexis, of Russia, when he was in the West.

THE INDIANS THAT APPEAR ARE ALSO REAL SAVAGE CHIEFTAINS.

THE SCOUTS ARE REAL SCOUTS.

After the drama a grand trial of skill between the Scouts and Indians lasting thirty minutes.

BRENHAM WEEKLY BANNER, DECEMBER 12, 1879

May Cody

The excitement among the small boys and many of maturer growth was worked up to fever heat over the announcement that the veritable "Buffalo Bill" was coming. Last night the gallery of the opera house was crowded to its utmost capacity, while the parquette was well filled, the attraction being Buffalo Bill and his combination in "May Cody," a thrilling drama of frontier life, the scenes save the first being laid out in Mormondom and the drama itself hanging on the Mountain Meadow massacre for which John D. Lee, the leader of the "Danites" was executed by shooting two years ago last spring. It is a very vivid illustration of Mormon iniquity, perfidy and crime and is worth more by its life-like portrayal of what Mormonism really is, towards awakening the sentiment of the people against the hideous and monstrous practices of those strange and deluded people than all the lectures, books and speeches put together. The portrayal is so vivid as to give the audience almost an ocular demonstration of Mormon doings.

We will not attempt to give a criticism, but will say that every scene of every act is thrilling and emotional. Buffalo Bill (Hon. W. F. Cody) in the different characters he represents fully sustained his reputation and was greeted with hearty applause. Having himself acted the characters he simulates on the stage, he could not well be otherwise than natural; without going into further particulars suffice to say that the entire company were all well up in their parts and the entire piece went off smoothly and to the intense satisfaction of the immense audience. This company will draw crowded houses wherever they go.

Program Notes for *The Red Right Hand; or, Buffalo Bill's First Scalp for Custer,* by Prentiss Ingraham

DECEMBER 1876–JANUARY 1877

107. Program notes for *The Red Right Hand; or, Buffalo Bill's First Scalp for Custer,* 1876. Buffalo Bill Historical Center, Cody, Wyoming. MS6.3061.01-04.

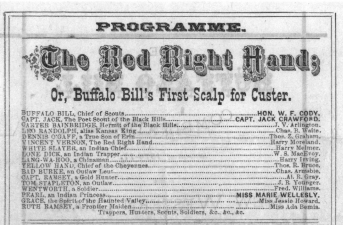

PROGRAMME.

The Red Right Hand;

Or, Buffalo Bill's First Scalp for Custer.

BUFFALO BILL, Chief of Scouts...HON. W. F. CODY.
CAPT. JACK, The Poet Scout of the Black Hills.........................CAPT. JACK CRAWFORD.
CARTER BAINBRIDGE, Hermit of the Black Hills..............................J. V. Arlington.
LEO RANDOLPH, alias Kansas King...Chas. B. Waite.
DENNIS O'GAFF, a True Son of Erin..Thos. Z. Graham.
VINCENT VERNON, The Red Right Hand...Harry Moreland.
WHITE SLAYER, an Indian Chief...Harry Melmer.
LONE DICK, an Indian Trapper..W. S. MacEvoy.
LANG-WA-HOO, a Chinaman..Harry Irving.
YELLOW HAND, Chief of the Cheyennes..Thos. R. Bruce.
BAD BURKE, an Outlaw Lieut...Chas. Arnable.
CAPT. RAMSEY, a Gold Hunter...Al. R. Gray.
TOM STAPLETON, an Outlaw..J. R. Younger.
WENTWORTH, a Soldier...Fred. Williams.
PEARL, an Indian Princess...MISS MARIE WELLESLY.
GRACE, the Spirit of the Haunted Valley.................................Miss Jessie Howard.
RUTH RAMSEY, a Frontier Maiden...Miss Ada Bemis.
Trappers, Hunters, Scouts, Soldiers, &c., &c., &c.

SYNOPSIS.

ACT FIRST.

SCENE 1st.—The Haunted Valley in the Black Hills. Red Hand at the Grave of Boyd Bernard. "Hark!" Appearance of Grace, the Spirit of the Valley. Oh, Horror! horror!" Pearl pursued by Indians. "Back! back! you red fiends!" "Bill to the rescue. Red Hand meets Bill. "Hold on, pard!" What! Bill Cody?" Hermit of the hills. "My rifle failed me, but this will not!" "Hello, Santa Claus!" "By heaven I will keep my vow!" Bill and Hermit. Struggle for Life. "Back! back! this must not be!" "Red Hand, you are doomed!" Appearance of the Spirit of the Valley. Come! come! or we are lost!" Tableau.

ACT SECOND.

SCENE 1st.—Indian Encampment. White Slayer and his warriors. Appearance of the hermit. "White Slayer is false; you have said it!" "White Slayer never breaks his word." SCENE 2d.— Dennis and Lang-wa-hoo. "We must be near the place where the gould b." Christening of Lang by Dennis. Lang called after a French Juke. Meeting of Lone Dick with Bill and Red Hand. SCENE 3d.—Captain Ramsey and his party surprised by Indians. Bill and Red Hand to the rescue. SCENE 4th.—Pearl on Bill's trail. "Yes, those are his foot prints." "I will guard him from danger." SCENE 5th.—Bill's encounter with a bear. Terrible struggle. Pearl surprised. "Oh, heaven, is he dead?" "My heart will break."

ACT THIRD.

SCENE 1st.—Bill and Red Hand on the trail. Lone Dick. SCENE 2d.—Dennis and Lang-wa-hoo. "Spare us! spare us!" "Me like Melican man! no killie!" SCENE 3d.—Pearl. "They shall not be caught asleep." Kansas King. "I mean you no harm." Hermit and White Slayer. SCENE 4th.—Bad Burke meets Pearl. "You are in my power." Bill to the rescue. Burke surprised. "Who are you?" "A man always ready to defend a helpless woman." Terrible knife fight. Bill kills Bad Burke. Pearl's warning of danger. Dennis and Lang pursued by Ind:ans. "Oh, save us! save us!" "Good'ee Ginjince, me lik'ee all sam'ee Melican man!" Bill and Red Hand's encounter with the Indians. Tableau.

ACT FOURTH.

SCENE 1st.—The Outlaw's plot. Dennis as a spy. Lone Dick on Bill's trail. Bill surprises Dick. Outlaw's attempt to capture Kansas King. A struggle. Retreat of Kansas King and the outlaws. SCENE 2d.—Ruth Ramsey and Kansas King. "I will never be your wife!" "You are in my power!" Pearl rescues Ruth. "I will kill you!" SCENE 3d.—The Haunted Valley. "I'll solve this mystery if I die in the attempt." Grace attempts to kill Red Hand, Death of Grace. "Grace, I forgive you." Tableau.

ACT FIFTH.

SCENE 1st.—Pearl and Lone Dick. Dennis' story of the Hermit and Kansas King. SCENE 2d.— Knife combat between Hermit and Kansas King. Hermit receives a death wound. Red Hand's story of his past life. "You are my son!" Kansas King a prisoner. Death of the Hermit. SCENE 3d.—The scouts. Bill gets orders to start at once and guide the 5th Cavalry to Indian Creek. Dennis and Lang anxious for the war path. SCENE 4th.—Encampment of General Merritt's old 5th U.S. Cavalry. The song "Tenting on the old camp ground to-night." Dennis and Lang sing. The Alarm. The "Old 5th" to the front. Couriers pursued by Yellow Hand and his warriors. Bill kills Yellow Hand. The first scalp for Custer. Finale—Allegorical Tableau.

The evening's Performance commencing with Miss MARIE WELLESLY'S Laughable Sketch,

SKETCHES IN INDIA.

SALLY.......................... MARIE WELLESLY. | Sir Matthew...............................H. Melmer
Tom Tape ....T. Z. Graham | Lady Scrags............................ Jessie Howard

THE INDIAN WAR.

SPECIAL DESPATCH TO THE NEW YORK HERALD.

Fort Laramie, July 22d, 1876.

THE INDIANS APPEAR.

At daybreak on Monday morning Lieutenant King commanding the outposts to the southeast, sent in word that the war parties were coming over the ridge from the direction of the reservation. Joining him at the advanced post, General Merritt found the report correct. The command noiselessly mounted and was massed under the bluffs, a quarter of a mile to the rear, out of sight of the Indians. At six o'clock the Indians were swarming all along the ridge to the southeast, some three miles away. Suddenly a party of eight or ten warriors came dashing down a ravine which led directly under the hill where Lieutenant King, with his six men, were watching.

WAITING FOR SCALPS.

The object was as suddenly apparent. Two horsemen, unconscious of the proximity of the foe, had ventured out ahead of the train, and were making rapidly for the creek. They were couriers with dispatches to the command. The Indians, utterly ignorant of the rapid move of the Fifth, were simply bent on jumping on the couriers and getting their scalps. "Buffalo Bill," chief of the scouts, lay on the hill with King, and instantly sprang to his horse down off the hill.

"All of you keep out of sight," said the General. "Mount now, and when the word is given, off with you."

Then turning to the officer of the picket, said:

"Watch them, King. Give the word when you are ready."

Crouching behind the little butte, Bill and his party of two scouts and six soldiers were breathlessly waiting; half way up was the General and his staff. The Lieutenant lay at the crest watching the rapidly advancing foe. Down they came nearer and nearer, the sun flashing from their brilliantly painted bodies and their polished ornaments. Then, just as they are dashing by the front of the hill, King shouts:

"Now, lads, in with you."

With a rush and a yell the troopers are hurled upon the Indians' flank, not fifty yards away.

THE FIRST REDSKIN SHOT.

General Merritt springs up to see the attack just as a tall Indian reeled in his saddle, shot by Corporal Wilkinson, of K company. An answering bullet whistled by the General's head, when King—still on the watch—sung out,

"Here they come by the hundreds."

The reserve Indians came swarming down from the ridge to the rescue. Company K was instantly ordered to the front. But before it appeared from behind the bluff, the Indians, emboldened by the rush of their friends to the rescue, turned savagely on Buffalo Bill and the little party at the outpost.

CODY KILLS YELLOW HAND.

The latter sprang from their horses and met the daring charge with a volley. Yellow Hand, a young Cheyenne brave, came foremost, singling Bill as a foeman worthy of his steel. Cody coolly knelt, and, taking deliberate aim, sent his bullet through the chief's leg and into his horse's head. Down went the two, and, before his friends could reach him, a second shot from Bill's rifle laid the redskin low.

A GRAND SURPRISE.

On came the others, bent on annihilating the little band that opposed them, when, to their amazement, a long blue line popped up in their very front, and K Company, with Colonel Mason at its head, dashed at them. Leaving their dead, the Cheyennes scattered back, helter skelter, to the ridge, but their fire was wild and their stand a short one. Company after company debouched from behind the bluff, and, utterly disheartened, the Indians rushed for the reservation, leaving behind all their provisions. General Merritt pursued them till night, when the whole command went into camp at the agency.

—The Combination will shortly appear in this City. See Daily Papers, Street Bills, &c.

—The celebrated Winchester Repeating Rifles are the ones used by Mr. Cody (Buffalo Bill), both on the plains and the stage.

—Broadway was almost blocked yesterday in the vicinity of the theatre where Buffalo Bill and his Combination are holding forth, the cause being the free exhibition in the lobby of the Scalp, Gun, Bridle, Pistols, &c. &c., worn by the Cheyenne Chief, Yellow Hand, and captured by the chief of scouts. —*N. Y. Herald.*

—"Capt. Jack killed and scalped an Indian a mile from the column during the engagement of yesterday afternoon."

This scalp was received in Omaha yesterday, and is now in possession of the writer. —*Omaha Daily Bee.*

—The Scalp, War Bonnet, Gun, Shield, Bridle, Blankets, Pistols and Lance of Yellow Hand, the Cheyenne Chief killed by Buffalo Bill, July 17th, 1876, will be on exhibition on the day of the arrival of Combination in the city, free of charge.

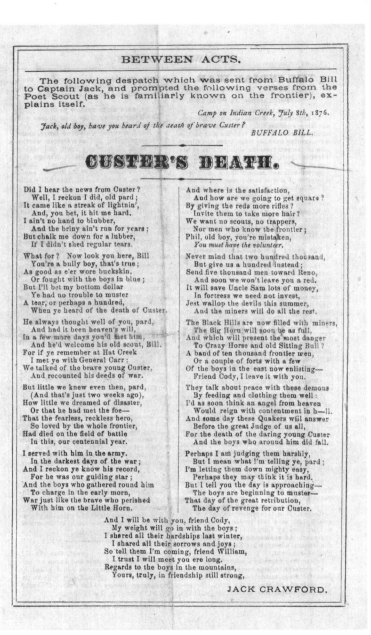

BETWEEN ACTS.

The following despatch which was sent from Buffalo Bill to Captain Jack, and prompted the following verses from the Poet Scout (as he is familiarly known on the frontier), explains itself.

Camp on Indian Creek, July 8th, 1876.

Jack, old boy, have you heard of the death of brave Custer?

BUFFALO BILL.

CUSTER'S DEATH.

Did I hear the news from Custer?
 Well, I reckon I did, old pard;
It came like a streak of lightnin',
 And, you bet, it hit me hard.
I ain't no hand to blubber,
 And the briny ain't run for years;
But chalk me down for a lubber,
 If I didn't shed regular tears.

What for? Now look you here, Bill
 You're a bully boy, that's true;
As good as e'er wore buckskin,
 Or fought with the boys in blue;
But I'll bet my bottom dollar
 Ye had no trouble to muster
A tear, or perhaps a hundred,
 When ye heard of the death of Custer.

He always thought well of you, pard,
 And had it been heaven's will,
In a few more days you'd met him,
 And he'd welcome his old scout, Bill.
For if ye remember at Hat Creek
 I met ye with General Carr;
We talked of the brave young Custer,
 And recounted his deeds of war.

But little we knew even then, pard,
 (And that's just two weeks ago),
How little we dreamed of disaster,
 Or that he had met the foe—
That the fearless, reckless hero,
 So loved by the whole frontier,
Had died on the field of battle
 In this, our centennial year.

I served with him in the army.
 In the darkest days of the war;
And I reckon ye know his record,
 For he was our guiding star;
And the boys who gathered round him
 To charge in the early morn,
War just like the brave who perished
 With him on the Little Horn.

And where is the satisfaction,
 And how are we going to get square?
By giving the reds more rifles?
 Invite them to take more hair?
We want no scouts, no trappers,
 Nor men who know the frontier;
Phil, old boy, you're mistaken,
 You must have the volunteer.

Never mind that two hundred thousand,
 But give us a hundred instead;
Send five thousand men toward Reno,
 And soon we won't leave you a red.
It will save Uncle Sam lots of money,
 In fortress we need not invest,
Jest wallop the devils this summer,
 And the miners will do all the rest.

The Black Hills are now filled with miners,
 The Big Horn will soon be as full,
And which will present the most danger
 To Crazy Horse and old Sitting Bull?
A band of ten thousand frontier men,
 Or a couple of forts with a few
Of the boys in the east now enlisting—
 Friend Cody, I leave it with you.

They talk about peace with these demons
 By feeding and clothing them well:
I'd as soon think an angel from heaven
 Would reign with contentment in h—ll.
And some day these Quakers will answer
 Before the great Judge of us all,
For the death of the daring young Custer
 And the boys who around him did fall.

Perhaps I am judging them harshly,
 But I mean what I'm telling ye, pard;
I'm letting them down mighty easy,
 Perhaps they may think it is hard.
But I tell you the day is approaching—
 The boys are beginning to muster—
That day of the great retribution,
 The day of revenge for our Custer.

And I will be with you, friend Cody,
 My weight will go in with the boys;
I shared all their hardships last winter,
 I shared all their sorrows and joys;
So tell them I'm coming, friend William,
 I trust I will meet you ere long.
Regards to the boys in the mountains,
 Yours, truly, in friendship still strong,

JACK CRAWFORD.

NOTES

Editor's Introduction

1. According to Joy Kasson, this image "shows the power of Cody's identification with the buffalo and suggests some of the ways in which the Wild West offered its audiences memories of American nature that could be balanced against the claims of progress" (235). Paul Fees refers to the same image in the *American Experience* documentary "Buffalo Bill" to suggest the level of Cody's celebrity at the turn of the century.

2. Slotkin, Richard. *Gunfighter Nation: The Myth of the Frontier in Twentieth-Century America*, 61.

3. Cody, *The Life of Hon. William F. Cody*, 32.

4. Cody, *The Life of Hon. William F. Cody*, 144.

5. Cody, *The Life of Hon. William F. Cody*, 69.

6. Cody, *The Life of Hon. William F. Cody*, 200.

7. Cody, *The Life of Hon. William F. Cody*, 73.

8. Cody, *The Life of Hon. William F. Cody*, 74.

9. Cody, *The Life of Hon. William F. Cody*, 74.

10. Greene *Battles and Skirmishes of the Great Sioux War, 1876–1877*, xv–xvi.

11. Cody, *The Life of Hon. William F. Cody*, 195.

12. For a paradigmatic example of this pattern see Mary Rowlandson's *Captivity and Restoration* narrative, which begins in the midst of an Indian attack on the author's frontier village in 1675. The account offers no details about the broader context of King Philip's War and depicts the settlers as Christian martyrs in the hands of a merciless heathen.

13. Cody, *The Life of Hon. William F. Cody*, 35.

14. Cody, *The Life of Hon. William F. Cody*, 43.

15. Cody, *The Life of Hon. William F. Cody*, 43.

16. Cody, *The Life of Hon. William F. Cody*, 301.

17. Cody, *The Life of Hon. William F. Cody*, 40.

18. Louis Warren takes this argument further, suggesting that Cody represents an evolutionary advance on Hickok in an incipient age of mass culture celebrity. Hickok inspires Cody's eventual career path, but Cody transcends Hickok because of fundamental differences in temperament. See *Buffalo Bill's America: William Cody and the Wild West Show*, 62–67.

19. Coined by Sacvan Bercovitch in *Emerson: Prophecy, Metamorphosis, and Influence*, it refers to the tendency in autobiographical writing to foreground the self as an ideal of American citizenship.

20. *Wheeling Register*, October 1, 1884.

21. Many of Twain's western-themed stories were published in the 1867 collection *The Celebrated Jumping Frog of Calaveras County*.

22. Cody, *Story of the Wild West and Campfire Chats*, 700.

23. Cody, *Story of the Wild West and Campfire Chats*, 700.

24. Cody, *Story of the Wild West and Campfire Chats*, 700.

25. Benjamin Franklin, *The Autobiography*, 1.

26. Terrence Whalen suggests that Barnum credits his success to a "pervasive environment of humbug" in a way that unsettles his mid-Victorian readership while offering a trenchant critique of American mass culture. See *The Life of P. T. Barnum*, xi.

27. Leslie Stephen, *Hours in a Library*, 4:185.

28. Louis Warren's *Buffalo Bill's America* represents the most rigorous effort to date to clarify the historical record. Warren addresses these as well as many other incidents and assesses their credibility against the historical record.

29. In the autobiography, Cody mistakenly refers to his opponent as Yellow Hand, a mistranslation that stuck in press accounts and in Cody's stage reenactments.

A Note on the Text

1. Don Russell, ed., *The Life of Hon. William F. Cody, Known as Buffalo Bill*, ix–x.

2. Warren, *Buffalo Bill's America*, 7.

Introductory

1. Freight wagons pulled by teams of oxen and traveling in large groups for safety. Also called prairie schooners. Prior to the advent of the railroad

in the late 1860s these wagons, which could carry thousands of pounds of goods, were the primary system for transporting supplies on the frontier.

2. Gen. Eugene Asa Carr (1830–1910) obtained the rank of Union brigadier general during the Civil War. He was active in the Plains Indians Wars in the 1860s and 1870s, leading campaigns against the Sioux at the Big Horn and in the Yellowstone campaign in 1876. Endorsements like this one played a vital role in Cody's path to celebrity. Cody repeatedly drew upon testimonials from figures such as Generals Carr and Sheridan throughout his show career to authenticate his frontier persona.

3. William Bedford Royall (1825–1895) began his military service during the war with Mexico and obtained the rank of major in the Union Army during the Civil War. He held that rank during his association with Cody although Cody refers to him by his honorary rank of colonel.

4. Cody later staged the Battle of Summit Springs as part of Buffalo Bill's Wild West and utilized General Carr's version of the event in the show program.

1. Childhood

1. Cody was actually born February 26, 1846.

2. Martha Cody (half-sister), 1835–1858; Julia Cody, 1843–1928; Sam Cody, 1841–1853; Eliza Cody, 1848–1902; Laura Ella (called both Helen and Nellie) Cody, 1850–1911; Mary Hannah (called May) Cody, 1853–1926; Charles Cody, 1855–1865. Parents: Mary Ann Laycock Cody, 1827–1863; Isaac Cody, 1811–1857.

3. Also known as "gold fever" and associated with the California gold rush.

4. The deadfall trap is a simple mechanism involving three notched sticks in the shape of the number four, which suspend a rock or other weight (or, in the case of the illustration, a box) until triggered by an animal.

5. The Whig political party was founded in the early 1830s and active until the mid-1850s. The party's influence was undermined by factionalism, especially over the expansion of slavery. Isaac Cody, like many of his northern Whig counterparts, opposed the expansion of slavery into the territories for economic reasons. The party was largely defunct at the time of this incident.

6. Prior to 1854 Kansas was designated as Indian Territory. The region experienced a significant influx of eastern Indian tribes, including the Kickapoos, in the wake of the Indian Removal Act of 1830.

7. A reservation under the management of the Bureau of Indian Affairs in the Department of the Interior.

8. Established in 1827 by Col. Henry H. Leavenworth to supply and protect westbound migrants, Leavenworth became the Kansas Territory's first incorporated community in 1855. It was the head of the Santa Fe and Oregon trails.

2. Early Influences

1. William Selby Harney (1800–1889) was a U.S. Cavalry officer who commanded troops in early Indian wars against the Seminoles and Sioux. He also served under Gen. Winfield Scott in the War with Mexico and held the rank of brigadier general at the start of the Civil War. Although Harney gained a reputation for brutality during the Battle of Ash Hollow (1855), after the Civil War he was deeply involved in negotiating peace treaties and advocating for the fair treatment of Indians.

2. Overland trails used as primary routes of westward migration in the 1840s through the 1860s. Although Cody is correct in claiming the California Trail ran through northeastern Kansas, the Mormon Trail was farther north in southern Nebraska.

3. Named for business partners Alexander Majors and William Hepburn Russell (and William B. Waddell), this firm handled most of the government-contracted freight to military forts in the west during the 1850s and 1860s.

4. The U.S. government built dozens of forts to facilitate trade and enforce peace between warring Plains Indians and, later, between Natives and white settlers. The 1850s witnessed a rapid expansion of military forts along the frontier as settlement increasingly encroached on Indian Territory.

5. A religious group founded in 1830, the Mormons began westward migration to the Rocky Mountain region in 1846 following the death of their leader, Joseph Smith Jr., and continued throughout the 1860s. Lead by Smith's successor, Brigham Young, the majority of Mormon pioneers

settled in the Utah territory. The primary Mormon migration route passed through Iowa, Nebraska, and Wyoming into Utah.

6. A bacterial infection usually brought on by unsanitary eating or drinking conditions.

7. A frolicsome adventure, a spree (from the OED).

8. Secured with a lariat: a rope used to lasso or picket horses (from the OED).

9. Also spelled tipis, tepees, and teepees.

10. Usually included two larger living or working spaces separated by an open space or hallway.

11. Part of the Algonquin group, the Kickapoo Tribe relocated to Kansas from Indiana as part of a settlement with the U.S. government after the War of 1812.

12. Mexican cowboy.

3. Boy Days in Kansas

1. Plural of beef, as in beef cattle.

2. Spelled Potawatomi, this Native tribe was displaced to the plains from Michigan, Illinois, and Indiana in the mid-1840s.

3. Kansas military post established in 1853 to protect people and goods on the California and Santa Fe trails.

4. The Nebraska-Kansas Act of 1854 created two new territories and applied the principle of popular sovereignty by allowing settlers to determine the status of slavery in each territory. This act repealed provisions of the 1820 Missouri Compromise.

5. This was a proxy war, also known as "Bleeding Kansas," between pro-slavery elements and anti-slavery Free-Staters in the Kansas Territory. The conflict arose in the wake of the Nebraska-Kansas Act of 1854. The population burgeoned as activists from both sides moved into the region while militia groups conducted raids against opposing communities. Although violence waned after 1858, the sovereignty question was not settled until Kansas was admitted as a free state in 1861, three months before the outbreak of the Civil War.

6. James Henry Lane (1814–1866), a U.S. congressman from Indiana, resettled in Kansas and became a U.S. senator and a Union general during

the Civil War. He was one of the leaders of the abolitionist movement in Kansas.

7. A free-state stronghold.

8. A political organization formed to counter pro-slavery actions in the territorial legislature, it eventually merged with the Republican Party.

9. A meeting of the territorial legislature which proposed a state constitution allowing slavery (and was boycotted by free-state supporters).

10. Andrew Horatio Reeder (1807–1864) was the first governor of the Kansas Territory.

11. A term denoting a band of horses or mules, used in Louisiana and Texas by the caravans that crossed the prairies (from the OED).

4. Youthful Experiences

1. Located in present-day Nebraska, Fort Kearny was established in 1848 as a supply depot for travelers bound for California and the Pacific Northwest. Located on the south bank of the Platte River it quickly became one of the key posts on the Oregon Trail, with approximately thirty thousand emigrants passing through in 1849 alone.

2. In what became known as the Utah War, Gen. William S. Harney and later Col. Albert Sydney Johnston (1803–1862) were charged by Pres. James Buchanan with leading U.S. troops to establish federal control over Mormon settlers in the Utah region. Motivated by conflicts over the Mormon cultural and political system, territorial boundaries, and relations between Mormons and Native tribes, the Utah Expedition involved few casualties but entailed high political and financial costs on both sides. The conflict lasted from May 1857 until July 1858.

3. A muzzle-loading rifle.

4. A bugle call used to wake military personnel.

5. A type of cannon or field gun known in the nineteenth century for its mobility and flexibility of use.

6. Fed by tributaries originating in northeastern Colorado, the Republican River runs east through southern Nebraska and into north-central Kansas.

5. In Business

1. The Battle of Ash Hollow was fought on September 2 and 3, 1855. It was motivated by the conflict over the 1851 Treaty of Laramie and in

retaliation for a massacre of U.S. troops, known as the Grattan Massacre, on August 19, 1855. General Harney led seven hundred U.S. troops against a Brulé Sioux village near Ash Hollow, Nebraska. Over one hundred Native men, women, and children were killed. Cody's experience with Native Americans is largely defined by his encounters with the Cheyennes and Sioux. Among the most militant of the Great Plains tribes, the Cheyennes were closely allied with the Arapaho Indians. They actively resisted the encroachment of white settlers through the 1860s and 1870s. By the mid-1880s the majority of Cheyenne tribes were forced to accept reservation life. Among the largest and most powerful of the northern Great Plains tribes, the Sioux repeatedly challenged the U.S. military in the 1860s and 1870s. The Battle of the Little Bighorn (1876) and the Wounded Knee Massacre (1890) are among the prominent episodes in the history of that conflict. Cody would later feature Sioux warriors in his Wild West exhibition.

2. James Butler Hickok (1837–1876). Hickok would also achieve notoriety as a frontiersman. Like Cody, he worked as an army scout, lawman, and, briefly, stage actor.

3. George Armstrong Custer (1839–1876). A lieutenant colonel during the Civil War, he achieved lasting notoriety for his death and defeat at the Battle of Little Bighorn in 1876. Custer's death was one of the most sensational incidents of the Plains Indian Wars in terms of national media attention. Cody later incorporated Custer's Last Stand into his Wild West exhibition.

4. *My Life on the Plains* by George A. Custer (1874).

5. Joseph Smith Jr., the founder and leader of the Mormon Church until his death in 1844. Smith died before Cody was born in 1846. Cody may be referring to Lot Smith, a Mormon leader who received some press attention for his participation in the Utah War.

6. A Mormon vigilante group formed in Missouri in 1838. The term was later associated with Mormon resistance to federal forces during the Utah War.

6. Hard Times

1. Built in 1834 at the junction of the North Platte and Laramie rivers. Originally a fur trading post, it was an important stop for travelers

on the Oregon Trail. It was sold to the U.S. government and made a military post in 1849.

2. Breech loading involves loading ammunition from the breech or rear-end of the barrel instead of through the muzzle. The needle gun gets its name from the long firing pin which looks like a needle.

3. During the First War of Indian Independence in 1857, then referred to as the Indian Mutiny, rebel troops laid siege to the city of Lucknow, eventually overcoming British forces. Legend associates the Scottish military song "The Campbells Are Coming" with the rescue of the besieged British.

4. Whiskey.

5. A river flowing from central Nebraska into Kansas, it is the largest tributary of the Kansas River.

6. The Pike's Peak area of the Rocky Mountains was part of the western Kansas territory in 1859 when the gold rush reached its peak. An estimated one hundred thousand people were drawn to the area in pursuit of gold.

7. Jules Beni operated a trading post and stagecoach station. He was suspected of robbing stagecoaches and was reportedly killed by Jack Slade in an 1861 gunfight.

8. Joseph Alfred Slade (1824–1864), aka "Jack Slade," was a gunfighter responsible for the death of Jules Beni, among others. He was lynched by vigilantes in 1864 near Virginia City, Montana.

9. The Pony Express mail service, formed by the freighting company Russell, Majors, and Waddell, continued in operation from April 1860 to October 1861. A horseback relay system carried mail from between St. Joseph, Missouri, and Sacramento, California. Riders exchanged horses every ten to fifteen miles over a seventy-five- to one-hundred-mile route. The ten days required to cover eighteen hundred miles was expedient at the time but rendered obsolete by the advent of the telegraph.

7. Accidents and Escapes

1. Rain-in-the-Face (ca. 1835–1905) was among the Sioux leaders who participated in the Battle of the Little Bighorn.

2. Pneumonia.

8. Adventures on the Overland Road

1. Owned by Ben Holladay, this stagecoach mail service ran between Atchison, Kansas, and Salt Lake City in the 1860s. The service was discontinued when the transcontinental railroad was completed in 1869.

10. Questionable Proceedings

1. Jayhawkers, also known as "Red Legs," were an active militia group which targeted pro-slavery Missourians during the period leading up to the outbreak of the Civil War. Under the leadership of Charles R. Jennison they conducted raids against pro-slavery settlements and communities in 1861 and 1862 that were marked by indiscriminate violence and theft. They disbanded after Jennison was ousted in 1862 but reformed in 1863 under the leadership of George Hoyt and continued raids in Missouri.

2. A large freight forwarder formed in 1859 to carry goods between Denver and Ft. Leavenworth.

3. The 1861 incident that inspired this tale was mythologized in a *Harper's Weekly* feature that brought Hickok to the attention of a national readership. The incident involved a dispute with a Kansas rancher, David McCanles, who visited the relay station where Hickok worked to demand payment for land he had sold Hickok's employer. Hickok, then known as "Duck Bill," reportedly shot and killed McCanles and injured two of his ranch hands with gunfire. The two were then killed by Hickok's co-workers. Hickok and two others were brought to trial for murder but acquitted for acting in self-defense.

4. This rare example of a quick-draw pistol duel took place on July 21, 1865. Hickok was later acquitted based on self-defense.

11. A Soldier

1. The Kiowas and Comanches were allied Plains Indians tribes who resisted encroachment of white settlers and eastern tribes until the 1867 Treaty of Medicine Lodge. Thereafter, a majority resettled in southwestern Oklahoma.

2. Flowing generally southeast through Colorado, Kansas, Oklahoma, and Arkansas, this river is one of the largest tributaries of the Mississippi River.

3. A Union-supported militia group formed in the early 1860s and associated with the Jayhawkers. The group's name comes from the red sheepskin leggings worn by many of them.

4. Johnny Fry (1840–1863) was known for being the first Pony Express rider to carry westbound mail, leaving St. Joseph, Missouri, on April 3, 1860.

5. Military irregulars or guerilla groups; bush-fighters. Although bushwhackers were active on both sides of the conflict, Cody only applies the label to fighters on the Confederate side.

6. Included Cole, Jim, John, and Bob Younger; this group originated as Missouri bushwhackers but turned to bank robbery after the Civil War. Later known as the James-Younger Gang, it counted Jesse and Frank James among its members. While participants in the gang would vary, they continued robberies until 1876.

7. *The Battle of Brice Crossroads* was fought on June 10, 1864, between the Union's brigadier general Samuel Davis Sturgis (1822–1889) and the Confederacy's major general Nathan Bedford Forrest (1821–1877). Although greatly outnumbered, Forrest's forces routed the Union contingent.

8. Price's Raid or Price's Missouri Expedition represented the Confederate Army's attempt to regain control of Missouri while undermining Abraham Lincoln's reelection prospects. Led by Confederate major General Sterling Price (1809–1867), the campaign came to an end on October 23, 1864. In *The Battle of Westport* (present-day Kansas City, Missouri) Union forces under Maj. Gen. Samuel R. Curtis (1805–1866) defeated Price's troops.

9. Slang for "secessionist"—a nickname for Civil War Confederate soldiers.

10. John McNeil (1813–1891). A Union brigadier general, McNeil was known for his brutality. He achieved national notoriety for the Palmyra Massacre in which he ordered the executions of ten Confederate prisoners. John Sappington Marmaduke (1833–1887) was a Confederate major general who was captured at the Battle of Mine Creek and held captive until the end of the war. He later served as the twenty-fifth governor of Missouri (1884–1887.

11. Alfred Pleasonton (1824–1897) was a Union major general. In 1864

he commanded Union forces to two major victories that led to the end of the Civil War in Missouri.

12. A Wedding

1. Militia conflict between free-state advocates and pro-slavery elements from Missouri.

2. Winfield Scott Hancock (1824–1886) was a Union major general. After the Civil War he was made head of the Department of the Missouri, which included oversight of Missouri, Arkansas, Kansas, and Indian Territory.

3. George Augustus Armes (1844–1919) served with Gen. Winfield Scott Hancock during the Civil War. He published a memoir in 1900 that included an account of Cody killing a buffalo; it was titled *Ups and Downs of an Army Officer.*

4. More than 186,000 African American men served in the Union Army. The U.S. military sent six all-black regiments to the western frontier in 1866. They were assigned infantry and cavalry service. The nickname "Buffalo Soldiers" referred to these troops.

13. A Millionaire

1. Construction of the Kansas Pacific Railroad began as part of a federal contract with Union Pacific to connect St. Joseph, Missouri, and Denver.

2. To reduce (the line of a road, railway, or canal) to levels or practicable gradients (from the OED).

3. A circular shed for locomotives, with a turn-table in the center (from the OED).

4. Arta Lucille Cody Thorp (1866–1904).

5. A machine (or scoop) drawn by horses or oxen for excavating ditches, canals, etc., for leveling and making roads, or for raising and removing soil, dirt, weeds, etc., a short distance (from the OED).

6. Lucrezia Borgia (1480–1519) was a Renaissance Italian noblewoman known for her role (as partner in three strategic marriages) in the political intrigues of her powerful family. Victor Hugo's opera about Borgia was touring the U.S. at about this time.

14. Earning a Title

1. An abbreviation for "Messieurs."

2. Out of fight; disabled from fighting (from the OED). Properly spelled "hors de combat," Cody highlights his bilingual pun with the addition of the parenthetical letter.

3. Christopher "Kit" Carson (1809–1868) was a legendary frontiersman, trapper, and Indian agent. He is noted for guiding John C. Fremont on several expeditions through the Rocky Mountains in the 1840s. Carson City, Nevada, is named after him.

15. Champion Buffalo Killer

1. William Averill Comstock (1842–1868), aka "Medicine Bill," was the grand-nephew of James Fenimore Cooper. According to Helen Cody Wetmore, among the stakes in the Buffalo-killing contest was the right to use the nickname "Buffalo Bill." See *Last of the Great Scouts*, chap. 16.

2. A breech-loading rifle popular during the Civil War among Union soldiers and commonly used for buffalo hunting.

3. [Cody's note:] Poor Billy Comstock was afterwards treacherously murdered by the Indians. He and Sharpe Grover visited a village of Indians, supposed to be peaceably inclined, near Big Spring Station, in Western Kansas; and after spending several hours with the redskins in friendly conversation, they prepared to depart, having declined an invitation to pass the night there. It appears that Comstock's beautiful white-handled revolver had attracted the attention of the Indians, who overtook him and his companion when they had gone about half a mile. After surrounding the two men they suddenly attacked them. They killed, scalped and robbed Comstock; but Grover, although severely wounded, made his escape, owing to the fleetness of the excellent horse which he was riding. This sad event occurred August 27, 1868.

16. A Courier

1. Satanta (?–1878), a Kiowa war chief, helped negotiate the Medicine Lodge Treaty in 1867 and became known as the "Orator of the Plains." Lone Wolf (?–1879), Kicking Bird (?–1875), and Satank (1810–1871) were all notable Kiowa leaders.

2. William Babcock Hazen (1830–1887). A Union major general in the Civil War, he was among the more controversial officers in the postbellum army. In 1880 he was appointed Chief Signal Officer of the U.S. Army by Pres. Rutherford B. Hayes.

3. Wagons designed as a touring caravan, often called "prairie wagons" (from the OED).

4. Although "How" became a generic "Indian" term, "Hau" is actually a Lakota Sioux greeting meaning "Hello." The warriors confronting Cody are Kiowas.

5. Gen. Philip Henry Sheridan (1831–1888). Eventual commanding general of the U.S. Army, Sheridan was commanding officer of the Department of the Missouri when he met Cody. He coordinated major campaigns against Plains tribes in the mid-1870s.

6. The Fort Hays–Fort Dodge Road was Fort Hays's main connection to the Santa Fe Trail, which stretched 780 miles from Independence, Missouri, to Santa Fe, New Mexico, its shortest distance.

7. An officer who assists a general in his military duties, including conveying his orders and procuring him intelligence (from the OED).

8. A mounted sentry placed in advance of the outposts of an army to observe the movements of the enemy (from the OED).

17. An Appointment

1. The Dog Soldiers were one of several warrior societies who led the resistance to the U.S. military during this period. Although Cody is right to associate them with the Cheyennes, they had grown increasingly separate from Cheyenne society since the 1830s as the two groups' political objectives diverged.

2. George Alexander Forsyth (1837–1915) was a U.S. brigadier general. In 1868 he organized fifty frontiersman to serve as scouts in Indian Territory.

3. A scion of one of America's most prominent families, Frederick H. Beecher (1841–1868) served with distinction for the Union Army during the Civil War. Thanks to his leadership during the battle, Beecher Island was posthumously named in his honor. The Battle of Beecher Island is also known as the Battle of Arickaree Fork.

4. Henry Ward Beecher (1813–1887), the brother of Harriet Beecher Stowe, was a prominent American Congregationalist minister and reformer.

5. Indicates that the officer holds a higher rank temporarily. It was a common practice during the Civil War to offer honorary promotions of this kind for distinguished service.

6. As opposed to Regular Army, the Volunteer Army was called up during wartime.

7. A tributary of the North Fork of the Republican River, the Arickaree originates in Colorado and flows east through Kansas into southwestern Nebraska.

8. Roman Nose or Woqini (ca. 1835–1868) was a prominent Cheyenne warrior belonging to the Crooked Lance warrior society. Although he was not a Dog Soldier as Cody implies, like many Cheyennes he became more militant in the wake of the Sand Creek Massacre of 1864, and led multiple attacks against settlers and U.S. troops along the Oregon Trail. His death was a significant setback to Cheyenne resistance, which received a fatal blow the following year at the Battle of Summit Springs.

18. Scouting

1. A division of the U.S. Army with headquarters in Omaha, Nebraska.

2. Henry Monk (1826–1883) was a legendary stagecoach driver. Cody alludes to a popular story recounted in Mark Twain's novel *Roughing It* (1872) in which Horace Greeley, the prominent newspaper editor and political reformer, is subjected to a bruising ride after demanding more speed from Monk. Major Brown paraphrases Monk's reply.

19. A Tough Time

1. The mess-wagon carried food and provisions.

2. To attach chains to a vehicle so as to slow it (from the OED).

3. "Hard tack" is a simple bread or biscuit made from flour and water. It is relatively nonperishable, which made it suitable as a staple among the military during the Plains Indians Wars.

4. A dark-skinned person of any race (from the OED).

5. Adobe Walls, a trading post in the Texas Panhandle, was the site

of Kit Carson's last significant battle against members of the Apache, Kiowa, and Comanche tribes in 1864.

6. Maj. Andrew Wallace Evans led a contingent as part of the Canadian River Expedition of 1868. The purpose of the campaign was to force militant Cheyennes and Arapahos back to their reservation.

7. Something very pleasant or pleasurable to deal with; something to be eagerly appropriated; a prize, a treat (from the OED).

8. A stake used for tethering animals.

9. One who follows an army or lives in a garrison town and sells provisions to the soldiers (from the OED).

20. An Exciting Chase

1. Railroad.

2. A bugle call alerting the guard to assemble.

3. The site of a massacre in November 1864 involving the Colorado Territory Militia, led by Col. John Chivington, setting upon a peaceful village of Cheyennes and Arapahos in southeastern Colorado Territory. A number of less-militant Cheyenne leaders were killed in the attack, which shifted the balance of power to more aggressive leaders such as Tall Bull, whose Dog Soldiers had resisted treaties that allowed further encroachment of white settlers.

4. An outlaw of some notoriety in Wyoming and Nebraska in the 1860s and 1870s. In 1877 he was captured and convicted for robbing stagecoaches, and served his sentence in the Nebraska State Prison until 1883.

21. A Military Expedition

1. Sharing meals.

2. A bugle call.

3. A large bottle often enclosed in a wicker basket with a handle.

4. [Cody's note:] Major North is now my partner in a cattle ranch in Nebraska.

5. Frank North (1840–1885) was commissioned an officer of the Pawnee Scouts in 1864. He was known for his facility with the Pawnee language. He later joined Cody's Wild West Show in 1883.

6. Belden, *The White Chief: or, Twelve Years Among the Wild Indians of the*

Plains (1870). James Sanks Brisbin (1837–1892), who later wrote biographies of Ulysses Grant and James Garfield, edited Belden's diary to produce this work. George P. Belden (1844?–1871).

7. A breech cloth or loin cloth.

8. The U.S. Government and the Pawnees enjoyed largely peaceful relations throughout the nineteenth century, with Pawnees frequently serving as scouts during the Plains Indians Wars.

22. A Desperate Fight

1. A platform or net mounted on two poles and dragged by hand or behind a horse.

2. Tall Bull's death in, the Battle of Summit Springs on July 11, 1869, brought an end to the Dog Soldiers' militaristic influence among the Cheyennes. The Cheyennes were subsequently moved to Lakota reservation land in the Dakota Territory.

3. Tall Bull (1830–1869) was a chief of the Dog Soldiers. In the wake of the 1864 Sand Creek Massacre, Tall Bull's warrior society was bolstered by the support of the Cheyennes, such as Roman Nose, as well as some Arapahos. Competing accounts have suggested that Tall Bull was killed by Maj. Frank North while trapped in a nearby ravine and that Cody had shot another Indian riding Tall Bull's horse.

4. The Whetstone Agency was created in 1868 as part of the Fort Laramie treaty ending Red Cloud's War. A reservation for the Brulé Sioux, the agency was named for its proximity to Whetstone Creek. With subsequent relocations the name was changed to the Spotted Tail Agency in 1874. It was named for Brulé Sioux chief Spotted Tail (1823–1881).

5. Ned Buntline was the pseudonym of the dime novelist Edward Zane Carroll Judson (1813–1886). The title "Colonel" came from his term of service with the Union Army during the Civil War. In addition to his prolific writing career, Judson was an editor, temperance lecturer (although he drank heavily himself), and political activist (most notably for the nativist Know-Nothing Party). Judson's colorful past included multiple suits for bigamy, arrests for an unprovoked shooting, desertion from the Union Army, and inciting the Astor Place Riot, the latter leading to a year in jail. He would introduce Buffalo Bill to a national audience with

Buffalo Bill, the King of the Border Men, a serialized story published in *New York Weekly* in 1869. Buntline's story was adapted for the stage in February 1872 at New York's Bowery Theater, with John B. Studley originating the role of Buffalo Bill. Buntline went on to write three more Buffalo Bill dime novels and the first Buffalo Bill drama starring the actual Buffalo Bill, *The Scouts of the Plains*.

23. Administering Justice

1. Possibly the British illustrator Arthur Boyd Houghton (1836–1875).

2. Scalp.

3. [Cody's note:] Since traveled with me in my Dramatic Combination as interpreter for Sioux Indians. [Editor's note:] Nelson, who was an experienced hunter and trapper, would continue with Cody for many years, performing various roles in the Wild West exhibition including stage driver and cowboy. His Sioux wife and their children accompanied the tour and performed as well.

4. [Cody's note:] Near the lonely camp where I had so long been laid up with a broken leg, when trapping years before with Dave Harrington.

5. Another term for justice of the peace.

6. A legal document which enforces the return of wrongfully taken property.

7. The Yale College Scientific Expedition of 1871, led by Othniel Charles Marsh (1831–1899), was seeking further remains of a previously discovered Pterosaur.

8. [Cody's note:] A favorite expression of the Professor's.

24. Hunting Expeditions

1. James Gordon Bennett Jr. (1841–1918) was publisher of the *New York Herald*, which was founded by his father, James Gordon Bennett Sr. (1795–1872). Leonard W. Jerome (1817–1891) was a New York financier and grandfather of Winston Churchill. Henry Eugene Davies (1836–1894) was a Union brigadier general but he retired from the military after the war to pursue a career in law. Davies wrote a biography of General Sheridan and also published an account of the 1870 hunting trip with Buffalo Bill, titled *Ten Days on the Plains*. John Schuyler Crosby (1839–1914) was a Union

Army officer who after the war served on General Sheridan's staff during the Plains Indian campaigns; he later served as governor of Montana Territory from 1882 to 1884. Anson Stager (1825–1885) was a Union Army general in the Civil War and chief of the military telegraph service; he co-founded Western Union and was the first president of the Western Electric Manufacturing Company.

2. Fashionable.

3. Nelson Buck and a party of ten to twelve surveyors were killed in late summer 1869 by a band of Sioux. The surveyors initiated the violence when they killed several Indian scouts in advance of the main party. There appear to have been three main skirmishes, and settlers found remains and pieces of surveying equipment for many years afterward. Newspapers of the time used the Buck Massacre as accusatory evidence that the Sioux did not maintain peace treaties.

25. Hunting with a Grand Duke

1. Grand Duke Alexei Alexandrovich (1850–1908), the fourth son of Tsar Alexander II, toured the United States for three months, November 1871 to February 1872. His travels took him from Boston to New Orleans and the American press covered every stage of the journey.

2. A train of followers, attendants, or servants; a retinue (from the OED).

3. A luck stroke, a fluke (from the OED).

4. Edward Otho Cresap Ord (1818–1883) was a Union major general. He commanded the Deparment of the Platte from 1871 to 1875.

26. Sight-Seeing

1. A musical and cultural society.

2. First produced in 1866, *The Black Crook* was the first piece of modern musical theater. It opened at Niblo's Garden on Broadway and ran for 474 performances.

27. Honors

1. John Burwell "Texas Jack" Omohundro (1846–1880) was originally from Virginia but made his way west after the Civil War. He first went to work in Texas but came north to Kansas with a trail drive and eventually found work as a scout at Fort McPherson.

2. Windham Wyndham-Quin (1841–1926), the fourth Earl of Dun-raven, later acquired land in Colorado and attempted to set up a game preserve. In 1925 he published an account of his hunting experiences titled *Hunting in the Yellowstone or On the Trail of the Wapiti with Texas Jack in the Land of Geysers.*

3. Literally an early form of bicycle, but figuratively suggests that he was the life of the party.

4. Elmer S. Dundy (1830–1896) was a Nebraska judge; he served as a member of the Nebraska territorial council (1858–1862), as justice of the Nebraska territorial supreme court (1863–1867), and as U.S. district judge for Nebraska (1868–1896). He is known for presiding over the 1879 trial of Standing Bear in which the Ponca chief was deemed a person under the meaning of habeas corpus.

5. Cody appears to have initially won the election, but his opponent, D. T. Ashburn, finally claimed the seat after votes from one county surfaced that the county clerk had sent to the wrong place.

28. An Actor

1. Orra Maude Cody (1872–1883).

2. Short for supernumerary: A person employed in addition to the regular company, who appears on the stage but does not speak (from the OED).

3. Niblo's Garden had a 3,200-seat capacity.

29. Starring

1. John M. Burke (?–1917), also known as "Arizona John." Burke later worked for over thirty years as a press agent with the Buffalo Bill Combination and Buffalo Bill's Wild West. He is credited with playing a major role in creating Buffalo Bill's celebrity through his manipulation of the press and his use of innovative marketing techniques.

2. A gambling game at cards in which the players bet on the order in which certain cards will appear when taken singly from the top of the pack (from the OED).

3. The murder took place on August 2, 1876. McCall was later convicted and executed on March 1, 1877.

4. William Frank "Doc" Carver (1851–1927) was working as a dentist

in Fort McPherson when he first met Cody. He moved to North Platte and developed his skills as a marksman, later becoming a full-time performer. In 1883 he partnered with Cody in his first attempt at the exhibition business. The "Wild West: Hon. W. F. Cody and Dr. W. F. Carver's Rocky Mountain and Prairie Exhibition" only lasted one season before the two men parted ways, eventually becoming bitter rivals.

5. Moses Embree Milner (1829–1876), who notably served as chief of scouts for Gen. George A. Custer.

6. Manufactured by the Sharps Rifle Company, these rifles were noted for power and long-range accuracy.

7. A Cheyenne chief (?–1904), he participated in the Indian victory at the Battle of the Little Bighorn and helped secure a Cheyenne reservation in traditional Cheyenne country. A renowned military tactician.

8. Affiliated with the Cheyennes, the Arapahos occupied lands in present-day Colorado, Wyoming, Nebraska, and Kansas along the Platte and Arkansas Rivers.

30. A Return to the Plains

1. George Crook (1828–1890) was a Union major general who later led campaigns against the Sioux and Apaches. He commanded the Department of the Platte from 1875 to 1882 and again from 1886–1888.

2. Reservation for Oglala Sioux, Northern Cheyennes, and Arapahos in the 1870s Wyoming Territory.

3. Wesley Merrit (1834–1910) was a Union major general and a distinguished cavalry officer. He led the Fifth Cavalry in the Battle of Slim Buttes (1876) and oversaw the investigation into the death of Custer at the Battle of the Little Bighorn.

4. A combination of Cheyenne and Lakota forces led by Chiefs Gall and Crazy Horse defeated the five companies under Custer's command through a combination of surprise and numerical superiority.

5. Short for aide-de-camp.

6. A Cheyenne subchief. "Yellow Hand" was a mistranslation of his name; his actual name was "Yellow Hair."

7. John Wallace "Captain Jack" Crawford (1847–1917) was an Irish immigrant who came west after the Civil War and served as an army

scout during the Plains Indians Wars. He would later follow Cody into show business, performing with Cody's Buffalo Bill Combination in 1877. Although Cody helped advance Crawford's careers in both scouting and stage acting, the two parted ways acrimoniously after Crawford was injured in a stage accident. He also worked as a correspondent for the *Omaha Bee*. His collected verse was published in 1879 as *The Poet Scout: Being a Selection of Incidental and Illustrative Verses and Songs.*

8. Abstains from alcohol.

9. Nelson Appleton Miles (1839–1925) was a Union brigadier general during the Civil War and was subsequently involved in most of the major campaigns in the Plains Indians Wars. The 1879 edition repeatedly confused Nelson Miles with Anson Mills, referred to as Colonel Mills in the previous chapter. Anson Mills (1834–1924) served as a cavalry officer under General Crook during the 1876 campaign against the Sioux. During a lengthy military career he distinguished himself as the inventor of an improved cartridge belt adopted by the military.

31. Dangerous Work

1. A good fellow, one whom one approves for his genuine good qualities (from the OED).

2. On September 11, 1857, a group of Arkansas emigrants were slaughtered in Mountain Meadows, Utah Territory, by Mormon militiamen and members of the Paiute Indian tribe. Approximately 120 immigrants were killed. Although the event received some media coverage at the time, national interest was much greater in the 1870s, when new testimony came to light and one of the leaders of the attack was put on trial and executed. Cody's play capitalizes on the sensationalism surrounding the media coverage and modifies the story by incorporating his sister's abduction by Mormon leader John D. Lee (Buffalo Bill rescues her by disguising himself as an Indian).

32. Conclusion

1. John T. Ford (1829–1894) was a well-known theater manager, and the owner of Ford's Theatre at the time of Abraham Lincoln's assassination.

2. Carl Schurz (1829–1906) was a German immigrant who served as

a Union Army general in the Civil War and a U.S. senator from Missouri. He played a significant role in Pres. Rutherford B. Hayes's cabinet as secretary of the interior and presided over an era of civil service reform and the institution of anti-corruption measures in the Office of Indian Affairs.

3. Prentiss Ingraham (1845–1904) was a colonel in the Confederate Army. He later worked as an advance agent for Cody's Wild West show and wrote many Buffalo Bill dime novels.

Appendix 2. Letters

1. Julia Cody Goodman (1843–1928), sister to William F. Cody.

2. Rochester, New York, was the Cody family home in 1876.

3. Kit Carson Cody was born in 1870 and named after the famous scout, Kit Carson (1809–1868). Kit Cody died on April 20, 1876, from scarlet fever.

4. Cody repeats "he" after a page break.

5. The Codys had two daughters at this time: Arta Lucille (born December 1, 1866) and Orra Maude (born January 1, 1872).

6. Lulu is Cody's wife, Louisa Frederici Cody.

7. Cody's sisters: Lida is Eliza Alice Cody (1848–1902); Nellie is Laura Ellen (Helen) Cody (1850–1911); May is Mary Hanna Cody (1853–1926).

8. The Skirmish at Warbonnet Creek took place on July 18. It involved troops from the U.S. Fifth Cavalry and Cheyennes from the Red Cloud Agency in northwest Nebraska.

9. Moses Kerngood was a family friend who owned a clothing store in Rochester.

10. Brev. Maj. Gen. Wesley Merritt took command as Colonel of the Fifth Cavalry (replacing General Carr) on July 1.

11. Brig. Gen. George Crook (1828–1890) played a central leadership role in the Great Sioux War of 1876–77. As commander of the Department of the Platte he led the Big Horn and Yellowstone expedition in 1876.

Appendix 3. Cody and Celebrity

1. A mountain pass in the Rocky Mountains of north-central Colorado.

2. A military fort located in South Dakota established in 1863.

3. The Bighorn River is located in northern Wyoming. The North Platte River originates in northern Colorado and runs through eastern Wyoming into western Nebraska.

4. Spotted Tail (1823–1881) was a Brulé Lakota chief known for his efforts to mitigate conflicts between the Sioux and the U.S. Military.

SELECT BIBLIOGRAPHY

Barnum, Phineas T., edited by Terence Whalen. *The Life of P. T. Barnum, Written by Himself*. Urbana: University of Illinois Press, 2000.

Brown, Bill. Introduction to *Reading the West: An Anthology of Dime Westerns*. Bedford–St. Martin's, 1997. 1–40.

Buffalo Bill. *Story of the Wild West and Camp-Fire Chats by Buffalo Bill*. St. Louis: Holloway, 1888.

Buntline, Ned [E. Z. C. Judson]. *Buffalo Bill: The King of the Border Men*. Davenport IA: Service Press, 1869; rpt. 1987.

Burke, John M. *"Buffalo Bill" from Prairie to Palace: An Authentic History of the Wild West, with Sketches, Stories of Adventure, and Anecdotes of "Buffalo Bill," the Hero of the Plains*. Chicago: Rand, McNally, 1893.

Carter, Robert A. *Buffalo Bill Cody: The Man Behind the Legend*. New York: Wiley, 2002.

Cody, William F., and Don Russell. *The Life of Hon. William F. Cody, Known as Buffalo Bill, the Famous Hunter, Scout, and Guide : An Autobiography*. Lincoln: University of Nebraska Press, 1978.

Cronon, William, George Miles, and Jay Gitlin, eds. *Under an Open Sky: Rethinking America's Western Past*. New York: W. W. Norton, 1992.

Custer, George Armstrong. *My Life on the Plains: Or, Personal Experiences with Indians*. New York: Sheldon, 1874.

Davies, Henry Eugene. *Ten Days on the Plains*. New York: Crocker, 1871.

Etcheson, Nicole. *Bleeding Kansas: Contested Liberty in the Civil War Era*. Lawrence: University Press of Kansas, 2004.

Foote, Stella A. *Letters from "Buffalo Bill"*. El Segundo CA: Upton, 1978.

Franklin, Benjamin. *The Autobiography of Benjamin Franklin*. Edited by Leonard W. Labaree. New Haven: Yale University Press, 1964.

Goodrich, Thomas. *Black Flag: Guerrilla Warfare on the Western Border, 1861–65*. Bloomington: Indiana University Press, 1995.

Gordon, Sarah Barringer. *The Mormon Question: Polygamy and Constitutional Conflict in Nineteenth-Century America*. Chapel Hill: University of North Carolina Press, 2002.

Gray, John S. "Fact Versus Fiction in the Kansas Boyhood of Buffalo Bill." *Kansas History* 8 (Spring 1985): 2–20.

Greene, Jerome A. *Battles and Skirmishes of the Great Sioux War, 1876–1877: The Military View*. Norman: University of Oklahoma Press, 1993.

Hall, Roger. *Performing the American Frontier, 1870–1906*. New York: Cambridge University Press, 2001.

Hedren, Paul L., and Don Russell. *First Scalp for Custer: The Skirmish at Warbonnet Creek, Nebraska, July 17, 1876, with a Short History of the Warbonnet Battlefield*. Glendale CA: Arthur H. Clark, 1980.

Johannsen, Albert. *The House of Beadle and Adams and Its Dime and Nickel Novels: The Story of a Vanished Literature*. 3 vols. Norman: University of Oklahoma Press, 1850–1862.

Kasson, Joy S. *Buffalo Bill's Wild West: Celebrity, Memory, and Popular History*. New York: Hill and Wang, 2000.

Lamar, Howard R., ed. *The New Encyclopedia of the American West*. New Haven: Yale University Press, 1998.

Leonard, Elizabeth Jane, and Julia Cody Goodman. *Buffalo Bill, King of the Old West: Biography of William F. Cody, Pony Express Rider, Buffalo Hunter, Plains Scout & Guide, Master Showman*. Edited by James Williams Hoffman. New York: Library Publishers, 1955.

Limerick, Patricia Nelson. *The Legacy of Conquest: The Unbroken Past of the American West*. New York: Norton, 1987.

Miller, Darlis A. *Captain Jack Crawford: Buckskin Poet, Scout, and Showman*. Albuquerque: University of New Mexico Press, 1993.

Milner, Clyde A., II, Carol A. O'Connor, and Martha A. Sandweiss, eds. *The Oxford History of the American West*. New York: Oxford University Press, 1994.

North, Luther. *Man of the Plains: Recollections of Luther North, 1856–1882*. Edited by Donald F. Danker. Lincoln: University of Nebraska Press, 1961.

Rohrbough, Malcolm J. *Days of Gold: The California Gold Rush and the American Nation*. Berkeley: University of California Press, 1997.

Russell, Don. *The Lives and Legends of Buffalo Bill*. Norman: University of Oklahoma Press, 1979.

Sagala, Sandra K. *Buffalo Bill on Stage*. University of New Mexico Press, 2008.

Slotkin, Richard. *The Fatal Environment: The Myth of the Frontier in the Age of Industrialization, 1800–1890*. Norman: University of Oklahoma Press, 1998.

———. *Gunfighter Nation: The Myth of the Frontier in Twentieth-Century America*. Norman: University of Oklahoma Press, 1998.

———. *Regeneration through Violence: The Mythology of the American Frontier, 1600–1860*. Norman: University of Oklahoma Press, 2000.

Smith, Henry Nash. *Virgin Land: The American West as Symbol and Myth*. Cambridge: Harvard University Press, 1971.

Tompkins, Jane. *West of Everything: The Inner Life of Westerns*. New York: Oxford University Press, 1992.

Turner, Frederick Jackson. *Rereading Frederick Jackson Turner: "The Significance of the Frontier in American History" and Other Essays*. New Haven: Yale University Press, 1998.

Twain, Mark. *Roughing It*. Berkley: University of California Press, 1996.

Unruh, John David. *The Plains Across: The Overland Emigrants and the Trans-Mississippi West, 1840–60*. Urbana: University of Illinois Press, 1982.

Utley, Robert Marshall. *The Indian Frontier of the American West, 1846–1890*. Albuquerque: University of New Mexico Press, 1984.

Walker, Ronald W., Richard E. Turley, and Glen M. Leonard, eds. *Massacre at Mountain Meadows: An American Tragedy*. New York: Oxford University Press, 2008.

Warren, Louis S. *Buffalo Bill's America: William Cody and the Wild West Show*. New York: Alfred A. Knopf, 2005.

West, Elliott. *The Contested Plains: Indians, Goldseekers, and the Rush to Colorado*. Lawrence: University Press of Kansas, 1998.

Wetmore, Helen Cody. *Last of the Great Scouts: The Life Story of Colonel William F. Cody*. Chicago: Duluth Press, 1899.

White, Richard. *"It's Your Misfortune and None of My Own": A New History of the American West*. Norman: University of Oklahoma Press, 1993.

White, Richard, and Patricia Nelson Limerick. *The Frontier in American*

Culture: An Exhibition at the Newberry Library, August 26, 1994–January 7, 1995. Ed. James Grossman. Berkeley: University of California Press, 1994.

Wilmeth, Don B., and Christopher Bigsby, eds. *The Cambridge History of American Theatre.* 2 Vols. New York: Cambridge University Press, 1998.

Wrobel, David M. *Promised Lands: Promotion, Memory, and the Creation of the American West.* Lawrence: University Press of Kansas, 2002.

INDEX

Cody, Laura Ellen/Ella (Helen, Nellie), 19, 374, 424, 428, 458, 495ch1n2, 504ch15n1, 514app2n7
Cody, Louisa. *See* Frederici, Louisa
Cody, Martha, 19, 97, 495ch1n2
Cody, Mary Ann, 19, 23, 28, 41, 43, 48, 50, 51, 53, 54, 55–59, 63, 67, 68–69, 75–76, 97, 104–5, 107, 115–16, 141, 144, 152, 495ch1n2
Cody, Mary Hannah (May), 19, 374, 424, 428, 495ch1n2, 514app2n7
Cody, Samuel, 19, 21–23, 24, 495ch1n2
Cody's Creek, 251
Cold Springs, 79
Comanche Indians, 151, 205, 221, 501ch11n1, 507ch19n5
Comstock, Billy, 197–200, 504ch15n1, 504ch15n3
Coon Creek, 225
Court House Rock NE, 79
Crane, John (Martha Cody's husband), 97
Crawford, Jack, 406–10, 51ch30n72
Crazy Woman's Fork, 121, 396
Cricket, Captain, 136, 139
Crook, Gen. George, 399–401, 406, 410, 411–13, 418, 420–21, 451, 512ch30n1, 514app2n11
Crook, J. J., 165
Crosby, Col. J. Schuyler, 327, 330, 464–65, 509ch24n1
Curtis, Dick, 205, 214–15, 227
Curtis, Major, 367
Custer, Gen. George A., 80, 82, 166–68, *168*, 349, 400, 407–10, 499ch5n3. *See also* Battle at the Little Big Horn
"Custer Massacre." *See* Battle at the Little Big Horn

Davies, Gen. H. E., 327, 337–38, 509ch24n1

Deadwood SD, 281, 393
DeBar, Ben, 424
DeBar's Opera House, 383
Deer Creek, 338, 423
Denver Jim, 211–12
Department of the Missouri, 231, 290, 503ch12n2, 505ch16n5
Department of the Platte, 239, 265, 283, 290, 304, 340, 357, 512ch30n1, 514app1n11
Devil's Gate WY, 79
Dismal River, 294, 374, 424, 428
Dog Soldier Indians, 231, 234, 505ch17n1, 505ch17n8, 507ch20n3, 508ch22n2–3
Doniphan NE, 51
the Dramatic Combination, 418, 429, 509ch23n3
Duncan, Brevet Brig. Gen. and Lt. Col. Thomas, 291, 311, 315–16
Dundy, Judge, 371, 375, 511ch27n4
Dunraven, Earl of, 368–69, 396, 510ch27n2

Echo Canyon, 79
Elephant Rock, 246
Ellsworth KS, 171
Emory, Brevet Maj. Gen. W. H., 311, 320, 327, 463
Enabling Act of Kansas Territory, 44

the *Far West* (steamship), 415, 417, 418, 423
Farley, Jack, 273, 275–76
Fitzhugh, General, 327, 330–33, 464–65
Ford, John T., 429, 513ch32n1
Forrest, Gen. Nathan Bedford, 153, 502ch11n7
Forsyth, Gen. George A., 232, 234, 236, 239, 343–44, 400, 505ch17n2
Fort Abraham Lincoln ND, 417

In the Papers of William F. "Buffalo Bill" Cody series

Four Years in Europe with Buffalo Bill
By Charles Eldrige Griffin
Edited and with an introduction by Chris Dixon

The Life of Hon. William F. Cody, Known as Buffalo Bill
By *William F. Cody*
Edited and with an introduction by Frank Christianson